CELEBRATIONS AND ATTACKS

OTHER BOOKS BY IRVING HOWE

Trotsky (Modern Masters Series)
World of Our Fathers
The Critical Point
Decline of the New
Steady Work: Essays in the Politics of Democratic Radicalism,
    1953-1966
Thomas Hardy: A Critical Study
A World More Attractive
The American Communist Party: A Critical History
    (with Lewis Coser)
Politics and the Novel
William Faulkner: A Critical Study
Sherwood Anderson: A Critical Biography
The U.A.W. and Walter Reuther (with B.J. Widick)

IRVING HOWE

Celebrations

AND *Attacks*

Thirty Years of Literary
and Cultural Commentary

HORIZON PRESS NEW YORK

Acknowledgment is gratefully made to the following publications and publishers for permission to reprint materials in this book: *Partisan Review, Commentary, The Nation, The New Republic, The New York Review of Books, The New York Times Book Review, Yale Review, Dissent, Harper's Magazine, Midstream*, Avon Books, The New Republic Book Company, New Directions.

For Sarah and Bernard Rosenberg

INTRODUCTION

This book contains a selection of my shorter critical writings composed during the past thirty years, what might be called my "selected short subjects." Any such gathering of fugitives is likely to raise the famous question of "unity," though it seems in the very nature of this kind of book that it cannot have a closely-defined unity of subject-matter. Its unity consists in the fact that it was all written by one person and may therefore reveal a chart of intellectual development, diversity of interests, and perhaps also discontinuities. It is the kind of book in which one picks and chooses, stays to enjoy or moves ahead to quarrel. Besides, I think the whole matter of "unity" somewhat tiresome.

A number of these pieces have been included because I enjoyed writing them and therefore hope it may give readers pleasure to read them. Some of the briefer items are here because it is interesting to see how a critic confronts important new books. Others touch on literary and cultural issues that remain significant into the late seventies and will no doubt continue to be during the next decade. In printing my notices of the work of writers like Crawford Power, John Williams, and George Konrad I want to bring valuable but insufficiently-known books to the attention of literate readers. And in a few instances I have thought pieces worth reprinting because they seemed to me well done. There are said to be critics who write best when hemmed in by space limitations; at times, perhaps, I am one of these.

I have divided the book into three parts, roughly according to the last three decades; but no claim is made, of course, that these parts "represent" the decades or provide a chronicle of their literary and cultural experiences. Perhaps all they represent is my own work and interests—and even that not completely, since during these years I have published several other collections of essays on literary, cultural and political topics (*Politics and the Novel, A World More Attractive, Steady Work, Decline of the New,* and *The Critical Point.*)

Occasionally I have trimmed passages of digression, spots of polemic and other matter no longer interesting; but in no case have I changed opinions or judgments, nor made any substantial revision of substance. After a few pieces I have added postscripts that amplify or qualify.

The selections are framed by two larger essays. "Strangers" is a semi-autobiographical venture into informal cultural history that may help give this book perspective; "Literature and Liberalism" sums up recurrent interests.

Finally, a word of thanks to my publisher Ben Raeburn. To be literate, to be a lover of books, to be ready to take chances with writers he cares about: what more could anyone ask of a publisher?

I.H.
May 1978

CONTENTS

Introduction   7

Strangers   *11*

THE FIFTIES

A Negro in America (Ralph Ellison)   *29*

The Stories of Bernard Malamud   *32*

The Suburbs of Babylon (Philip Roth)   *35*

Mailer's Political Novel (Norman Mailer)   *39*

The Snopes Saga (William Faulkner)   *41*

In the Day of a False Messiah (Isaac Bashevis Singer)   *49*

The Stories of Isaac Babel   *53*

Tomato or Cucumber? (Alain Robbe-Grillet)   *59*

Culture and Radicalism (Richard Chase)   *62*

Anti-Semite and Jew (Milton Hindus)   *68*

Henry James as Latter-Day Saint   *72*

God, Man and Stalin (Whittaker Chambers)   *80*

THE SIXTIES

Richard Wright: A Word of Farewell   89

The Salinger Cult (J. D. Salinger)   93

Flannery O'Connor's Stories   97

Treacheries of Faith (Crawford Power)   102

A Fine Novel of Academic Life (John Williams)   109

Doris Lessing: No Compromise, No Happiness   112

The Stories of Pirandello (Luigi Pirandello)   118

George Eliot in Her Letters   127

The Country of the Pointed Firs (Sarah Orne Jewett)   132

Robert Frost: A Momentary Stay   135

A Neglected American Poet (Frederick Tuckerman)   145

Literature on the Couch (Leslie Fiedler)   150

The Wounds of All Generations (Ernest Hemingway)   155

Southern Agrarians and American Culture   161

Endgame: The Fate of Modernism (Renato Poggioli)   166

W. E.B. DuBois: Glory and Shame   170

THE SEVENTIES

Delmore Schwartz: An Appreciation   183

George Konrad: The Traffic of Suffering   189

The Plebeian Realism of James Hanley   192

The Poetry of Isaac Rosenberg   195

Privacy for Joyce? (James Joyce)   202

Lillian Hellman and the McCarthy Years   206

Lionel Trilling: Sincerity and Authenticity   213

A Man of Letters (Edmund Wilson)   221

Octavio Paz: Mexican Modernist   225

Tribune of Socialism (Norman Thomas)   230

The Holocaust and Moral Judgment (Lucy Dawidowicz)   234

Literature and Liberalism   239

Books Discussed   255

STRANGERS

Being an American, we have been told repeatedly, is a complex fate, and being an American writer still more so: traditions ruptured, loyalties disheveled. Yet consider how much more complex, indeed, how utterly aggravating, it could have been to grow up in an American subculture, one of those immigrant enclaves driving itself wild with the clashing hopes that it would receive the new world's blessing and yet maintain a moment of identity neither quite European nor quite American. The rise and fall of such subcultures is said to be intrinsic to the American experience, and no doubt it is. But when one looks into conventional accounts of our literature, it is hard to find much evidence that our writers ever felt themselves to be strangers in the land—though about their estrangement from the cosmos everyone speaks. It is hard to find evidence of that deep, rending struggle which marked those writers who had to make, rather than merely assume, America as their native ground.

The whole of our literary history for the past century might be reworked so as to encourage a richer sense of what cultural influence really signifies—a sense, for example, that it is not enough simply to trace lines of continuity, since these lines are blocked, distorted, and even obliterated by recurrent outcroppings of transported Europe. Toward such a history I would here offer a few words, based not on hard evidence, of which we have little, but on recollections of the

experiences shared by a generation of American Jewish writers. I will
use the first person plural, though with much uneasiness, since I am
aware that those for whom I claim to speak are likely to repudiate that
claim and wish to provide their own fables of factuality. Here, in any
case, is mine.

Lines of connection from writer to writer are never as neat or as
"literary" as historians like to make out. Between master and disciple
there intervene history, popular culture, vulgarization, organized
forgetting, decades of muck and complication. Still, if only to ease my
argument, we may agree that for writers like Robinson and Frost,
Ralph Waldo Emerson towered as an ancestor imposing and authoritative, sometimes crippling, and that he figured for them not merely
through the books they picked up at home or had to read in school, but
through the very air, the encompassing atmosphere, of their culture.
How much of "transcendentalism" remains in their writing everyone
can estimate on his own, since no one has yet found a scale for weighing
weightlessness; but that the pressures of this weightlessness are at
work upon their writing seems beyond dispute. Despite inner clashes
and discontinuities, American culture moves from the generation of
Emerson to that of Robinson and Frost, as a bit later, that of Crane and
Stevens, with a more or less "natural" or spontaneous rhythm. There is
a passing on of the word.

But for young would-be writers growing up in a Jewish slum in New
York or Chicago during the 'twenties and 'thirties, the main figures of
American literature, as well as the main legends and myths carried
through their fictions and stories, were not immediately available.
What could Emerson mean to a boy or girl on Rivington Street in 1929,
hungry for books, reading voraciously, hearing Yiddish at home, yet
learning to read, write, and think in English? What could the tradition
of American romanticism, surely our main tradition, mean to them?

Together with the poems of Browning and Tennyson, such young
people took in the quasi- or pseudo-Emersonian homilies their Irish
teachers fed them at school. They took in the American legends of an
unspoiled land, heroic beginnings, pioneer aloneness, and individualist success. All of these had a strong, if sometimes delayed,
impact. In the course of this migration of myth from lady teachers to
immigrant children there had, however, to occur twistings, misapprehensions. Besides, we immigrant children did not come as empty
vessels. We had *other stories*. We had stories about legendary endurance in the Old World; stories about the outwitting of cruel priests;
stories about biblical figures still felt to be contemporaries though by
now largely ripped out of their religious setting; stories about endless

martyrs through the ages (while America seemed to have only one martyr and he, in beard and shawl, had a decidedly Jewish look).

These stories of ours were the very material out of which cultures are made, and even as we learned to abandon them with hurried shame and to feign respect for some frigid general who foolishly had never told a lie, or to some philosopher of freedom who kept slaves, we felt a strong residue of attachment to our own stories. We might be preparing to abandon them, but they would not abandon us. And what, after all, could rival in beauty and cleverness the stories of Isaac and Ishmael, Jacob and the angel, Joseph and his brothers?

Raised to a high inclusiveness, a story becomes a myth. It charts the possibilities and limits for the experience of a people, dramatizing its relations with the universe. We are speaking here of *possession:* that which we know, or remember, or remember that we have been forgetting. We are speaking about those tacit gestures, unseen shrugs, filaments of persuasion which form part of subverbal knowledge. We are speaking of that which is irrevocable. By way of the simplest illustration, let me choose not some high-flown piece of poetry or rhetoric but a little folk story, the merest anecdote, about Chelm, the legendary town into which the Jews have wisely packed all their foolishness.

They asked a Jew of Chelm: "What would you do if you found a million rubles in the market place and knew who had lost them? Would you withstand the temptation and return the money?"

The Jew of Chelm answered, quick as a flash: "If I knew the money was Rothschild's I'm afraid I couldn't withstand the temptation and would not return it. But if I knew the million rubles belonged to the poor *shammes* [sexton] of the old synagogue, I'd return it to the last penny."

Part of what it meant to be a would-be American Jewish writer was that a fragile anecdote like this one offered a rich store of implications, a vista of multiplied ironies, each irony grappling onto the back of the other; it meant being able to see a whole cultural style, indeed, a whole cultural fate in this one little story; and it meant, also, being obliged to respond to it through the eyes of one's father, even if one were devoting one's deepest energies to battle against that father.

For a time, then, we tried to reconcile our stories with the American stories. The two of them would coexist in our minds, awkwardly but fruitfully, and we would give to the one our deep if fading credence and to the other our willed if unsure allegiance.

With American literature itself, we were uneasy. It spoke in tones that seemed strange and discordant. Its romanticism was of a kind we could not really find the key to, for while there were figures of the

Jewish past who had striking points of kinship with the voices of Concord, we had largely been deprived of the Jewish past. (When the comparison was first made between Whitman's poetry and the teachings of Hasidism, it came from a Danish critic, Frederick Schyberg; but most of us, who ought to have noticed this immediately, knew little or nothing about Hasidism, except perhaps that it was a remnant of "superstition" from which our fathers had struggled to free themselves.)

Romanticism came to us not so much through the "American Renaissance" as through the eager appropriations that East European Jewish culture had made in the late nineteenth century from Turgenev and Chernyshevsky, Tolstoy and Chekhov. The dominant outlook of the immigrant Jewish culture was probably a shy, idealistic, ethicized, "Russian" romanticism, a romanticism directed more toward social justice than personal fulfillment. The sons and daughters of this immigrant milieu were insulated from American romanticism by their own inherited romanticism, with the differences magnified and the similarities, for a time, all but suppressed.

American romanticism was more likely to reach us through the streets than the schools, through the enticements of popular songs than the austere demands of sacred texts. We absorbed, to be sure, fragments of Emerson, but an Emerson denatured and turned into a spiritual godfather of Herbert Hoover. This American sage seemed frigid and bland, distant in his New England village—and how could we, of all generations, give our hearts to a writer who had lived all his life "in the country"? Getting in touch with the real Emerson, whoever *that* might be—say, with the Emerson radiant with a sense of universal human possibility yet aware enough, at least in his notebooks, of everything that might thwart and deny—this was not for us a natural process of discovering an ancestor or even removing the crusts of misconstruction which had been piled up by the generations. It was a task of rediscovering what we had never really discovered and then of getting past the barriers of sensibility that separated Concord, Massachusetts from the immigrant streets of New York.

These were real barriers, significant differences of taste and value. What could we make of all the talk, both from and about Emerson, which elevated individualism to a credo of life? Nothing in our tradition, little in our experience, prepared us for this, and if we were growing up in the 'thirties, when it seemed appropriate to feel estranged from whatever was "officially" American, we could hardly take that credo with much seriousness. The whole complex of Emersonian individualism seemed either a device of the Christians to lure us into a gentility that could only leave us helpless in the worldly struggles ahead, or a bit later, when we entered the phase of teen-age Marxism, it seemed a mere reflex of bourgeois ideology, especially that distinctive American form which posited an "exceptionalist" destiny for the New World.

Perhaps a more fundamental way of getting at these matters is to say that we found it hard to decipher American culture because the East European Jews had almost never encountered the kind of Christianity that flourished in America. The Christianity our fathers had known was Catholic, in Poland, or Orthodox, in Russia, and there was no reason to expect that they would grasp the ways or the extent to which Protestantism differed. We knew little, for instance, about the strand of Hebraism running through Puritan culture—I recall as a college student feeling distinct skepticism upon hearing that the Puritan divines had Hebrew. (If they had Hebrew, how could they be gentiles?) It was only after reading Perry Miller and Edmund Wilson in later years that this aspect of American Protestant culture came alive for me. All that was distinctive in Protestant culture, making it, for better or worse, a radically different force in confrontation from Catholicism or Eastern Orthodoxy, we really could not grasp for a long time. We read the words but were largely deaf to the melody.

For most of us, individualism seemed a luxury or deception of the gentile world. Immigrant Jewish culture had been rich in eccentrics, cranks, and individualist display; even the synagogue accepted prayer at personal tempos, coming to a conclusion with about the same nicety of concord one finds in certain American orchestras. But the idea of an individual covenant with God, each man responsible for his own salvation; the claim that each man is captain of his soul (picture those immigrant kids, in white shirts and middy blouses, bawling out, "O Captain, My Captain"); the notion that you not only have one but more than one chance in life, which constitutes the American version of grace; and the belief that you rise or fall in accord with your own merits rather than the will of alien despots—these residues of Emersonianism seemed not only strange but sometimes even a version of that brutality which our parents had warned was intrinsic to gentile life. Perhaps our exposure to this warmed-over Emersonianism prompted us to become socialists, as if thereby to make clear our distaste for these American delusions and to affirm, instead, a heritage of communal affections and responsibilities.

Then, too, Jewish would-be writers found the classical Americans, especially Emerson and Thoreau, a little wan and frail, deficient in those historical entanglements we felt to be essential to literature because inescapable in life. If we did not yet know we surely would have agreed with Henry James's judgment that Emerson leaves "a

singular impression of paleness" and lacks "personal avidity." Born, as
we liked to flatter ourselves, with the bruises of history livid on our
souls, and soon to be in the clutch of new-world "avidities" that would
make us seem distasteful or at least comic to other, more secure,
Americans, we wanted a literature in which experience overflowed,
engulfed, drenched. So we abandoned Emerson even before encountering him, and in later years some of us would never draw closer
than to establish amiable diplomatic relations.

Hardest of all to take at face value was the Emersonian celebration of
nature. Nature was something about which poets wrote and therefore
it merited esteem, but we could not really suppose it was as estimable
as reality—the reality which we knew to be social. Americans were said
to love Nature, though there wasn't much evidence of this that our
eyes could take in. Our own tradition, long rutted in *shtetl* mud and
urban smoke, made little allowance for nature as presence or refreshment. Yiddish literature has a few pieces, such as Mendele's "The
Calf," that wistfully suggest it might be good for Jewish children to get
out of the *heder* (school) and into the sun; but this seems more a
hygienic recommendation than a metaphysical commitment. If the talk
about nature seemed a little unreal, it became still more so when
capitalized as Nature; and once we reached college age and heard that
Nature was an opening to God, perhaps even his phenomenal mask, it
seemed quite as far-fetched as the Christian mystification about three
gods collapsed into one. Nothing in our upbringing could prepare us to
take seriously the view that God made his home in the woods. By now
we rather doubted that He was to be found anywhere, but we felt
pretty certain that wherever He might keep himself, it was not in a
tree, or even leaves of grass.

What linked man and God in our tradition was not nature but the
commandment. Once some of us no longer cared to make such a link-
age, either because we doubted the presence of God or the capacity of
man, we still clung to the commandment, or at least to the shadow of
its severities, for even in our defilements it lay heavily upon us.

I think it ought to be said that most of us were decidedly thisworldly,
in that sardonic Yiddish style which, through the genius of a Sholom
Aleichem or occasionally a Peretz, can create its own darkly soothing
glow. Our appetites for transcendence had been secularized, and our
messianic hungers brought into the noisy streets, so that often we
found it hard to respond to, even to hear, the vocabulary of philosophical idealism which dominates American literature. Sometimes this
earthboundedness of ours was a source of strength, the strength of a
Delmore Schwartz or a Daniel Fuchs handling the grit of their experience. Sometimes it could sour into mere candy-store realism or sadden

into parkbench resignation. If the imagination soared in the immigrant slums, it was rarely to a Protestant heaven.

I am, of course, making all this seem too explicit, a matter of words. It went deeper than words. We had grown up, for instance, with the sovereign persuasion which soon came to seem our most stringent imprisonment: that the family was an institution unbreakable and inviolable. Here, though we might not yet have known it, we were closer to the Southern than to the New England writers. For where, if you come to think of it, is the family in Emerson, or Thoreau, or Whitman? Even in Melville the family is a shadowy presence from which his heroes have fled before their stories begin. And where is the family in Hemingway or Fitzgerald? With Faulkner, despite all his rhetoric about honor, we might feel at home because the clamp of family which chafed his characters was like the clamp that chafed us. When we read Tolstoy we were witness to the supremacy of family life; when we read Turgenev we saw in Bazarov's parents a not-too-distant version of our own. But in American literature there were all these strange and homeless solitaries, motherless and fatherless creatures like Natty and Huck and Ishmael. Didn't they know where life came from and returned to?

Glance at any significant piece of fiction by an American Jewish writer—Schwartz's "America, America," Malamud's "The Magic Barrel," Bellow's "The Old System"—and you will see that the family serves as its organizing principle, just as in Jewish life it had become the last bulwark of defenselessness. Even in the stories of Philip Roth, which herald and perhaps celebrate the break-up of immigrant culture, there is finally a crabbed sort of admiration for the family. The Jewish imagination could not so much as conceive a fiction without paying tribute, in both senses of the word, to the family.

We had, to be sure, other and more positive reasons for keeping an uneasy distance from American literature. We felt that together with the old bedclothes, pots and pans that our folks had brought across the ocean, they had also kept a special claim on Russian culture. Tolstoy, Turgenev, Chekhov—though not the sensationalist and anti-Semite Dostoevsky—were very close to us. They had been liberally translated into Yiddish and read by the more advanced Jewish youth of Eastern Europe. Breathing moral idealism, they spoke for humanity at large; they told us to make life better and, as it seemed to us then, what better word could literature tell? The works of these masters revealed a generosity of spirit at the very moment that the spirit of the East European Jews was straining for secular generosity. In the devotion of the Yiddish-speaking intelligentsia to Tolstoy, Turgenev, and Chekhov it almost came to seem as if these were *Jewish* writers! Tolstoy presented some problems—perhaps we regarded him as a Jew for Jesus.

But the other two, they were ours! I remember Isaac Rosenfeld, the
most winning of all American Jewish writers, once explaining to me
with comic solemnity that Chekhov had really written in Yiddish but
Constance Garnett, trying to render him respectable, had falsified the
record. Anyone with half an ear, said Rosenfeld, could catch the tunes
of Yiddish sadness, absurdity, and humanism in Chekhov's prose—and
for a happy moment it almost seemed true.

Coming as strangers who possessed, so to say, the Russian masters,
we could afford to be a little cool toward the American ones. What was
Dreiser to Tolstoy, Anderson to Turgenev, and the sums of all American short stories to one by Chekhov? These Russians formed a moral
dike guarding the immigrant Jewish intelligentsia and then their children from the waves of American sensibility and myth. Like the Yiddish culture from which we had emerged, we were internationalist in
our sentiment before we were part of *any* nation, living in the exalted
atmospheres of European letters even as we might be afraid, at home,
to wander a few streets away.

The situation was further complicated by the fact that the young
would-be Jewish writers were themselves only tenuously connected
with the Jewish culture from which they had emerged. They were
stamped and pounded by the immigrant experience, but that was
something rather different from the Jewish tradition. Brilliant and vital
as the immigrant experience may seem to us now, it was nevertheless a
thinned-out residue of the complex religious culture that had been
built up over the centuries by the East European Jews. A process of
loss was being enacted here—first, the immigrant culture was estranged from its Old World sources, and second, we were estranged
from the immigrant culture. Especially were we estranged from—in
fact, often ignorant of—those elements of religious mysticism and enthusiasm, ranging from the Cabalists to Hasidism, which had wound
their way, as a prickly dissidence, through East European Jewish life.
It was, for many of us, not until our late teens that we so much as heard
of Sabbatai Zevi or Jacob Frank, the false messiahs who had torn apart
the life of the East European Jews in the seventeenth and eighteenth
centuries. Even as the fierce self-will of the immigrant culture kept us
at a certain distance from American literature, so did it also screen out
"reactionary" elements of the Jewish past.

I sometimes think that respectful gentile readers have been badly
gulled by the American Jewish writers into believing that they, the
writers, possess a richer Jewish culture than in fact they do. The truth
is that most of the American Jewish writers are painfully ignorant of the
Jewish tradition. When they venture to use a Yiddish phrase they are
liable to absurd mistakes. There is a delicious bit revealing this con-

dition in a story by Irvin Faust about a Brooklyn boy who has gone for a
season to Vermont and is asked by the farmer's daughter, "Myron, talk
Jew to me." He has to scramble in his memories to find a phrase: "Ish
leeba Dick."

> "Oh," Rita Ann moaned softly, "say that again."
> "Ish . . . leeba . . . Dick."
> "Oooh. What's it mean?"
> This I remembered, at least to a point. "I love you . . . Dick."

The work of the American Jewish writers represented an end, not a
beginning—or perhaps more accurately, its end was in its beginning. It
was a sign of the break-up of Jewish community and the crumbling of
Jewish identity; it spoke with the voice of return, nostalgia, retrospec-
tion, loss. And even if we chose to confine our sense of Jewish experience to the immigrant milieu, something that would already constitute
a major contraction, many of these writers didn't even command that
milieu in a deep, authentic way. Abraham Cahan, Henry Roth, and
Daniel Fuchs did command it, with their very bones; Delmore
Schwartz and Michael Seide made wry poetry out of their boyhood
recollections; Saul Bellow recreated the immigrant world through
ironic scaffoldings and improvisations; Bernard Malamud, by some
miracle of transmutation, summoned in English an occasional true
replica of the Yiddish story. But the work of many American Jewish
writers is filled not only with cultural and linguistic errors; it suffers,
importantly, from a gross sentimentalism, a self-comforting softness,
with regard to the world they suppose themselves to be representing
or reconstructing. Especially is this true of those younger writers who
are, so to say, exhausting the credit of their grandfathers' imaginations,
making of the East Side a sort of black-humored cartoon, half-Chagall,
half-Disney. By now it is clear that the world of our fathers, in its brief
flare of secular passion, gave the American Jewish writers just enough
material to see them through a handful of novels and stories. The
advantages of remembered place soon gave way to the trouble of having lost their place. Which is why so many of the American Jewish
writers seem to enter the second half of their careers as displaced
persons: the old streets, the old songs, have slipped away, but the
mainstream of American life, whatever that may be, continues to elude
their reach. America, it turns out, is very large, very slippery, very
recalcitrant.

For the American Jewish poets, whom I have largely ignored here,
things may yet turn out more favorably. Once milieu and memory are
exhausted, Jewishness can take on the strangeness of a fresh myth, or
at least myth rediscovered; that myth need have no precise location, no

street name or number; and the Bible may lose its tyranny of closeness and become a site to be ransacked. Something of the sort has happened in the last few decades among Yiddish writers, the novelists and story-tellers among them finding it more and more difficult to locate their fictions in a recognizable place, while precisely an awareness of this dilemma has yielded the poets a rich subject.

But now I must retrace my steps and make things a little more complicated. For if I've been talking about the pressures that kept us at a certain distance from American literature, it must surely be remembered that there were other pressures driving us, sometimes feverishly, toward it.

With time we discovered something strange about the writing of Americans: that even as we came to it feeling ourselves to be strangers, a number of the most notable writers, especially Whitman and Melville, had also regarded themselves as strangers, though not quite in the blunt and deprived way that we did. Whitman saw himself as a poet-prophet who necessarily had to keep a certain distance from his culture—a stranger in the sense proposed by Georg Simmel, that is, a potential wanderer who "has not quite lost the freedom of coming and going," so that even when "fixed within a particular spatial group . . . his position in this group is determined, essentially, by the fact that he has not belonged to it from the beginning, that he imports qualities into it. . . ." The Whitman who has often been seen as "furtive," the wanderer of the streets who comes into touch with everyone but remains close to no one, is a stranger, making of that condition the metaphysical coloring of his *persona*.

In the early years of the immigrant culture, Whitman was the most popular American writer (except perhaps Poe) among Yiddish readers and writers; there are odes addressed to him in Yiddish and some rough translations of his shorter poems. One reason for this affection was that to the Yiddish-speaking immigrant intelligentsia Whitman seemed really to *mean* it when he invited everyone to make himself at home in the New World. They detected in Whitman an innocence of soul which touched their own innocence; they heard in his voice strains of loneliness which linked with their own loneliness; they saw him as the American who was what Americans ought to be, rather than what they usually turned out to be. They may have been misreading him, but, for their purposes, very usefully.

By the time our turn came—I mean, those of us who would be writing in English—Whitman had lost some of his charm and come to seem portentous, airy, without roots in the griefs of the city, not really a "modern" sensibility. In 1936 "Crossing Brooklyn Ferry" might not speak very strongly to a boy in the slums, even one who had often crossed the Staten Island ferry on Saturday nights; it would take several decades before the poem could reveal itself in its grandeur, this time to the aging man that boy had become. But probably not until the late 'thirties or early 'forties did there come into our awareness another American writer who seemed to speak to us as comrade to comrade, stranger to stranger. Herman Melville was a "thicker" writer than Whitman, "thicker" with the pain of existence and the outrage of society, a cousin across the boundaries of nationality and religion who seemed the archetypal young man confronting a world entirely prepared to do him in. Had we known *Redburn* in time, we might have seen Melville as the tenderfoot only a step or two away from the greenhorn, and we would have been enchanted by the great rhetorical outpouring in that book where Melville welcomes immigrants, all peoples. to the American fraternity. We would have seen the young Melville as a fellow who had to work in a ship—I was about to say, in a shop—where he was hooted at because he wanted to keep some of the signs of his delicate youth. And we would have seen him as a writer who bore the hopes, or illusions, that we were bearing about the redemptive possibilities of "the people."

But the Melville book that we knew was, of course, *Moby Dick*, quite enough to convince us of a true kinship. Melville was a man who had worked—perhaps the only authentic proletarian writer this country has ever known—and who had identified himself consciously with the downtrodden plebes. Melville was a writer who took Whitman's democratic affirmations and made them into a wonderfully concrete and fraternal poetry. If he had been willing to welcome Indians, South Sea cannibals, Africans, and Parsees (we were not quite sure who Parsees were!), he might have been prepared to admit a Jew or two onto the *Pequod* if he had happened to think of it.

The closeness one felt toward Melville I can only suggest by saying that when he begins with those utterly thrilling words, "Call me Ishmael," we knew immediately that this meant he was not Ishmael, he was really Isaac. He was the son who had taken the blessing and then, in order to set out for the forbidden world, had also taken his brother's unblessed name. We knew that this Isaac-cum-Ishmael was a mama's boy trying to slide or swagger into the world of power; that he took the job because he had to earn a living, because he wanted to fraternize with workers, and because he needed to prove himself in the chill of the world. When he had told mother Sarah that he was leaving, oh, what a tearful scene that was! "Isaac," she had said, "Isaac, be careful," and so careful did he turn out to be that in order to pass in the gentile world he said, Call me Ishmael. And we too would ask the world to call us Ishmael, both the political world and the literary world, in whose chill we also wanted to prove ourselves while expecting that finally we would still be recognized as Isaacs.

The stranger who wore Redburn's hunting jacket and subjected himself to trials of initiation on Ahab's ship, this stranger seemed "one of us," as we could never quite suppose the heroes of Cooper or Twain or Hawthorne were "one of us." These remained alien writers, wonderful but distant, while Melville was our brother, a loose-fish as we were loose-fish.

To be a loose-fish seemed admirable. Alienation was a badge we carried with pride, and our partial deracination—roots loosened in Jewish soil but still not torn out, roots lowered into American soil but still not fixed—gave us a range of possibilities. Some we seized. The American Jewish writers began developing styles that were new to American literature. That we should regard ourselves as partisans of modernism, defenders of the European experimentalists against middle-brow sluggards and know-nothing nativists—this followed a pattern already established in America. Decades earlier the first struggling painters to escape from the immigrant Jewish milieu, figures like Abraham Walkowitz and Max Weber, had leapt across their worthy American contemporaries in order to become pupils at the School of Paris. That, simultaneously, we should respond with pleasure and draw upon the styles of the popular Jewish entertainers, from Fanny Brice to the Marx Brothers, from Willie and Eugene Howard to S. J. Perelman—this too was made possible by the freedom of our partial deracination.

Not fixed into a coherent style, we could imitate many. Not bound by an enclosing tradition, we could draw upon many. It was a remarkable feat for Alfred Kazin, still under thirty and living in Brooklyn, to write a book called *On Native Grounds* in which he commandeered the whole of American prose fiction. It was a canny self-insight for Paul Goodman to declare his cousinship with Emerson and his American patriotism as a sign of anarchist desire, even though most of his friends, including myself, were not quite sure what he was up to. And it was a display of sheer virtuosity, the virtuosity of a savored freedom, for Saul Bellow to write in *Henderson the Rain King* a pure Emersonian fiction, quite as if he had finally wrenched loose from Napoleon Street and the Hotel Ansonia.

Imitation could not always be distinguished from improvisation. If I ask myself, where did the style of the *Partisan Review* essay come from—a style I have elsewhere described as "nervous, strewn with knotty or flashy phrases, impatient with transitions and other concessions to dullness, wilfully calling attention to itself as a form of outcry, fond of rapid twists, taking pleasure in dispute, dialectic, dazzle"—I think I know a few of the sources. The early Van Wyck Brooks may be one, Edmund Wilson another, and some Continental writers too. But I want also to add that *we made it up*, or rather, the writers of a decade earlier than myself, those who started out in the middle 'thirties, dreamed it out of their visions or fantasies of what a cosmopolitan style should be. They drew upon Eliot and Trotsky, perhaps also Baudelaire and Valéry, but finally they made it up: a pastiche, brilliant, aggressive, unstable.

It remains, then, an interesting question why it was that while the first literary passions of the American Jewish intellectuals were directed toward modernism, there was rather little modernist experimentation among the American Jewish writers of fiction. I have a few simple answers. In their imaginations these writers were drawn to Eliot and Joyce, Kafka and Brecht, but the stories most of them composed had little to do with the styles or methods of modernism. Modernism had come to America a decade earlier, in the 'twenties, with Hemingway and Faulkner, Eliot and Stevens, Crane and Williams. By the 'thirties, when the generation of Schwartz and Bellow began to write, experimentalism no longer seemed so very experimental; it was something one rushed to defend but also, perhaps, with some inner uneasiness. To the revolution of modernism we were latecomers.

But more. Reaching American literature with heads full of European writing yet also still held by the narrowness of experience in the cities, the American Jewish writers turned inevitably and compulsively to their own past, or to that feverish turf of the imagination they declared to be their past. It was the one area of American life they knew closely and could handle authoritatively, no more able to abandon it in memory than bear it in actuality. The sense of place is as overpowering in their work as, say, in the stories of Eudora Welty and Flannery O'Connor, soon becoming a sense of fate: hovering, lowering, confining, lingering, utterly imperious.

In the end, as we like to say, it was upon language that the American Jewish writers left their mark. Just as the blacks left theirs upon the vocabulary of American music, so the Jews brought to the language of fiction turnings of voice, feats of irony, and tempos of delivery that helped create a new American style— probably a short-lived style and brought to fulfillment in the work of a mere handful of writers, but a new style nonetheless. Style speaks of sensibility, slant, vision; speaks here of a certain high excitability, a rich pumping of blood, which the Jews brought with their baggage, a grating mixture of the

sardonic and sentimental, a mish-mash of gutter wisdom and graduate
school learning. I think it no exaggeration to say that since Faulkner
and Hemingway the one major innovation in American prose style has
been the yoking of street raciness and high-culture mandarin which we
associate with American Jewish writers.

Not, to be sure, all of them. There really is no single style that is
shared by these writers, and some—Delmore Schwartz in the artifice
of his anti-rhetoric, Michael Seide in the mild purity of his diction,
Tillie Olson in her own passionate idiom—clearly challenge the
generalizations I shall nevertheless make. For what I want to assert is
that the dominant American Jewish style is the one brought to a pitch
by Saul Bellow and imitated and modified by a good many others.

In the growth of this style one can see reenacted a pattern through
which our nineteenth-century writers created the major American
styles. Cooper and Hawthorne, though fresh in their matter, still
employed versions of formal Augustan prose; even as they were doing
so, however, a language of native storytellers and folkloristic colloquialism was being forged by the humorists of the Old Southwest and
the Western frontier; and then, to complete a much-too-neat triad,
Twain and Melville blended formal prose with native speech, the
heritage from England with the improvisations of American regions,
into a style that in Twain might be called purified demotic and in
Melville democratic extravagance.

A similar development, on a much smaller scale, has been at work in
the fiction of the American Jewish writers. The first collection of stories
by Abraham Cahan, *Yekl*, is written in a baneful dialect so naturalisti-
cally faithful, or intent upon being faithful, to the immigrant moment
that it now seems about as exotic and inaccessible as the argot of Sut
Lovingood. Cahan's major novel, *The Rise of David Levinsky*,
employs, by contrast, a flavorless standard English, the prose of an
earnest but somewhat tone-deaf student worried about proper usage.
More interesting for its mythic narrative line than for verbal detail, this
novel shows Cahan to be not quite in possession of *any* language, either
English or Yiddish, a condition that was common enough among the
immigrants and, in the case of their occasionally talented sons, would
become the shifting ground upon which to build a shifty new style. The
problem foreshadowed in Cahan's work is: how can the Yiddishisms of
East Side street talk and an ill-absorbed "correct" prose painfully ac-
quired in night school be fused into some higher stylistic enterprise?

One answer, still the most brilliant, came in Henry Roth's *Call It
Sleep*, a major novel blending a Joyce roughened to the tonalities of
New York and deprived of his Irish lilt with a Yiddish oddly transposed
into a pure and lyrical English but with its rhythms slightly askew, as if

to reveal immigrant origins. In Roth's novel the children speak a
ghastly, mutilated sort of English while the main adult characters talk in
Yiddish, which Roth renders as a high poetic, somewhat offbeat, English. Thus, the mother tells her little boy: "Aren't you just a pair of eyes
and ears! You see, you hear, you remember, but when will you know?
. . . And no kisses? . . . There! Savory, thrifty lips!" The last phrase
may seem a bit too "poetic" in English speech, but if you translate it
into Yiddish—*Na! geshmake, karge lipelakh!*—it rings exactly right,
beautifully idiomatic. Roth is here continuing the tradition of Jewish
bilingualism, in the past a coexistence of Hebrew as sacred and Yiddish
or Ladino as demotic language; but he does this in an oddly surreptitious way, by making of English, in effect, two languages, or by writing
portions of this book in one language and expecting that some readers
will be able to hear it in another.

Yet, so far as I can tell, Roth has not been a major stylistic influence
upon later American Jewish writers, perhaps because his work seems
so self-contained there is nothing much to do with it except admire.
Perhaps a more useful precursor is Daniel Fuchs, a lovely and neglected writer, especially in his second novel *Homage to Blenholt*,
where one begins to hear a new music, a new tempo, as if to echo the
beat of the slums.

This American Jewish style, which comes to fulfillment and perhaps
terminus with Bellow, I would describe in a few desperate phrases:

A forced yoking of opposites: gutter vividness and university refinement, street energy and high culture rhetoric.

A strong infusion of Yiddish, not so much through the occasional use
of a phrase or word as through an importation of ironic twistings that
transform the whole of language, so to say, into a corkscrew of questions.

A rapid, nervous, breathless tempo, like the hurry of a garment
salesman trying to con a buyer or a highbrow lecturer trying to dazzle
an audience.

A deliberate loosening of syntax, as if to mock those niceties of
Correct English which Gore Vidal and other untainted Americans hold
dear, so that in consequence there is much greater weight upon trans-
itory patches of color than upon sentences in repose or paragraphs in
composure.

A deliberate play with the phrasings of plebeian speech, but often
the kind that vibrates with cultural ambition, seeking to zoom into the
regions of higher thought.

In short, the linguistic tokens of writers who must hurry into articulateness if they are to be heard at all, indeed, who must scrape together
a language. This style reflects a demotic upsurge, the effort to give

literary scale to the speech of immigrant streets, or put another way, to create a "third language," richer and less stuffy, out of the fusion of English and Yiddish that had already occurred spontaneously in those streets. Our writers did not, of course, create a new language, and in the encounter between English and Yiddish, the first has survived far better than the second; but still, *we* have left our scar, tiny though it be, on *their* map.

The other day a gentle friend of mine remarked that in getting from City College in uptown Manhattan to the City University's Graduate Center at Forty-Second Street she had had a long *shlep*. She used this word without a trace of self-consciousness, and she was right, for what she had experienced was not quite an inconvenience nor even a drag, it was a *shlep*. The word in Yiddish bears a multitude of burdens, as if to take a New York subway comes, as indeed it does, to taking on the weight of the world. *Shlep* is becoming part of the American language and in the hard days ahead it can only help.

But there is more. There is the *shlepper*, in whom the qualities of *shlepping* have become a condition of character. There is a *shlep-penish*, an experience that exhausts the spirit and wearies the body. And as virtual apotheosis there is *shlepperei*, which raises the burdens of *shlepping* into a statement about the nature of the world. Starbuck unable to resist Ahab was a bit of a *shlepper*, Prufrock afraid to eat his peach made his life into a *shleppenish*, Herzog ground down by his impossible women transformed all of existence into sheer *shlepperei*.

Of such uncouth elements is the American language made and re-made. Upon such renewals does the American experience thrive. And if indeed our dream of a New World paradise is ever to be realized, this time beyond mere innocence, how can we ever expect to get there except through the club-foot certainties of *shlepping*?

THE FIFTIES

A NEGRO IN AMERICA

Ralph Ellison's *Invisible Man* is a searing and exalted record of a Negro's journey through contemporary America in search of success, companionship, and, finally, himself; like all our fictions devoted to the idea of experience, it moves from province to city, from naive faith to disenchantment; and despite its structural incoherence and occasional pretentiousness of manner, it is one of the most remarkable first novels we have had in years.

The beginning is nightmare. A Negro boy, timid and compliant, comes to a white smoker in a Southern town, there to be awarded a scholarship. Together with several other Negroes he is rushed to the front of the ballroom, where a sumptuous blonde tantalizes and frightens them by dancing in the nude. Blindfolded, the Negro boys stage a "battle royal," a free-for-all in which they pummel each other to the drunken shouts of the whites. "Practical jokes," humiliations, terrors—and then the boy delivers a prepared speech of gratitude to his white benefactors.

Nothing in the rest of the novel is quite so harrowing. The unnamed hero goes to his Southern college and is expelled for having innocently taken a white donor through a Negro gin-mill; he then leaves for New York, where he works in a factory, becomes a soapboxer for the Harlem Communists, a big wheel in the Negro world, and the darling of the

Stalinist bohemia; and finally, in some not quite specified way, after witnessing a frenzied riot in Harlem, he "finds himself."

Though immensely gifted, Ellison is not a finished craftsman. The tempo of his book is too feverish, and at times almost hysterical. Too often he tries to overwhelm the reader, and usually he does; but when he should be doing something other than overwhelm, when he should be persuading or suggesting or simply telling, he forces and tears.

Because the book is written in the first person singular, Ellison finds it hard to establish ironic distance between his hero and himself, between the matured "I" telling the story and the "I" who is its victim. And because the experience is so apocalyptic and magnified, it absorbs and then dissolves the hero; every minor character comes through brilliantly, but the seeing "I" is seldom seen.

The middle section of the novel, which concerns the Harlem Stalinists, is the only one that strikes me as not quite true. Writing with evident bitterness, Ellison makes his Stalinists so stupid and vicious that one cannot understand how they could ever have attracted him. I am ready to believe that the Communist Party manipulates its members with conscious cynicism, but I am quite certain that this cynicism is both more guarded and complex than Ellison assumes; surely no Stalinist leader would tell a prominent Negro member, "You were not hired to think"—even if that were what he secretly felt. The trouble with such caricature is that it undermines the intention behind it, making the Stalinists seem not the danger they are but mere clowns.

Equally disturbing is Ellison's apparent wish to be intellectually up-to-date. As his hero quits the Communist Party, he wonders: "Could politics ever be an expression of love?" This portentous and perhaps meaningless question, whatever its place in a little magazine, is surely inappropriate to a character who has been presented mainly as a passive victim of experience. Nor am I persuaded by the hero's final discovery that "my world has become one of infinite possibilities," his refusal to be the invisible man whose body is manipulated by various social groups. Though the unqualified assertion of individuality is at the moment a favorite notion of literary people, it is also a vapid one, for the unfortunate fact remains that in defining one's individuality one is very likely to stumble across social barriers that do not allow "infinite possibilities." It is hardly an accident that Ellison's hero does not even attempt to specify those possibilities.

These faults mar *Invisible Man* but do not destroy it. For Ellison has an abundance of that primary talent without which neither craft nor intelligence can save a novelist; he is richly, wildly inventive; his scenes rise and dip with tension, his people bleed, his language stings. No other writer has captured so much of the confusion and agony, the hidden gloom and surface gaiety of Negro life. His ear for Negro speech is magnificent: a sharecropper calmly describing how he seduced his daughter, a Harlem-street-vender spinning jive, a West Indian woman inciting her men to resist an eviction. The rhythm of the prose is harsh and tensed, like a beat of harried alertness. The observation is expert: Ellison knows exactly how the antagonism between American and West Indian Negroes works itself out in speech and humor. For all his self-involvement, he is capable of extending himself toward his people, of accepting them as they are, in their blindness and hope. And in his final scene he has created an unforgettable image: "Ras the Destroyer," a Negro nationalist, appears on a horse, dressed in the costume of an Abyssinian chieftain, carrying spear and shield, and charging wildly into the police—a black Quixote, mad, absurd, unbearably pathetic.

Some reviewers, from the best of intentions, have assured their readers that this is a good novel and not merely a good Negro novel. But of course *Invisible Man* is a Negro novel—what white man could ever have written it? It is drenched in Negro life, talk, music; it tells us how distant even the best of the whites are from the black men that pass them on the streets; and it is written from a particular compound of emotions that no white man could possibly simulate. To deny that this is a Negro novel is to deprive Negroes of their one basic right: the right to cry out their difference.

Postscript

In this piece, as in several others to come, I use the term "Negro" rather than "black." When I wrote my review of Ralph Ellison's book, the word "black" would have seemed an insult. Conventions of courtesy change, of course, and it seems appropriate that in the seventies one should say "black." Nevertheless, I also think it would be a mistake—a violation of the historical spirit—retroactively to change "Negro" to "black" in pieces written during the fifties and sixties.

THE STORIES OF BERNARD MALAMUD

It is very hard to describe the stories in *The Magic Barrel* with any sort of exactness—and not because they are so weird or exotic but because they are genuinely original. Part of the shock of pleasure in reading them comes from the discovery that one's initial response is mistaken. One reacts, first of all, to Malamud's painfully familiar setting: the Jewish immigrant neighborhood of the depression years. Here, predictably, are the Jewish grocery-man dragging in cases of milk each morning, the Jewish baker slowly expiring over his ovens. Somewhat later in time comes the Jewish graduate student fumbling his way through Rome, eager to grasp knowledge of the Gentile world yet perversely oppressed by a strange Jew, an archetypal *nudnik*, who in his unqualified shamelessness represents the claim that each Jew has on all others: the claim of trouble.

Malamud's stories bring back, for a page or two, memories of half-forgotten novels: the cramped, grey, weepy aura of "American Jewish" fiction. But then one learns that Malamud is not so easily "placed," and that if it is legitimate to admire the care with which he summons the Jewish immigrant world, an important reason is that he treats it as no writer before him—except perhaps Daniel Fuchs—has ever done.

For in each of Malamud's best stories something surprising happens: it is as if the speed of the movie reel were crazily increased, as if the characters leapt clear of the earth, as if a Chagall painting snapped into motion and its figures, long frozen in mid-air, began to dip and soar. The place is familiar; but the tone, the tempo, the treatment are all new.

In what way? Malamud, as it seems to me, moves not to surrealism or fantasy but to a realistic fable in which the life cycle is exhausted at double-time: a wink, a shrug, a collapse. Everything—action, dialogue, comment—is sped up, driven to a climax in which a gesture compresses and releases an essential meaning, and the characters, hurtling themselves across a dozen pages, rise to a fabulous sort of "Yiddish" articulateness of gesture and speech.

Now, in any obvious sense this is not realism at all: the stories seldom plot along accumulating incidents, and they frequently diverge from strict standards of probability in order to leap-frog to dramatic moments of revelation. Nonetheless, their essential economy, the psychological pattern to which they remain loyal, can be called "realistic": for they aim at verisimilitude in depth, they are closely responsive to a serious public morality, they wish ultimately to indicate that this is the way things *really* are. Malamud spurs the realistic story to a pace so feverish as to leave behind the usual stylizations of realism, but the moral and psychological intentions that are typical of realistic stories continue to operate in his work.

This is a procedure with obvious dangers. Partly they are inherent ones, since his stories usually involve gambling everything on one or two paragraphs; partly they seem the result of a manner that Malamud shares with a good many other recent American Jewish writers: a jazzed-up, slap-dash, knock-em-down-and-hit-em-again approach to language and action. In his inferior stories Malamud depends too much on hard and flashy climaxes, so that the most beautiful aspect of his novel *The Assistant*—its hum of contemplativeness, its quiet humane undertone—is not to be found here. And too often Malamud's stories seem excessively brilliant on the surface, a ruthless dash for effect, and then one has the feeling that one is being bullied and blinded by a virtuoso.

But these are incidental faults, and at his best Malamud has worked out for himself a kind of story that is spectacularly successful. In "The Loan," Kobotsky, an impoverished Jew, comes to his old friend Lieb, an aging and harassed baker, to ask for some money. Years ago they had quarreled, but still a spark of feeling survives. Among his other troubles Lieb now has a second wife, Bessie, who shares with him the tears of poverty and adds some salt of her own. Kobotsky begs for his loan on the ground that his wife is sick, but Bessie, who must make the final decision, remains unmoved; then Kobotsky tells the truth, his wife has been dead for five years and he wants the money to buy a long overdue stone for her grave. Bessie, who can identify with a wife in a grave more easily than with a wife in a hospital, begins to weaken. Gathering force and lyricism, the story now speeds along to its climax:

through a device I shall not disclose, Malamud achieves another reversal, this time to show that Bessie's heart has again hardened and Lieb will not be able to help his friend. The last paragraph:

Kobotsky and the baker embraced and sighed over their lost youth. They pressed mouths together and parted forever.

Now by any usual standard this ending is melodramatic and most improbable: Jews like Kobotsky and Lieb do not press mouths together. But in the story the ending works, since it embodies what Malamud could neither have represented through ordinary realism nor risked stating in his own right: the beauty of defeat as a kind of love. And the reason it works is that Malamud has prepared for surprise by leading us so surely from one moment of suppressed intensity to another that the burst of pressure which creates the final excitement also dissolves any lingering expectations of ordinary realism. It is for similar reasons that one does not find it disturbing that in the superb title story a matchmaker who has arranged for a meeting between a rabbinical student and his (apparently) sluttish daughter, should watch them on the sly, chanting "prayers for the dead." Such incidents, in Malamud's stories, are not symbolic; they are synoptic.

At his best, then, Malamud has managed to bring together that sense of the power of external circumstance which so overwhelmed writers a few decades ago and the concern of more recent writers for the gratuitous sign that declares a man's humanity even as it is being crushed. The settings contribute an atmosphere of limitation, oppression, coercion: man is not free. The action and language preserve, through the renewing powers of imagination, the possibility of freedom.

Malamud is one of the very few American writers about whom it makes sense to say that his work has a distinctly "Jewish" tone. He writes as if the ethos of Yiddish literature, the quiver of *menshlichkeit*, had, through a miraculous salvage, become his possession. And he preserves this heritage with an easiness, a lack of self-consciousness, that makes most American Jewish writers seem local colorists exploiting accidental associations. Malamud can grind a character to the earth, but there is always a hard ironic pity, a wry affection better than wet gestures of love, which makes him seem a grandson of the Yiddish writers. How this has happened I cannot say, for my guess would be that Malamud does not have a close knowledge of Yiddish literature; but perhaps the moral is that for those who know why to wait, the magic barrel will reappear.

THE SUBURBS OF BABYLON

What many writers spend a lifetime searching for—a unique voice, a secure rhythm, a distinctive subject—seem to have come to Philip Roth totally and immediately. At 26 he is a writer of narrow range but intense effects. He composes stories about the life of middle-class American Jews with a ferocity it would be idle to complain about, so thoroughly do they pour out of his own sense of things.

Mr. Roth's stories in *Goodbye, Columbus* do not yield pleasure as much as produce a squirm of recognition: surely, one feels, not all of American Jewish life is like this, but all too much of it is becoming so. Anyone who might object to these stories insofar as they are "reports" about a style of life cannot do it on the ground that Mr. Roth is hard-spirited—for given his material what else can he be?—or that he is unskilled—for, like so many other young writers these days, he has quickly absorbed the lessons of modern craftsmanship, perhaps a bit too quickly. If one is to object to these stories on nonliterary grounds, out of a concern for the feelings or reputation of middle class American Jews, it can be done only by charging that, in effect, Mr. Roth is a liar. And that, I am convinced, he is not.

Like any lively new writer, Mr. Roth takes his place in a tradition and, because he has something fresh to say, helps extend and transform it. But, for reasons I shall come to, he may be helping to collapse it. There is by now a considerable number of novelists and story writers who take as their dominant concern the moral and psychic consequences of the great transformation in American Jewish life: the transformation from proletarian immigrant poverty to middle class suburban comfort, which has all too often meant, from tragi-comic intensities to a dreary slackness. It is a theme which allows for as full a play of satire and as rich a notation of manners as the contrast between established gentry and ambitious climbers in the 19th Century English novel. Yet it has seldom been worked with anything like a similar success, mainly because American Jewish writers have been caught up in a crippling problem of involvement. The subject proves to be both terribly close—finally, it's about one's mama and papa—and frustratingly transient—it has all occurred within a few decades and now it's almost over, the conflicts of value and generation resolved badly, the memories curdled, the pain dulled.

In the title story of *Goodbye, Columbus*—it's really a short novel—Mr. Roth focuses upon a Jewish young man in Newark, Neil Klugman, who works in a public library to see himself through college, lives with his plain, anxious Aunt Gladys (she, relic, goes to Workmen's Circle picnics) and as his name ("Cleverfellow") suggests, is a budding intellectual. One gathers that in some sense Neil is a version of the author, yet Mr. Roth, to his credit, presents Neil with a matter-of-fact detachment which eliminates chances for self-pity.

Neil meets up with Brenda Patimkin, a sleek and likable Radcliffe girl, the daughter of a Jewish *alrightnik*, which is to say, a manufacturer of sinks who used to sweat in the Newark slums but having made his pile, now lives in a green suburb. There follows a nervous summer romance between Neil and Brenda, through which Mr. Roth skillfully—I suppose the word had better be, ruthlessly—charts the varieties of amiable vulgarity, *arriviste* snobbism and sheer mindlessness to be found in the world of the Patimkins. Mr. Roth is more tender, though equally successful, at evoking the eager heavy sexuality of the girl as it registers upon and stirs up the ambitious boy. Brenda's sense of social place enables her, somewhat like Daisy Buchanan in *The Great Gatsby*, to come through unscathed from the break-up of the affair, for it is this sense of social place—of money, family, security— which permits her to take emotional risks without quite knowing that they are risks.

(*"The rich are different,"* said Fitzgerald. *"Yes, they have more money,"* answered Hemingway, thinking he had scored a knockout when he had merely swung wild. For what in America could so make for a sense of "difference" as having more money?)

The best parts of "Goodbye, Columbus," done with a deadpan malicious accuracy, are those in which Mr. Roth sketches the manners and morals of the Patimkins. It is harsh but alas, true, the father barging through life with his rough, mean sentimentality, the mother coolly quizzing Neil as to whether he is Orthodox, Conservative or Reform, and the brother, more gentile than the gentiles, fulfilling the bonehead pattern of the All-American boy.

To the uninformed reader all of this might seem to verge on caricature, but I think it is ferociously exact. Indeed, that is the trouble: it is too exact, too close to surface realities, there is not enough imaginative transformation. Mr. Roth is dedicated to a kind of mimetic revenge, with the result that about two thirds of the way through "Goodbye Columbus" one feels a drop of interest. For anyone familiar with the Patimkin world the outcome of the story is as predictable as the life of one's cousin.

In Mr. Roth's other stories, arresting as they are, one finds similar difficulties. The main reason for this repeated drop of interest is that Mr. Roth is a writer concerning whom the much-abused adjective "compulsive" seems really to apply. All of his stories use their subjects as targets; all drive openly to moral conclusions, hammered out with aggressive intent; and as Alfred Kazin has remarked, some of them are too easily absorbed in the "points" they make, leaving little to contemplate except these "points."

Given Mr. Roth's skill and intelligence, why should this be so? I think a possible answer may be that in his stories he cannot find sufficiently energetic and supple forces to resist the spiritual corrosion of Jewish middle-class life. That he personally has discovered some basis for resistance is obvious from the fact that he writes at all; but he does not manage to embody this resistance with enough vigor in the stories themselves.

Perhaps the reason for this is that Mr. Roth, while emotionally involved with his subject, is one of the first American Jewish writers who finds, so far as I can judge, almost no sustenance in the Jewish tradition. Writers like Daniel Fuchs, Delmore Schwartz and Bernard Malamud have also dealt harshly with the life of middle-class American Jews, but to one or another extent the terms of their attack have been drawn from memories of Jewish childhood and family life, from the values of the Jewish tradition. Mr. Roth, however, finds little here to sustain him; he does not remember or think it significant that Neil's Aunt Gladys may once have been a Yiddishist firebrand or a trade union enthusiast; and for this, I suppose, he can hardly be blamed: the memory *is* growing dim.

It is possible that this signifies the end of a tradition, the closing of an arc of American Jewish experience. If so, that is a saddening thought, since it is hard to see what new sources of value are likely to replace the

Yiddishist tradition and the American Jewish *milieu* at its best, against which many of us rebelled but which, by shaping the nature of our rebellion, helped to give meaning to our lives.

Still, none of this should detract from Mr. Roth's achievement. Nor should it give an inch of encouragement to those in the "Jewish community" who have begun to mutter against his book as an instance of "self-hatred."

Postscript

The above was written as a review of Philip Roth's first and, I think, his best book. A dozen or so years later I did an essay on Roth's work as a whole, much more sharply critical in judgment; it appears in my book *The Critical Point*. Perhaps there are some points of conflict between the early review and the later essay; perhaps not. But nowhere is it written that critics cannot or should not modify their opinions as time goes by.

MAILER'S POLITICAL NOVEL

At the drop of a memory, literary people will tell you that the critics of the thirties sinned in judging novels by political rather than esthetic standards. Some of these very people are now attacking Norman Mailer's *Barbary Shore* on grounds that are almost entirely political, and in a few reviews attacking with nasty invective and bad faith. Only Maxwell Geismar has discussed the book with the considerateness that a gifted writer like Mailer deserves. *Barbary Shore*, as it happens, is a bad novel, but not because Mailer has chosen to express, or employ, an unpopular political outlook.

Apparently Mailer has taken to heart the dubious notion that naturalism is "exhausted" and Kafkaesque symbolism the only recourse for a serious novelist. *Barbary Shore* is crammed with symbols and can be read as a political allegory, but it does not do the first things a novel should: create dramatic tension and arouse interest in its characters. Since one cannot become involved with the weird collection of disembodied voices Mailer has brought together in a Brooklyn rooming-house, one does not care what they "stand for." The meaning of symbols in a work of art matters only when they enchant, disturb, or otherwise arouse us in their own right.

Another trouble here is that Mailer writes badly. His lumpy and graceless prose is strewn with quasi-intellectual chatter and stiff with echoes of radical jargon, "progressive" journalism, and WPA living-newspaper skits. Once a writer has been exposed to such influences it is hard for him to develop a style, but there is no evidence in *Barbary Shore* that Mailer is even aware of the problem.

Because its action is merely a lifeless posturing and its prose is savorless, the political message of *Barbary Shore* does not seem to me very impressive. And for another reason: if the critic has no business judging a work of art in terms of political opinion, he has every right to judge the *quality* of its thought. Though I roughly agree with Mailer's position of intransigent socialism, I find myself embarrassed by his crude formulations and the tone of pious, apocalyptic certainty with which he delivers them. It is one thing to say that capitalism and Stalinism are both reactionary societies and that a political identification with the first may lead to a political victory of the second; but it is sheer cant to suggest that the absolute dictatorship of Russia and the limited but real democracy of the United States are, or are soon likely to be, "two virtually identical forms of exploitation."

I cavil at Mailer's tone not because doubt is necessarily good "in itself" or because the sort of "open mind" some liberals affect is particularly admirable. It is simply that if one is to try to remain a radical these days and not surrender to cynicism or weariness or atomic hysteria, one *must* be torn by doubts, one must reexamine every scrap of doctrine and every step of action to see where and why things went wrong, one must engage in the "soul-searching" that is scorned equally by the kind of dogmatic Marxist who is content to have predicted catastrophes he did not avert and by the kind of complacent liberal who now boasts, after years of guilt over his timidity, that he was never "taken in." (The kind of liberal, I mean, who has discovered that "the end does not justify the means" but is reconciled to the probability of an atom war.)

The trouble is that Mailer has come to his radicalism a little late: he does not really know in his flesh and bones what happened to the socialist hope in the era of Hitler and Stalin, and that is why he can refer so cavalierly to democracy and carry on like a stale pamphleteer. He is sincere and he is serious; I admire his courage in writing a book he must have known would bring him grief and attack. But I can only say that his relation to his material, like his presentation of it, is not authentic. Otherwise he would not seem so sure.

THE SNOPES SAGA

The Snopeses have always been there. No sooner did Faulkner come upon his central subject—how the corruption of the homeland, staining its best sons, left them without standards or defense—than Snopesism followed inexorably. Almost anyone can detect the Snopeses, but describing them is very hard. The usual reference to "amorality," while accurate, is not sufficiently distinctive and by itself does not allow us to place them, as they should be placed, in a historical moment. Perhaps the most important thing to be said about the Snopeses is that they are what comes afterwards: the creatures that emerge from the devastation, with the slime still upon their lips.

Let a world collapse, in the South or Russia, and there appear figures of coarse ambition driving their way up from beneath the social bottom, men to whom moral claims are not so much absurd as incomprehensible, sons of bushwhackers or *muzhiks* drifting in from nowhere and taking over through the sheer outrageousness of their monolithic force. They become presidents of local banks and chairmen of party regional committees, and later, a trifle slicked up, they muscle their way into Congress or the Politburo. Scavengers without inhibition, they need not believe in the crumbling official code of their society; they need only learn to mimic its sounds.

In a prefatory note to *The Mansion*, the novel which completes the Snopes trilogy, Faulkner says that he has been working on this clan

41

since 1925. We can well believe it. The Snopeses have appeared in earlier books, *Sartoris* and *Sanctuary*, which contain snatches of portraiture or anecdote later to be worked up in *The Hamlet*, *The Town* and *The Mansion*. One would speculate that by the mid-twenties, after Faulkner had returned to Mississippi from World War I, the originals of Snopesism, red-neck rascals and demagogues, had come to the social forefront. Perhaps it was some shock of perception, some encounter with an adulterated (because real-life) model of Flem or I.O. or Ike Snopes, which first prompted him to look back into the fate of the homeland, mulling over the collapse of the Sartorises and Compsons which left the field open for Flem Snopes and his plague of relatives.

In Faulkner's version—it is simply grounded in historical reality—the South by the turn of the century had come to resemble a social vacuum. The homeland drifted in poverty and xenophobia, without social direction or moral authority. Traditional relationships had decayed but there were no workable new ones. Into this vacuum, with a shattering energy, came the Snopeses. And insofar as they are both its sign and product, Faulkner's description of them in *The Hamlet* as "sourceless" is brilliant.

Most of *The Hamlet*, published in 1940, was written during the previous ten or twelve years, and together with *Go Down, Moses*, brings to a close Faulkner's great creative period. It is a comic extravaganza, half family chronicle and half tall tale, strung together in loosely-related episodes that portray the swarming of the Snopeses upon Frenchman's Bend, a hamlet in a rich river-bottom, "hill-cradled and remote," at the southern rim of Yoknapatawpha county. By the end of the book Flem Snopes, who had begun as a clerk in the village store, is ready to leave for Jefferson, the town where he will become a bank president and then owner of a splendid mansion.

Flem towers over the book, a figure with a marvellous energy for deceit, an almost Jonsonian monomania in pursuit of money. In Flem, Faulkner has embodied the commercial ethos with a grotesque purity, both as it represents the power of an undeviating will and as it appears in its ultimate flimsiness. This *tour de force* depends upon Faulkner's refusal to make Flem "human," his steadiness in holding Flem to an extreme conception which, violating verisimilitude, reaches truth. Though Flem stands for everything Faulkner despises and fears, he is treated in *The Hamlet* with a comic zest, a sheer amazement that such a monster could exist or even be imagined. The danger is real, but the battlefield still confined, and opposed to Flem there stands as a mature antagonist, if in the end a defeated one, the humane sewing-machine agent V. K. Ratliff. One of the few "positive" characters in Faulkner's novels who is utterly convincing and neither hysterical nor a canting windbag, Ratliff provides an aura of security for the book. His very presence makes possible a sustained comic perspective upon the Snopes invasion, and in its own right speaks for the possibilities of civilized existence. Seventeen years intervened between *The Hamlet* and *The Town,* years of a slowly mounting crisis in Faulkner's career. The more he kept reassuring us that man would "endure," the less assurance his own work showed. Though the novels he wrote in the forties and fifties contain many fine and even brilliant parts, they are on the whole forced, anxious and high-pitched, the work of a man, no longer driven, who now drives himself. *Intruder in the Dust* launches the marvellous Negro curmudgeon Lucas Beauchamp, but goes utterly dead with pages of barren Southern oratory. *Requiem for a Nun* contains some exquisite rhapsodic interludes, but in the central sections, so clearly meant to be dramatic, it falls into inert statement. *The Fable,* which may come to hold a place in Faulkner's work analogous to *Pierre* in Melville's, is a book noble in conception but incoherent in execution. What went wrong? In all these works there is a reliance upon a high-powered rhetoric which bears the outer marks of the earlier Faulkner style, but is really a kind of self-imitation, a whipped-up fury pouring out in wanton excess. There is a tendency to fall back upon hi-jinks of plot, a flaunting arbitrariness and whimsicality of invention—as if Faulker, wearied of telling stories and establishing characters, were now deliberately breaking his own spell and betraying an impatience with his own skill. Consciously or not, he seems to be underscoring the incongruity between the overwrought, perhaps incommunicable seriousness of his intentions—his having reached a point where language seems no longer to suffice—and the triviality of the devices to which he turns.

There is, further, an apparent disengagement, perhaps even a disenchantment with the Yoknapatawpha locale which had fruitfully obsessed him in the past. Faulker has now entered the familiar workaday world in which you and I live, at least one part of him has, the man you see in the photographs dressed in a natty grey topcoat; and no longer is it possible to imagine him, like Balzac, calling on his deathbed for a doctor—"get old Doc Peabody!"—from his own novels. His creative journey, begun with the nihilism of the twenties in *Soldier's Pay,* has led him, not as his conservative critics have maintained, to the strength of a traditionalist morality but to the more perilous edge of the nihilism of the fifties.

Faulkner has become our contemporary. He can no longer work within his established means; one senses a bewilderment and disorientation spreading through his pages, by which the subject of his earlier novels now becomes the force constraining his later ones. How else can one explain the frantic verbal outpourings of Gavin Stevens, the character so disastrously his *alter* ego? Anyone with a touch of feeling, to say nothing of respect, must respond to this new Faulkner who so evidently shares our hesitations and doubts. But in truth this is no longer the man who wrote *The Sound and the Fury,* not even the one who wrote *The Hamlet.*

By the time he turned back to the Snopeses, completing the trilogy in the last few years, Faulkner could sustain neither his old fury nor his old humor. Both, to be sure, break out repeatedly in *The Town* and *The Mansion;* there are sections which, if torn out of context, read nearly as well as anything he has done in the past. But they have to be torn out of context. Nor is the difficulty to be found in the over-all design of the trilogy. That, on the contrary, is superb. Faulkner sees how Flem Snopes must assume the appearance of respectability, which in turn will rob him of a portion of his demonic powers and pinch him into an ordinary helplessness. Faulker also sees how Flem, though safe from attack by the "traditionalist" moral leaders of the county, must meet his destruction at the hands of a Nemesis from within his tribe: Mink Snopes, a pitiful terrier of a man who spends 38 years in jail because, as he believes, Flem has failed him, and who knows that the meaning of his life is now to kill Flem.

Indeed, one can anticipate scores of critical essays which will trace the ways in which each incident in the trilogy contributes to the total scheme, and which thereby will create the false impression that a satisfying congruence exists between the conceptual design and the novels as they are. (This, I think, is the single greatest weakness of American criticism today: that, in its infatuation with the ideas of literary structure as a system of thematic strands, it fails to consider performance, execution as the decisive measure.) Yet, as regards *The Town* and *The Mansion,* such a congruence is not to be found, for only fitfully do these novels fulfill the needs and possibilities of Faulkner's over-all design.

Let me cite an example. One of the Snopeses, Cla'ence, goes in for politics and in 1945, running for Congress, suddenly declares himself an opponent of the KKK. This shrewd maneuver, apparently made in response to the changing atmosphere of the South, greatly upsets Ratliff and Gavin Stevens, who fear that the minority of "liberal" Yoknapatawpha citizens will now be taken in. Ratliff then arranges that, at a picnic in Frenchman's Bend, a gang of dogs should mistake Cla'ence for a familiar thicket which they visit regularly each day—and this dampening of the candidate makes him so ridiculous that he must withdraw from the race. For as Uncle Billy Varner, the Croesus of Frenchman's Bend, says: "I ain't going to have Beat Two and Frenchman's Bend represented nowhere by nobody that ere a son-a-bitching dog that happens by cant tell from a fence post."

Simply as an anecdote, this comes off beautifully. Faulkner can tease this sort of joke along better than anyone else, just as he knows the mind of a grasping little demagogue like Cla'ence Snopes better than anyone else. But in the context of the trilogy the incident is damaging, since it suggests that the threat of Snopesism can easily be defeated by the country shrewdness of a Ratliff—an assumption which all the preceding matter has led us gravely to doubt and which, if we do credit it, must now persuade us that the danger embodied by the Snopeses need not be taken as seriously as the whole weight of the trilogy has seemed to argue. The incident is fine, and so is the over-all pattern; but their relationship is destructive.

There are other, more important difficulties. Through both *The Town* and *The Mansion* Flem Snopes moves steadily toward the center of Yoknapatawpha economic power. The meaning of this is fully registered, but Flem himself, as a represented figure, is not nearly so vivid in these novels as in *The Hamlet*. Partly this seems due to a flagging of creative gifts, so that, for the first time, one feels Faulkner is dutifully completing a cycle of novels rather than writing for the sheer pleasure and immediate need of writing. Partly it is due to his propensity for avoiding the direct and dramatic, for straining the action through the blurred—and blurring—consciousness of the insufferable Stevens and the mediocre young Charles Mallison. Partly it is the result of a genuine literary problem: that Faulkner, having set up Flem with such a perfection of malevolence in *The Hamlet*, now faced the difficult task of finding ways to dispose of him, as a character, in the two later books. Apparently aware of this problem, Faulkner tries to outflank it in *The Mansion* by keeping Flem in the background as a figure whom we barely see, though his impact upon the other characters is always felt. That Flem Snopes, of all the memorable monsters in American literature, would end up seeming shadowy and vague—who could have anticipated this?

Faulkner has made the mistake of softening Flem; he verges at times on sociological and psychological explanations of Flem's behavior; and he even shows a few traces of sympathy for Flem, which is as unfortunate as if Ben Jonson broke into tears over Volpone. When the Flem we see—or, alas, more often hear about—is "the old fishblooded son of a bitch who had a vocabulary of two words, one being No and the other Foreclose," all is for the best in the best of Faulknerian worlds; but when it is a Flem who becomes still another item in the omniverous musings of Gavin Stevens, then he suffers a fate worse than even he deserves. The greatest trouble, finally, with *The Mansion*, as with *The*

Town, is that Faulkner feels obliged to give a large portion of his space
to material that does not directly involve the Snopeses. Again, there is
a conflict between the design of the trilogy and what Faulkner can
bring off at the moment of composition. The trilogy requires that a new
force of opposition to the Snopeses be found, since they have moved to
the town where, presumably, Ratliff can no longer operate with his
accustomed assurance. In both *The Town* and *The Mansion* Ratliff
suffers a sad constriction, all too often playing straight-man to Gavin
Stevens. For the new force of opposition to the Snopeses, as the
Faulker *afficionado* can sadly predict, now comes largely from Stevens, the District Attorney with a degree from Heidelberg and a passion for rant. Stevens not only speaks the underbaked wisdom that has
become Faulkner's specialty since his Nobel Prize speech in Stock-
holm; he also betrays how deluded Faulkner is in his notion of what an
intellectual can or should be.

The middle section of *The Mansion* deals with Stevens' relation to
Linda Snopes, stepdaughter of Flem and daughter of Eula Varner
Snopes, whom Gavin had worshipped in vain throughout *The Town*.
Linda has left Jefferson; married a Jewish sculptor in New York; gone
off to the Spanish Civil War, where she suffered a puncture of her
eardrums; returned to Jefferson as a member of the Communist Party;
and now loves Gavin (also in vain), "meddles" with the Negroes, and
shares a home with Flem in cold silence, until her schemes lead to
Mink being freed from jail, destroying Flem and thereby avenging the
suicide of her mother. Gavin loves Linda too, but once more in vain.
For reasons that two readings of the novel do not yield to me, they fail
to marry or do anything else that might reasonably be expected from a
man and a woman in love, except to purr sympathetically at each other.
Very likely some exegetes will discover or infer a reason for this curious
situation, but that will not be at all the same as justifying it in the novel.

In any case, this whole section is poorly managed and frequently
tedious. The New York locale, Linda's venture into Communism, the
snooping of an FBI man—these are not matters that Faulkner can
handle with authority. The relationship between Gavin and Linda,
never allowed to settle into quiet clarity, elicits at most a mild pity,
since Faulkner seems unable to face up to whatever remnants of
Southern "chivalry," romantic ideology or plain ordinary repression
drive him to think of love as a grandiloquent "doom." The truth, I
suspect, is that Faulkner cannot treat adult sexual experience with a
forthright steadiness, despite the frequency with which sex appears in
his earlier books as a symptom of disorder and violation. Only at the
end of the novel, as Stevens and Linda kiss goodbye and he slides his

hand down her back, "simply touching her . . . supporting her but-
tocks as you cup the innocent hipless bottom of a child," does Faulkner
break into that candor for which this whole section cries out. If the
Snopes trilogy, bringing together nearly the best and nearly the worst
in Faulkner's career, is both imposing and seriously marred, *The Mansion* taken more modestly, as a novel in its own right, has some superb
sections. Perhaps the reader who is not steeped in Faulkner's work and
cares nothing about its relation to his previous books is in the best
position to accept it with pleasure. For whenever Mink Snopes appears, the prose becomes hard, grave, vibrant, and Faulkner's capacity, as Malcolm Cowley has well put it, for "telling stories about men or
beasts who fulfilled their destiny," comes into full play. Like the con-
vict in *The Wild Palms*, Mink drives steadily toward his end, without
fear or hope, unblinking and serene.

Faulkner begins *The Mansion* by retelling a story told in *The Hamlet*, but with far greater depth of feeling. Mink Snopes, galled by the
arrogance of his wealthy neighbor Houston and himself full of a bitter
meanness as well as a bottom-dog dignity which draws the line beyond
which humiliation is not to be borne, finally kills Houston and stands
trial for murder. He expects Flem to rescue him, since for him, as for
all the other Snopeses, Flem is the agent, the connection between
their clan and the outer world. Flem, however, coldly abandons Mink,
and Mink, sentenced to prison, lives only for the day he can destroy
Flem. A stratagem of Flem's lures Mink into attempting an escape; his
sentence is doubled; but he waits patiently, sweating out his blood over
the state's cotton. At the age of 63, his body as puny as a child's, he
comes out a free man.

The portrait of Mink is beyond praise: a simple ignorant soul who
sees existence as an unending manichean struggle between Old Moster
(God) and Them (the world), with Them forever and even rightly and
naturally triumphant, always in control of events as they move along,
yet with Old Moster standing in reserve, not to intervene or to help
but to draw a line, like Mink himself, and say that beyond this line no
creature, not even a wretched little Mink, dare be tried. Mink's is the
heroism of the will, a man living out his need: what we might call his
destiny.

In the opening part of the novel, as well as in its brilliant final
pages—where Mink goes to Memphis to buy a gun, gets caught up in a
superbly-rendered revivalist sect led by Marine Sergeant Goodyhay,
mooches a quarter from a cop and supposes that this is one of those new
dispensations he had dimly heard described as the "WP and A" and
finally, as if in a pageant of fatality, returns to Jefferson to kill his

cousin—in these pages Faulkner is writing at very close to the top of his bent. It all quivers with evocation, the language becomes taut, and Faulkner's sense of the power of life as it floods a man beyond his reason or knowledge, becomes overwhelming. Here is Mink reflecting:

"In 1948 he and Flem would both be old men and he even said aloud: 'What a shame we cant both of us jest come out two old men setting peaceful in the sun or the shade, waiting to die together, not even thinking nor more of hurt or harm or getting even, not even remembering no more about hurt or harm or anguish or revenge,'— two old men not only incapable of further harm to anybody but even incapable of remembering hurt or harm. . . . But I reckon not, he thought, *Cant neither of us help nothing now. Cant neither one of us take nothing back.*"

And here is Mink approaching Jefferson after 38 years, as he rests on a truck:

"He was quite comfortable. But mainly he was off the ground. That was the danger, what a man had to watch against: once you laid flat on the ground, right away the earth started in to draw you back down into it. The very moment you were born out of your mother's body, the power and drag of the earth was already at work on you . . . And you knew it too."

Reading such passages in the fullness of their context, is like returning to a marvellous world that has gone a little dim, the world Faulkner made; and then all seems well.

IN THE DAY OF A FALSE MESSIAH

In the mid-seventeenth century, the east European Jews were decimated by the rebellion-pogrom of the Cossack leader Chmielnicki. Many of the survivors were then caught up in a religious enthusiasm that derived, all too clearly, from their total desperation. They began to summon apocalyptic fantasies, to indulge in long-repressed religious emotions which, paradoxically, were stimulated by the pressures of Cabbalistic asceticism.

As if in response to their yearning, a messianic pretender named Sabbatai Zevi appeared in eastern Europe. Everything that rabbinical Judaism had confined or suppressed found release in Sabbatai's movement: the temptation of the doctrine that faith alone will save, the impulse to evade the limits of mundane life by forcing a religious transcendence, the union of erotic with mystical appetites, the lure of a demonism which the very hopelessness of the Jewish situation rendered plausible. In 1665-6 Sabbatianism reached an orgiastic climax, whole communities, out of a conviction that the messiah was at hand, abandoning the Mosaic law and the inhibitions of exile.

Their hopes were soon smashed. Confronted with persecution by the Turkish Sultan, Sabbatai converted to Mohammedanism. Nonetheless, Sabbatianism survived for a time as a secret cult which celebrated Sabbatai as the apostate saviour, who had been required to descend to the depths of the world in order to emerge on the heights of salvation.

Satan in Goray, a short novel by Isaac Bashevis Singer translated from the Yiddish, shows the Jews of a small Polish town abandoning themselves, in a transport of mass delusion, to the false messiah. It is a remarkable book, brilliant, enigmatic. The author is one of the two or three most gifted living writers of Yiddish prose: his command of Yiddish idiom, his range of metaphor, his fierce short-breathed rhythms mark him as a virtuoso.

Like most Yiddish fiction, *Satan in Goray* is focussed on the community, its main theme, as its main "character," being the collective destiny of the Jews in exile. The norm of communal life is so deeply ingrained in the traditional Jewish imagination that any deviation will constitute a significant action for the Yiddish reader, one inherently possessing those potentialities for conflict and disaster that go to make up the idea of the dramatic. Goray, an obscure Jewish town in Poland, tries to reestablish its life after the Chmielnicki massacres, but people cannot go on as before, not even Jews trained in suffering and endurance. The Rabbi who warns against ecstasies born of mere desire is pushed aside. The town is overwhelmed by a millenial hysteria. First come the ascetics, who break down the sanctions of rabbinic law, and then the possessed and the depraved who experiment in sin and satanism with the justification that the dawn of the messianic age means the lapsing of the Commandments.

Singer has peopled his novel with a number of sharply-etched figures: a self-mutilating ascetic who brings the Sabbatian word to Goray and then expires in anguish when his hope is betrayed, a corrupt and dionysian ritual slaughterer who rules Goray in its moment of abandonment, and a haunting epileptic girl who symbolizes the martyrdom of the community, being married first to the ascetic, then to the ritual slaughterer, and finally entered by the spirit of a dead person.

Singer piles up local detail after detail, partly as a means of authenticating a novel that runs the risk of abstractness and rhetoric because of its concentration on collective life, and partly because he has an enormous interest in everything that is strange. But for all its local richness, the over-all structure of the book is rigidly economical. Singer makes the boldest elisions in his narrative, cuts through the usual packing of the Yiddish novel, and drives toward his climax with a furious energy. His materials are thoroughly traditional, but he himself is a modern writer who has learned the lessons of Flaubert and Turgenev. Yet because he remains partly attached to the Yiddish literary tradition, he can bring surprising resources to his work. At the climax of the novel, when the epileptic girl is being exorcised of the *dybbuk* and the tension has become almost unbearable, Singer suddenly turns to the meandering archaic mode of the old Yiddish tale, and the result is not merely a fascinating *tour de force* but the achievement of perspective and a kind of serenity.

Partly his power derives from an ability to hold in a delicate tension such contrary elements as the miraculous and the skeptical, the moral and the exotic. At times the style of *Satan in Goray* seems almost *as if* it were the style of a man possessed, so thoroughly does he give himself to the subject; yet he also maintains a rigorous distance, one is always aware of the *conditional* nature of his absorption in the Sabbatian experience. He bring to play upon Jewish life a mind that delights in everything that is antique and curious yet is drenched with the assumptions of modern psychology, and the result is a balance between the impulse to surrender to his subject and the temptation to deny it.

Jacob Sloan's translation is good, though it communicates more of the color than the pace of the original Yiddish. But I must quarrel with Mr. Sloan's introduction. He writes: "As Isaac Bashevis Singer . . . reminds us: once the core of faith is lost, Satan must triumph and the forces of evil overwhelm mankind." This gratuitous religiosity has nothing whatever to do with the novel, not even if one could bring a testimonial from the author proclaiming his piety. For the point of Singer's achievement is that it does not lend itself to any such obvious or pre-fabricated point: he accepts the Sabbatian episode as a human experience, tragic and absurd in its own terms, and not requiring any contemporary tags in order to validate it.

Still more questionable is Mr. Sloan's effort to assimilate the Sabbatian collapse to Twentieth century politics. "Like the people of Goray," he writes, "we too have found that . . . there are no simple and complete solutions to the tragic complications of being fallible human beings in an incomprehensible universe." This sentence, laden as it is with the overtones of our contemporary wisdom, indicates that Mr. Sloan has absorbed the message of Edmund Burke or, if one wants to get right up to date, of Russell Kirk; but it has nothing to do with *Satan in Goray*.

The events of our time are enacted by men who, whatever their disagreements, all accept in common the necessity for action *within* history. But the traditional Jewish judgment, which plays an implicit role in the development of Singer's novel, is that salvation cannot come through history. At the end of the archaic fable that climaxes *Satan in Goray*, the "moral"—toward which we may expect so sophisticated a writer as Singer to retain a certain ironic reserve—is stated: "Let none attempt to force the Lord: To end our pain within the world . . ." The heresy of false messianism is that in trying to force a premature apocalypse it enters not the realm of the sacred but the realm of the secular. Messianism is thus reduced to historical action, and historical action itself viewed largely as the province of the demonic. This, at least, is the working imaginative hypothesis of *Satan in Goray*, and regardless of whether Singer as a person fully agrees with it one thing should be clear: it has nothing in common with and should not be assimilated to, the problems of modern politics, all of which are rooted in the common assumption of secular historicity.

THE STORIES OF ISAAC BABEL

The publication of Isaac Babel's collected stories, coming at a time when the dominant political and cultural trends are deeply hostile to this kind of imagination, is cause for happiness. Most of the stories have appeared in one or another English version, but now to have them in their proper order and thereby to receive their accumulative impact is to know that Babel is not merely, as Maxim Gorky claimed, the most gifted prose writer of post-revolutionary Russia, but one of the literary masters of our century.

Born in 1894, Babel was raised in a lower-middle-class Jewish family in Odessa, and during the pre-revolutionary period, when he lived and starved in Moscow as a literary bohemian, he became a protegé of Gorky. After five years of fighting in the revolution and civil war, Babel returned to his writing and won immediate fame as the author of *Red Cavalry*, a book of breath-taking stories that drew from his experiences with a Cossack unit in Budenny's army. But as the Stalin dictatorship hardened its grip, Babel wrote less and less (he was not, in any case, very productive) and after a time he lapsed into silence.

In 1934 Babel made one of his rare public appearances, at the first Russian Writers' Congress, partly to join in the ritual of pledging loyalty to the regime, partly to explain his failure to publish. His performance was a remarkable political act. He practiced, said Babel, a new literary genre: he was "the master of the genre of silence." And in the midst of his praise for the regime and the party, he remarked, as if in passing, that they presumed to deprive writers of only one right, the right to write badly. "Comrades," he went on, "let us not fool ourselves: this is a very important right and to take it away from us is no small thing. . . . Let us give up this right, and may God help us. And if there is no God, let us help ourselves. . . ."

The right to write badly!—to write from one's own feelings, from one's own mistakes. It would be hard to imagine a more courageous, and a more saddening, gesture on the part of a writer whose every impulse was for the spontaneity, the freedom, the playfulness which his society denied. Babel, who was protected by Gorky and for whom, it is rumored, even Number One had a soft spot, suffered no immediate punishment, other than the continued silence he had imposed on himself. But in 1937 he was arrested and two or three years later died in a concentration camp. Except for a memorial note on Gorky which appeared in 1938, Babel remained silent to the end, the master of his genre.

The stories in *Red Cavalry* impress one in endless ways, but their primary impact is shock. Hard, terse, violent, gorgeously colored, they come upon one like disciplined explosions. Primitive Cossack ways jar against Babel's sophisticated consciousness; the random brutality that is the inheritance of centuries of blackness suddenly lifts itself to a selfless red heroism, and in the very moment of doing so helplessly corrupts the heroism; extremes of behavior, weaving into one another as if to spite all moralists, bewilder Babel as narrator and the reader as onlooker.

The stories turn upon Babel's struggle with a problem that cannot be understood unless it is seen both in the historical setting of the Russian Revolution and in the context of Babel's personal being as both intellectual and Jew. Though he was not, so far as we know, concerned with politics as ideological definition or power strategy, Babel understood with absolute sureness the problem that has obsessed all modern novelists who deal with politics: the problem of action in both its heroic necessity and its ugly self-contamination, the "tragic flaw" that is at the heart of an historical action which by virtue of being historical must to some extent be conceived in violence and therefore as a distortion and coarsening of its "self." But it must be stressed that Babel sees this problem not as a mere exercise in metaphysics: for him it is at the very center of choice. And it is in this sense, despite the virtual absence of explicit politics, that the stories in *Red Cavalry* are profoundly revolutionary: under the red heat of Babel's passion, creation and contemplation melt into one.

The problem of historical action also absorbs Malraux and Silone in their best novels, and in Bert Brecht's great poem "To Posterity" it receives its most exalted and most shameful expression, for here every word is bitterly true yet the poem itself is put to service as a rationale for Stalinism. For Babel, characteristically, the problem turns into one of personal assertion, his capacity to embrace and engage in, yet at some level of awareness to stand apart from, the most terrifying extremes of human conduct.

In his introduction, Lionel Trilling has raised, or I should say, abstracted, this problem into a kind of timeless moral dialectic. "In Babel's heart," he writes, "there was a kind of fighting—he was captivated by the vision of two ways of being, the way of violence and the way of peace, and he was torn between them." True as this is, I think it misses the center of Babel's concern, which was not so much the choice between "two ways of being" open to men in almost any circumstances and at almost any time, but rather the unbearable—unbearable because felt as entirely necessary—difficulties of being an artist committed to the fate of a desperate revolution. One very important side of Babel was a Bolshevik, or tried hard to be ("O regulations of the Russian Communist Party," begins one story, "You have laid headlong rails through the sour pastry of our Russian tales"), and precisely from this side of Babel came some of the energies and anxieties that give life to his work. Like it or not, we cannot blink this simple fact, nor the equally important fact that Babel, as a writer whose politics and esthetics meet in an appetite for extremes, does not lend himself very easily to those more reasonable modes of feeling which Mr. Trilling has designated as the Liberal Imagination. To deprive a writer of the immediacy, even the distracting immediacy, of his preoccupations is to lessen his capacity for disturbing and uprooting us.

Some of the most terrible stories in *Red Cavalry* are directed against Babel himself, against his inability to kill other men and his tragi-comic efforts to adapt himself to the ways of the Cossacks. The Jewish literary man, with spectacles on his nose and autumn in his heart, needs to prove to himself that, *given the historical necessity*, he can commit acts which for the Cossack are virtually second nature. But since he is also a writer of imaginative largesse, Babel in the course of "lending" himself to the Cossacks falls in love with their gracefulness of gesture and movement. (Mr. Trilling, linking Babel to Tolstoy, has some acute remarks on this.) Above all, Babel admires the Cossacks' sureness of manner, their unreflective absorption in inherited modes of life.

Yet he does not sentimentalize the Cossacks nor use them, as a modern literary man might, to sanction his own repressed aggressiveness. He remains in awed puzzlement before the ancient mysteries of their ways, and even when he achieves occasional rapport with them he does not pretend to understand them. But he grants them every possible human claim, and he trembles beneath the lash of their simple unqualified criticism.

In a magnificent five-page story called "The Death of Doglushov," a wounded Cossack, his entrails hanging over his knees, begs Babel to shoot him, but Babel, soft and scrupulous, funks it. A comrade of the wounded man does the job and then turns furiously upon Babel: "You guys in specs have about as much pity for chaps like us as a cat has for a mouse." In another five-page masterpiece, "After the Battle," a Cossack curses Babel for having ridden into battle with an unloaded revolver ("You didn't put no cartridge in. . . . You worship God, you traitor!") and Babel goes off "imploring fate to grant me the simplest of proficiencies—the ability to kill my fellow-men." And at the end of *Red Cavalry* another Cossack pronounces his primitive sentence upon Babel: "You're trying to live without enemies. That's all you think about, not having enemies."

As counterforce to the Cossacks Babel turns to the Polish Jews, squatting in their villages while opposing armies trample back and forth, passive and impervious to the clamor for blood. Even as he fights in the Red Army, Babel listens, with the attentiveness of a child, to Gedali, the Hassid who believes that "the Revolution means joy" and who wants "an International of good people." "I would like every soul to be listed," says Gedali, "and given first-category rations. There, soul, please eat and enjoy life's pleasures. Pan comrade, you don't know what the International is eaten with. . . ." "It is eaten with gun-powder," answers Babel, "and spiced with best-quality blood."

The Jews of Poland, with their "long bony backs, their tragic yellow beards," pierce through the taut objectivity of Babel's narrative and stir in him a riot of memories ("O the rotted Talmuds of my childhood!"). He goes back and forth from the Cossacks, strange, cruel and beautiful, to the ghetto Jews, who "moved jerkily, in an uncontrolled and uncouth way, but [whose] capacity for suffering was full of a sombre greatness . . ." If *Red Cavalry* is a paean, ambiguous but ardent, to the force of revolution, it is also an elegy for the dying ghetto, for "the Sabbath peace [which] rested upon the crazy roofs of Zhitomer."

Even to mention Babel's style is to involve one's self in a tangle of contradictions and frustrations. Gestures of bare violence turn abruptly, without preparation, into states of reflective quietness. Objectivity seems the dominant mode, yet few modern prose writers would dare indulge in such lyrical apostrophes and such laments as fill Babel's pages. We have been taught to value terseness and understatement; but in Babel terseness has nothing whatever to do with understatement, since it is actually the consequence of the boldest political and metaphysical generalizations. Indeed, hardly another writer of our time has succeeded so well in making the generalization, even the political slogan, so organically a part of his imagery. One moves in these stories with a dizzying speed from conceptual abstraction to primitive notation: Babel never permits the reader to rest in any mold of style or upon any level of perception, he always drives one from surprise to surprise. In some of the stories there is a surrender to sadness as complete as the urge to motion and violence that accompanies it. In other stories the event itself has been removed from sight, and the surface of the prose is devoted to a few wry ripples of talk and a few startling images of place and weather.

The best observation on Babel's style has been made by John Berryman, who has noted certain similarities to the style of Stephen Crane. In both writers there is an obsessive concern with compression and explosion, a kinesthetic ferocity of control, a readiness to wrench language in order to gain nervous immediacy. Both use language as if to inflict a wound. But the differences are also important. Babel, as Berryman goes on to mention, is warm, while Crane is cold. And more important, I think, Babel has a wider range of effects; by comparison, Crane seems a little stiff-jointed.

The two main literary sources upon which Babel seems to have drawn, Russian and Yiddish, flourished most in the 50 or 75 years directly before he began to write; he was one of those writers who spring up at the end of such a creative period and absorb its energies as if they were still at their fullest. The Chekhov strain in Russian literature is strongly evident in Babel's miscellaneous stories (though not so much in *Red Cavalry* or his other group called *Tales of Odessa*); one quickly recognizes the pathos, the warm skepticism of the older writer. The Yiddish literary influence is less likely to be noticed by American critics (Mr. Trilling pays no attention to it). But surely no one who has read Sholom Aleichem can fail to see that in Babel's Odessa stories there is a remarkable parallel of effect: the comic grasp of social relationships, the sardonic arguing with God, the attraction to the undersides of history. Compare Babel's bitter wit with Sholom Aleichem's impudent reverence in writing about Jewish fate.

[Babel]: "But wasn't it a mistake on God's part to settle the Jews in Russia, where they've had to suffer the tortures of Hell? Would it be bad if the Jews lived in Switzerland, where they'd be surrounded by first-class lakes, mountain air and nothing but Frenchmen? Everybody makes mistakes, even God."

[Sholom Aleichem]: "Apparently if He wants it that way, that's the way it ought to be. Can't you see? If it should have been different it would have been. And yet, what would have been wrong to have it different?"

Sometimes the richness of emotion, and often the very phrasing of his idiom, is understandable only in terms of Babel's relationship to Yiddish literature. In a story called "In the Basement" the vulgar-loving rebuke of a grandfather to a boy who tries to commit suicide ("My grandson . . . I'm taking a dose of castor oil, so as to have something to place on your grave") is given its true value and inflection only if one knows that in the Jewish mores suicide is taken to be not merely impious but shameful.

Lost as he often is in melancholia and sadness, perplexed and even a little betrayed as he sometimes is by violence, Babel—through his simple readiness to accept his own desires—makes upon life the most radical of demands: the demand for happiness. In his work one finds a straining toward a union of passion and tenderness, those two elements of feeling which Freud says have become dissociated in the life of modern man and which, because they are dissociated, tend to decline into aggressiveness and impotence. I do not say that Babel often achieves this union, only that he will not let anything, not even "the regulations of the Communist Party," distract him from straining toward it. In his work everything becomes eroticized, everything becomes animated: love and energy come closer.

There is a lovely little story by Babel in which he describes how a baby named Karl-Yankel (half Marxist-half Jew) is being fought over by the two sets of believers. Babel, watching the comic struggle, ends the story by telling himself, "It's not possible . . . it's not possible that you won't be happy, Karl-Yankel. It's not possible that you won't be happier than I."

TOMATO OR CUCUMBER?

Alain Robbe-Grillet's *The Voyeur* comes to us as an example of the "anti-novel novel," reinforced by an elaborate theoretical equipage. Robbe-Grillet writes that he wishes to dismiss "the old myth of 'depth,' " the assumption that a meaning is to be found in a depicted relationship between objects and/or events. *"Profundity,"* he writes in a sentence as shallow as it is sparkling, "has functioned like a trap in which the writer captures the universe to hand it over to society." What Robbe-Grillet wants is the chair and not the "signification" of the chair, for "the world is neither significant nor absurd. It *is,* quite simply." Quite simply!

Roland Barthes gives a more sustained explanation:

Description for Robbe-Grillet is always 'anthological'—a matter of presenting the object as if in a mirror, as if it were in itself a *spectacle,* permitting it to make demands on our attention without regard for its relation to the dialectic of the story . . . The object has no being beyond *phenomenon:* it is not ambiguous or allegorical . . . A slice of tomato in an automat sandwich, described according to this method, constitutes an object without heredity, without associations, and without references . . . and refusing with all the stubbornness of its *there*ness to involve the reader in an *elsewhere.* . . .

As one might expect, these writers look for support in certain kinds of contemporary painting which seem also to represent the object in its thereness, without volunteering any value other than that which may reside in the visual moment.

But one is entitled to wonder: what principle of selection guides Robbe-Grillet in choosing one object for description rather than another? (An "anthological" description obviously implies selection.) Why a tomato rather than a cucumber? From certain points of view, this is by no means a trivial choice. And is not the act of choice necessarily dependent upon some bias of meaning, with its "heredity" and "associations," regardless of whether the writer is aware of this fact? Barthes's apparently casual reference to the position of the slice of tomato—that it lies within an *automat* sandwich—supplies it, actually, with a complex series of "depth" associations, indeed, with an entire historical aura.

For a painting it may be enough that the principle of selection be the visual satisfaction that can be had simply from looking at a created object, though here too one might wonder whether the object can exist on the plane of *there*ness without leading the observer to some *elsewhere*. But things seem to be quite different in literature, among other reasons because the verbal description of the object, no matter how effective, can seldom be as complete and self-contained an aesthetic unit as a painting can.

The reality of Robbe-Grillet's writing is quite different from the claims of his theory. The compulsive anthologizing of events and objects directs our attention not to the surface of things, not to mere phenomena, but—it seems almost perverse—to possible clues as to meaning, response, emotion; and the fewer clues we have, the more are we driven to hunt for them. Nor is this comic shifting of direction unique in modern literature. When we read Virginia Woolf's *The Waves*, we are so thoroughly immersed in the flow of psychic sensation and reflection that we soon find ourselves seeking desperately for guide-points of event; we wish to make whole again the universe of conduct she has split into a radical duality. Reading *The Waves*, as it keeps immersing us in depth, turns our attention to surfaces; reading *The Voyeur*, which confines itself to surfaces, turns our attention to depth.

The Voyeur, in any case, is not merely an "anthologized" string of described objects; it has a plot of sorts. And no sooner is plot in evidence than there must be a recourse to ideas, preconceptions, inflections of emotion. So that it is simply not true, as Barthes writes, that "the work of Robbe-Grillet is susceptible to no thematic index whatever." Robbe-Grillet might protest that we are thrusting upon him that very incubus of meaning which he seeks to discard; but short of inflicting lobotomies upon his readers, he will have to put up with the fact that in coming to his books they inevitably bring with them an heredity. Joyce demanded that his readers give him their future; Robbe-Grillet, more extravagant, demands their past.

The novel itself is more interesting than the theories that surround it. Robbe-Grillet is skillful at evoking moods of anxiety (as one might expect in a writer distrustful of "depth"). Incidents repeat themselves crazily in the way they do in some experimental films, thereby creating a kind of epistemological disturbance; the chaotic mental references of his protagonist are presented as if they were actual happenings or as if they were indistinguishable from actual happenings. Though severely limited by the writer's programmatic avoidance of emotion, the result is a novel with moments of considerable power—but a power that is primarily psychological. All of which suggests that reality—in this case, the spontaneous human striving for a unity of perception and comprehension—has a way of revenging itself upon those who go too far in violating it.

CULTURE AND RADICALISM

At a time when so many American intellectuals have been turning to conservatism, the literary critic Richard Chase has moved in the opposite direction. Invoking the tradition of Randolph Bourne and the early Van Wyck Brooks, his book *The Democratic Vista* is a call for the reassertion of radical values in American culture—perhaps also in American politics. It is a tentative book, almost ingenuous in the exposure of its weaknesses; but both as a statement and a sign it seems to me valuable.

The Democratic Vista has won praise from the very people it attacks: reviewers for middle-brow magazines, literary academicians and young critics who seem to feel that Maturity is a goddess sprung full-blown from the brow of Morningside Heights. Every author enjoys praise and Mr. Chase deserves his share; but this kind of praise ought to give him some uneasy moments. For if you write a polemic and the people who are its targets say they like it, *something* is wrong.

Partly the curious amiability with which Mr. Chase's book has been received is due to the sponginess of American culture in the 50's. Dissident criticism, instead of arousing anger and firm response, is often disarmed by a process of bland assimilation; distinctions of opinion are erased by rhetoric, good will, and apathy. But the trouble seems also to arise from the book itself. Mr. Chase first announced his themes in a series of articles that were specific and sharp; in the book these have been rewoven into a dialogue among several characters, the leading one, Ralph Headstrong, speaking for the author and his antagonist, George Middleby, sounding like a smug version of some of the people who have since come along to praise *The Democratic Vista*. Now the dialogue as a form has its pleasantly old-fashioned attractions, and there are genuine advantages to its use in this book, where no pretense is made at creating "real" characters and the voices come through with awkward yet charming bookishness. But I wonder whether the consequent blurring of polemical edge isn't too great a price to pay.

At the same time, I feel uneasy about the harsh attacks to which the book has been subjected from the left, notably by Philip Green in the *New Republic* and Hilton Kramer in *Dissent*. Quick to catch out the obvious deficiencies of Mr. Chase's argument, these reviewers have not troubled to consider the *direction* of his thought, or the possibility that its direction may be more significant than its momentary point of rest; they have failed to see that the book matters as one of the first serious efforts by an American intellectual to reorient himself after the collapse of cold war moods and ideologies.

Through his *alter ego* Ralph Headstrong, Mr. Chase begins with a sharp criticism of contemporary American culture. He is keen at observing the boredom and purposelessness that lie just beneath the surface of so much "activity," the loss of zest and animation, the decline of culture into a sort of household convenience. And he asks the right questions: "Will it be possible to keep alive, in an atmosphere of growing conformity, a fruitful versatility of taste and opinion, or are all forms of expression and feelings, above the level of the mass media, being boiled down into a sort of middlebrow mush where all distinctions are lost? How are we to reconcile the American imagination as we find it in our literature—on the whole a literature of extremity, of brilliant fragments, of melodrama, humor, pastoral idyll and romance—with the mild, routine life of the new suburban America?"

It is in response to such questions that Mr. Chase advances his plea for "cultural radicalism," an attitude that would seem to include a continued loyalty to *avant-garde* experimentation, a willingness to think of human existence in extreme terms, an adherence to a radical democratic secularism, and a strong resistance to both mass culture and middlebrow *kitsch*. In the course of his argument Mr. Chase falls back upon the somewhat worn categories of highbrow, middlebrow, and lowbrow, acknowledging that it isn't always clear whether these refer to styles of life, attitudes toward culture, kinds of occupation, or trivialities of manner. Still, I think he is right in saying that, for all their looseness, the "brow" terms cannot easily be avoided in a discussion of

American culture. And by using them, Mr. Chase has reached a conclusion of the first importance: that our culture, as it recedes from high
and lowbrow intransigence, is settling at "some sort of middle ground
of taste and opinion, a general desire for passivity and rest . . . a fear of
the turmoil of the mind, a longing to escape conflict, a longing to
assuage all the vivid contradictions and anomalies that in the past have
engaged the American mind."

Some of the liveliest passages in the book occur when Ralph Headstrong elaborates on this view—passages about the changing nature of
American anti-intellectualism (less strident, more insidious), about the
way American universities are becoming indistinguishable from the
surrounding social landscape, about the peculiar temptations that
prosperity puts in the way of writers. Mr. Chase is also very good at
explaining why some of the views of his mentor, Van Wyck Brooks, no
longer hold. Forty-five years ago Brooks, finding himself troubled by
the chasm between the intelligentsia and the masses, felt that the goal
of a healthy democratic culture should be to bring together the standards of the cultivated minority and the vitality of the plebs. I think it
would be a sad mistake if intellectuals were to abandon once and for all
this idea of an "organic" culture; but as Mr. Chase explains, a more
immediate and urgent need—if only to make possible a later realization
of Brooks's goal—is to preserve a sharp sense of cultural seriousness
such as the prevalent middlebrow mind in America can't envisage, let
alone encourage.

As Mr. Chase's argument unfolds, there is some amusing by-play
between Headstrong and Middleby, but a by-play that reveals one of
the troubling faults of the book. Too many of its references are
those peculiar to an "in-group," and to get all of them you probably
have to be not only a reader of but also a contributor to *Partisan
Review*. Otherwise, you might never guess that a good part of Mr.
Chase's polemic has for its target the conservative "moderation" of
Lionel Trilling. Mr. Chase has dulled the force of his argument by
engaging in anonymous polemics and by resorting occasionally to a
Prufrockian archness of mannner. Now anonymous polemic is always a
dubious affair: it doesn't give your opponent a fair chance to strike back
and it leaves the outsider bewildered. But more important, his
approach helps to perpetuate the very gentility and flabbiness he
deplores. These days anyone who wants to advance radical ideas, be
they in relation to culture or politics, has to risk being charged with bad
manners.

Perhaps the best parts of the book are those in which Mr. Chase tries
to relate his desire for cultural radicalism with his views on the central
tradition of American literature. He is entirely committed to the idea

that the central impulse of American literature has been democratic, secular, radical, extremist, and "dialectical" (a term he uses to suggest a mixture of romantic and speculative views which, together, make for an "open" culture). The trouble, however, is that Mr. Chase's argument becomes, in the narrow sense, too *literary:* he tends to treat social and personal problems not in their own right but as they provide touchstones for the literary tradition. At times (to be just a little unfair) his radicalism seems to be asserted primarily as a means of preserving a close relationship to writers like Melville, Whitman, and Emerson. Were George Middleby a bit quicker on his feet, he might tell Headstrong to put these great men aside for a moment and to justify his views in strictly contemporary terms.

But the main difficulty in Mr. Chase's book concerns the relation in our day between politics and culture. At some points Mr. Chase writes as if "cultural radicalism" were a self-sufficient attitude compatible with the politics of "the liberal virtues—moderation, compromise, countervailing forces, the vital center, the mixed economy." Which is to say: radicalism in culture, the ADA in politics. If this is a fair deduction from Mr. Chase's argument, it seems necessary to ask: what *content* is a "cultural radicalism" divorced from radical politics to have?

The defense of standards, the assault upon middlebrow complacence, the willingness to look at life in tragic perspective—all excellent; but there is surely no reason to assume that these are confined to radicals. When men like Bourne and the early Brooks asserted a need for cultural radicalism, they were writing as socialists or near-socialists who believed that the need of the moment was to bring politics and culture into a closer relationship, not to pull them apart.

Now I can see one circumstance in which a "cultural radicalism" without an accompanying radical politics might be valid. Intellectuals may feel that they are living in a good and healthy society, one which deserves their basic loyalties, but that it is nevertheless their task to keep prodding it toward a higher level of cultural awareness. This would seem to be the way many American intellectuals now explain, or rationalize, their relationship to our society. Part of the time Mr. Chase writes in this spirit too, as when he tells us that "At present, in its immediate applications, radicalism is not political or economic. . . . For the moment, American politics and economics, on the domestic scene, appear impenetrable, mysterious and roughly successful." If this is true, then "cultural radicalism" has a consistent rationale; but I think it is very far from being true, and so, in his less relaxed moments, does Mr. Chase. At one point he suddenly drops his professional pose and bursts out with a rush of feeling: "It is time to ask ourselves if a fruitful and humane life will be possible at all in an America full of the flashy and insolent wealth of a permanent war economy, brutalized slums, rampant and dehumanizing Levittowns, race hatred, cynical exploitation, and waste of natural resources, government by pressure groups . . . vulgarization and perhaps destruction of our schools, not to mention the sporadic flash and fallout of 'nuclear devices.' Here are enemies enough. Here is the seedbed of new ideologies."

This is well said, and Mr. Chase's list of questions could be extended for pages. But if such questions are to the point, are not the "virtues" of "moderation, compromise, etc." seriously called into doubt? Do our politics and economy seem quite so mysteriously "successful" as American intellectuals were saying a few years ago? May there not be possible, tomorrow if not today, a new American radicalism which will push beyond the conventional liberal assumptions, yet will not compromise itself with the corruptions and fantasies of the 30's?

Mr. Chase is aware that he is in difficulties here and he even has George Middleby ask, for once, an intelligent question: "I don't see how you can force such a gap between what is, or should be, organic—between politics and culture. Isn't this just an academic stratagem to get yourself off the hook—to allow you, that is, to be radical in merely literary and cultural matters without mingling in the dangerous realities of politics?" To which Mr. Chase, through Headstrong, pointedly replies: "The forcer of the gap . . . is not I but history."

It is here that Mr. Chase's critics from the left ought to show a bit more modesty than they have, since it is here that he puts us on the spot. Denying in effect that there is any significant radical politics in America today (he is right), Mr. Chase would then add, I imagine, that the efforts of those intellectuals involved in a venture like *Dissent* are still essentially "literary." This is true enough, and there is no point in disputing it. All that can be said in turn to Mr. Chase is that the "literary" nature of intellectual radicalism is an undesired limitation under which we chafe and which we hope eventually to remove.

Mr. Chase's reviewers have noticed other difficulties in his book: an all-too-easy assumption that there exists a natural alliance between the literary *avant-garde* and political radicalism; an equally questionable assumption that the *avant-garde* is a "permanent movement" in modern culture (I think, to the contrary, that it has reached a point of at least temporary exhaustion). But it would be captious to end on a negative note. Mr. Chase's book seems to me an important sign of a certain shift in sentiment and opinion, still modest in its proportions, that is beginning to take place among American intellectuals. The worst of the cold war fanaticism has died out. The more vulgar varieties of anti-Communism have lost their appeal (indeed, a new danger is that of a sophisticated reconciliation with Communist power). The jeering scorn to which radicals have been subjected these past fifteen years has begun to soften a little. Faint beginnings can be discerned of a new worry, a new uneasiness. Mr. Chase's book provides a possible way for transforming these responses into ideas; and if some of us feel that it is not strong enough here or clear enough there, we ought to be grateful to him for raising the *problem* of radicalism once again, and in circles where it has become the fashion to dismiss it. We might also remember the old Jewish saying that there is more than one way of getting to paradise.

ANTI-SEMITE AND JEW

In the summer of 1948 Milton Hindus, then a young teacher of literature at the University of Chicago, made a strange journey. At some personal sacrifice, he went to Denmark to see Louis-Ferdinand Céline, the French novelist who had written anti-Semitic tracts prior to and early in the war and had been accused by the Resistance of collaborating with the Nazis. For some years Hindus had been Céline's most vocal American admirer and had helped him in many ways, from writing laudatory essays about his work to sending him food packages. Hindus' journey was strange not merely because he was a Jew visiting an apparently unrepentant anti-Semite, but because a major reason for his visit was his inability to reconcile himself to the idea that Céline was, in fact, an anti-Semite. In an introduction to an American reprint of Céline's novel *Death on the Installment Plan*, Hindus had speculated on the similarity between Céline's anti-Semitic pamphlets and Swift's "Modest Proposal," as Gide had previously taken Céline's rantings for satire. (Previously, however, in a tortured article for an Australian magazine, Hindus had written, "I, a Jewish Nationalist, find myself in the position of defending an anti-Semite in his anti-Semitism— that is where the complications of modern society have led us. Society has grown so complicated that we no longer know whom to blame.")

Now certain kinds of Jewish publicists will immediately consign Hindus to perdition with the pat phrase: Jewish self-hatred. But that phrase provides only a simple discharge of emotion, not an understanding of problems. And while I can hardly call myself a "defender" of Hindus, I want to get at what seems to me the heart of his problem—which is not his problem alone.

To do that, we must turn to Céline. Like Hindus, I greatly admire Céline's novels. Céline speaks for the underside of European society, the petty bourgeois crushed almost to *lumpen* status, the worker demoralized, the intellectual contemptuous of his own intellectuality. He represents the 20th-century underground man, fed up with ideas and ideologies, hating whatever is official, and despairingly aware of how incongruous is his overwrought consciousness in contrast with his feeble activity. In a brilliant essay on Céline's first novel, Léon Trotsky compared his protagonist with Poincaré. At first sight, this comparison may seem a piece of political forcing, but actually it reveals Céline's significance: Poincaré stands for the official cant of French society, Céline for the actual feeling at its base and in its interstices.

At the same time Céline is an aesthete (the crimes of Hitler, he told Hindus, were the result of bad taste) who fears and scorns his aestheticism. When Hindus showed him reviews of his books, for which he was probably ravenously hungry, Céline violently asserted his lack of interest in anything but "How much money will they bring me?" For all his great mimetic-literary gifts, Céline fears his mind, all mind; he is an intellectual suffering from an extreme case of self-disrespect, which is not necessarily incompatible with self-love. He is a romantic whose romanticism has curdled and who has no intellectual resources on which to fall back. Consequently the torrent of language in his novels, which is like a stream of noise designed to drown out the agonies of feeling and the burdens of thought.

Trotsky said something similar in political terms: "Céline will not write a second book with such an aversion for the lie and such a disbelief in the truth. The dissonance will resolve itself. Either the artist will make his peace with the darkness or perceive the dawn." Trotsky meant, of course, that anyone with so total a grasp of the decay of modern life would have to choose either fascism or socialism, and though one need not accept the political terms of his analysis, one must grant that he was right in insisting that Céline's dissonance is the dissonance of European society seeking resolution. Now it is to the credit of Milton Hindus that he sensed all this some years back, and therefore described Céline as a key artist of our time. But so great was his admiration for Céline's work that he literally could not bear the thought that Céline could sink to anti-Semitism. And so he went to Denmark to see for himself.

The Crippled Giant, the journal he kept during his visit, is a record of disillusionment. With a naivety that would be absurd were it not so pure, Hindus found to his horror that Céline was still an anti-Semite. "He [Céline] said . . . that the great crime of the Nazis was that they had awakened anti-Semitism without having any real program. . . . He knows that in writing a violent diatribe like *Bagatelles pour un massacre* in 1938 against the Jews, he was like a man screaming 'Fire' along with the Hitlerian maniacs in the crowded theater of Europe, but he sees his case *from within* and knows the train of causes that brought him to that act and therefore expects to be forgiven." And again: "I asked Céline if he blamed the Jews for getting France into the war, and he said no at first and then modified that with the statement that the Jews had a part in starting the war, but that their part was no larger than Hitler's." And this to a Jew who had been his most intrepid American defender and had journeyed thousands of miles to see him.

Céline is a very sick man. During his conversations with Hindus, he betrayed signs of extreme paranoia, was subject to irrational avarice, found great pleasure in humiliating his visitor, and showed a blatant callousness with respect to his own moral responsibility. Clearly his mentality reflects that of a broad stratum in Europe: a mentality driven to irrational, sadistic, and self-humiliating excesses. As Céline perceptively and sadly remarked of himself: "I'm like the porcupine—if I uncurl I'm lost."

Meanwhile Hindus suffered terribly. He developed tics in his eye, "unaccountable" pains in his legs and fingers. "My feelings toward Céline undergo as many alternations as do those of a disappointed lover." Finally, the disappointed lover rebelled, and began abusing Céline in his journal with as little dignity as Céline had abused him in conversation. Yet, in the end, enough love remained for Hindus to offer Céline whatever royalties he would make on the book, despite his recognition that "this man is across too great an abyss from me to be reached ever."

The Crippled Giant is written in a tone of melodramatic hysteria that might be tolerable if it announced something genuinely shocking (say, that Russia was a slave state at a time when most intellectuals supported Stalinism), but which seems inappropriate for a rather belated personal discovery. After all, Hindus, like any other reasonably intelligent person, should always have known what he so painfully learned: that a great writer can also be a great scoundrel.

Yet a particular significance lies in Hindus's experience: it is a classic instance of what might be called the "culture sickness" increasingly prevalent among American intellectuals and the intellectualized middle class. Hindus's previous inability to see the truth about Céline was based, I think, on an extreme overvaluation of literature at the expense of immediate personal and social experience: a writer as good as Céline—how *could* he be a fascist? This overvaluation, or misunderstanding, of culture is widespread in America today partly because of the failure of radical politics and the intellectuals' consequent sense of social powerlessness. As an intelligent man Hindus could easily have seen the simple truth about Céline, but his supreme attachment to literature would not let him. As long, however, as we are unable properly to distinguish between literature and experience, as long as we fail to acknowledge that a writer who provides us the deepest aesthetic satisfactions can also hold the most repugnant opinions and values, we shall muddle both our reading and our lives. How it is possible for a man to write the profoundest truth in one book and the vilest lies in another is indeed a heart-breaking question; but first we must acknowledge that it is a real question.

I am afraid that Hindus has not recovered from his "culture sickness," for toward the end of his book he begins to doubt the value of Céline's novels. But that is just to reverse his original error. The books stand, their value unimpaired by Céline's personal wretchedness. Hindus says that "Céline is a splinter in my mind that I've got either to absorb completely or eject completely." And there is the root of his trouble, as of his sad and humiliating experience—for loyalty to literature and to life requires that the splinter be neither ejected nor absorbed.

HENRY JAMES AS LATTER-DAY SAINT

The admirers of Henry James are not likely to feel lukewarm about *The American Henry James*. Quentin Anderson's approach, which transforms the novelist into a moral allegorist using the Swedenborgian symbols and assumptions of his father Henry Sr., was first offered in *Kenyon Review* in 1947; and since then his work has won the praise of such accomplished critics as Francis Fergusson, Lionel Trilling and (with major qualifications) F. R. Leavis. This is not a company to be contradicted unless one has good reasons, so I had better say at once that to my mind the reasons are not only good but urgent. Mr. Anderson's book is the product of enormous labor, skill, earnestness, and ingenuity; but it is a bad book. Turgid in style, perverse and willful in approach, it rests upon assumptions that must prove destructive to literary values and critical discriminations.

What strikes one upon first reading this book—it constitutes a radical criticism—is that even while staking out the largest claims for his thesis Mr. Anderson never states precisely what it is. We are to be persuaded that an important relationship exists between some of James's novels and the moral philosophy of his father; we are told that without grasping this relationship it is virtually impossible to make out the meaning of these novels; but we are not told, with sufficient rigor and exactness, what that relationship is supposed to have been. Mr. Anderson simply fails to confront the question: Was James consciously and systematically charting an allegorical equivalent of his father's system, or did the values of that system so infiltrate James's consciousness that, quite regardless of his will, they also dominate his novels? Nor is this a secondary question; for even, I think, those critics most rigid in dismissing the "intentional fallacy" would have to grant that as regards allegory the description of the genre is inseparable from the claim for intention.

For long stretches of his book Mr. Anderson "translates" the action of Jame's later novels—with much wrenching and twisting, which I shall specify later—into the vocabulary of the elder James. That such a shift from the son's marvelously complex and subtle vision to the eccentric husks of the father's doctrine must sadly impoverish and narrow some very great works of art is finally the crux of the matter; but at the moment I prefer to stress that this process of "translation," even if one could find it convincing and useful, does not necessarily tell us very much about the intellectual relationship presumed to have been present between father and son.

In Mr. Anderson's presentation the philosophy of James Sr., despite some frightful language, turns out to be as simple as most systems of nineteenth-century American romantic moralists: it is an account of the struggle between Love and Self, between morality as a spontaneous, unfettered, personally forged and endlessly renewed "style," on the one hand, and moralism as the institutional hardening and corruption of Selfhood, on the other. It would therefore almost be possible to "translate"—though for no good reason whatever—a number of other nineteenth-century American novels into the vocabulary of the elder James, since his ideas had much in common with the whole transcendentalist impulse of mid-nineteenth century America. The generation of writers of that time, Mr. Anderson himself declares, "tried to maintain . . . the moral and religious sanctions which, for their fathers and grandfathers, had been institutionalized. They tried to stuff into the self what the society had ceased adequately to represent." Good enough; but in this remark there is neither novelty—the point having been made most notably by Yvor Winters in his fine essay on James, which Mr. Anderson does not mention—nor warrant for reading *The Golden Bowl* as an allegory to which only the system of James Sr. provides the key. All that can reasonably be said, and many critics have said it, is that James absorbed a good deal of the moral idealism floating about in New England at the time and absorbed some of it, no doubt, from his father.

At some points, however, Mr. Anderson bids higher. "The younger son," he writes, "is, to my knowledge, the only man who has ever *used* the elder James's beliefs" (emphasis in original). What is more, Mr.

Anderson can speak of "the teasing way in which, throughout the prefaces, James refers to his emblems without ever announcing or classifying them." Not only, then, was James consciously working with his father's "emblems," but he was engaged in a "teasing" effort to obscure their presence and their meaning. Here Mr. Anderson approaches the Conspiracy Theory of Criticism, which gives us writers practicing a life-long mystification: Kafka secreting Freudian formulas in his work, Melville conducting a secret quarrel with God throughout his novels. It is an approach to literature which makes it very hard to distinguish between a novel and the Zohar.[1]

In any case, if it is Mr. Anderson's intention to say that James's *use* of his father's emblems is the central discovery of his book, then one would expect that some evidence might be offered to indicate that James also knew what Mr. Anderson knows he was doing. But not a line! Mr. Anderson feels obliged to quote from James's letters and autobiographies several statements gently disavowing interest in his father's system, as for example this one:

> It comes over me as I read . . . how intensely original and personal [his father's] whole system was, and how indispensable it is that those who go in for religion [But doesn't that phrase give away the whole show?—I.H.] should take some heed of it. I can't enter into it (much) myself—I can't be so theological nor grant his extraordinary premises, nor throw myself into conceptions of heavens and hells, nor be sure that the keynote of nature is humanity. . . .

This was written by James in 1885, and for those who are familiar with the elaborate kindliness of his letters, as well as the depths of his filial piety, the passage must surely seem all the more decisive as an intellectual dissociation. Mr. Anderson wrestles with it manfully, and declares that it shows the younger James to be "plainly uninformed" about his father's system—though why this is supposed to support his case that Henry Jr. "*used* the elder James's beliefs" escapes me.

Nor is there anything in the Notebooks concerning symbolic or allegorical intentions of a systematic kind, despite the fact that James discussed in them so many of his themes, methods and literary problems. (Swedenborg is not listed at all in the index to the Matthiessen-Murdock edition, while James Sr. makes his few appearances in a strictly personal capacity, never in regard to literary matters.) For James's utter silence concerning what is supposed to have been the dominant influence upon his novels—indeed, the conceptual system he "*used*" in structuring them—Mr. Anderson has a remarkable explanation: "the novelist was incapable of conveying information simply *as* information; he had to give a dramatic form to everything." In regard to literary topics this is hardly true, since James was avid for, and loved to note down, such information. But suppose it were true: why then did the novelist not give "dramatic form" to his memories—surely they would have been affecting—of having worked with his father's "emblems," just as he gave "dramatic form" in the prefaces and Notebooks to his memories of having worked with so many other elements of his experience and observation?

Perhaps the most astonishing aspect of Mr. Anderson's method is his treatment of those novels—*The Europeans, Washington Square, The Bostonians, What Maisie Knew* and *The Awkward Age*—which, he admits, cannot be squeezed into his scheme. He simply puts them aside, casts them off: they do not behave according to the rules laid down for "the American James." But when you are proposing a revolutionary approach to a great writer like James, an approach which renders most previous criticism obsolete, you can hardly dismiss so casually this dazzling list of masterpieces: it is as if one discovered the "key" to Dostoevsky but had to grant that the doors remained locked to *Crime and Punishment* and *The Possessed.*

As it happens, three of these James novels are set in America (which comes to three more than any among those Mr. Anderson does discuss), and one wonders how it is that precisely the novels with an American setting fail to be relevant to "the American James." More important, Mr. Anderson, in the course of dividing the novels into "emblematic" sheep and "non-emblematic" goats, fails to ask himself some essential questions: If *The Bostonians, Washington Square,* etc. fail to conform to what is supposed to be the central principle of James's vision, what other principle do they conform to? And if there is at work in these novels another, let us call it "alien" principle, what is its relation to the "emblematic" one that controls such books as *The Wings of the Dove* and *The Golden Bowl?* And finally, if such an "alien" principle is to be found in some of James's novels,[2] might it not be supposed that it also operates, however fitfully, in those novels Mr. Anderson has chosen to consider? For unless we assume James to have been hopelessly schizoid, it hardly seems plausible that he could have spent a lifetime writing from two utterly disconnected and opposing principles of composition that would each have no effect upon the work dominated by the other.

The image of James that emerges from Mr. Anderson's book is that of a painfully high-minded, idealistic, humorless and unworldly Professor of Moral Philosophy. James, we are told, celebrated "a vision of the moral life founded on personal freedom and unsupported by institutional props. . . ." His world "is one in which dramatic situations are always prior to fated conditions. . . ." "A conception of the world in which consciousness made all the differences exempted him from the tyranny of conditions, external compulsions and from the unblinking pressure of the unaware."[3] (Here, as elsewhere, Mr. Anderson seems to be talking about James as a novelist rather than as a person.) And finally, James was not trying "to cope with a threatening cultural situation in which, as a matter of fact, he was not involved."

Apart from that "unblinking pressure of the unaware," which sounds fine but tends to resist paraphrase, all of these statements can be examined and shown to be inaccurate or serious exaggerations. If James held "a vision of the moral life founded on personal freedom," then a "threatening cultural situation" would necessarily involve him, since it would be working in opposition to his "vision of the moral life"; and as James in his unsystematic way knew only too well, that is precisely what did happen. It is true of course that "a vision of the moral life founded on personal freedom" does inform his novels, but what Mr. Anderson refuses to recognize—in the interest of his thesis, but at great cost to the moral tension within the novels—is that there is also present in them a profound and often extremely painful sense of "the tyranny of conditions." What else endows them with their high drama? *What else could?* For without this awareness of the power of all that is external to the self, it may be doubted that James or anyone else could write novels at all.

But it is when one turns back to the novels themselves, while remembering Mr. Anderson's words, that one rubs one's eyes. Hyacinth Robinson, caught between Paris and the Sun and Moon café—is he in a dramatic situation prior to fated conditions? Isabel Archer, discovering that her very quest for unconditioned freedom leads her into a terrible subjection—is she exempt from the tyranny of conditions? Maggie Verver, desperately maneuvering to save her marriage—is she free from external compulsions?

Reading *The American Henry James* one would hardly suppose that novels, among other things but surely not as the least of them, are *performances;* that a writer like James could yield himself to a moment of spontaneity, could soften into his gift for play, even in his most freighted and solemn works; that he could put something into a novel because it seemed noteworthy as an instance of human conduct, quite without reference to its place in a symbolic scheme to be announced fifty or sixty years later; that, like every other novelist who ever wrote, he could be fascinated with human character in its own right and for its own sake, even if he was silly enough to speak of Russian novels as "fluid puddings"; and above all that James, ingrained nineteenth-century American as in one part of himself he was and habitual moralist as he also was, could ever be tempted by sophistication or worldliness or malice or even, perhaps, the sinister—temptations that might lead

him, as it has led almost everyone else, to like and admire a magnificent schemer like Kate Croy. If the bent of contemporary criticism is to
supply novelists with severe moral intentions, might it not also recognize how creative and life-renewing the relaxation of moral intentions
can be in a work of art? Like so many other critics of our time, Mr.
Anderson does not really read novels; he reads through or past them,
searching so obsessively for the figure that he quite chews up the
carpet.

And so it is that he summarizes the "emblematic themes":

The Ambassadors has for its subject the failure of the law, and its correspondent 'church' is New England's, here standing for the elder James's 'Jewish'
church. *The Wings of the Dove* treats the redemption of an individual by an
exemplary savior, Milly Theale; the correspondent church is 'Christian.' *The
Golden Bowl's* subject is the regeneration of mankind, and its correspondent
church is that of the new Jerusalem announced by Swedenborg.

Admittedly, quoting these summary sentences without providing
the material from the elder James upon which they are based, is to
make them seem more obscure than they need be or already are.[4] But
the objection to this sort of thing isn't that one can't make sense out of
such descriptions; it is that finally they have so little to do with literature. In Mr. Anderson's reading of the great trio of James's final period,
Prince Amerigo emerges as "the walking sum of history," Adam Verver
as "the Christ founding a new temple," Lionel Croy as "the Devil,"
Colonel Assingham as also "a devil of sorts." Mme. de Vionnet "turns
out to be a lovely lie" (whereas I had taken her for an attractive and
cultivated middle-aged woman painfully discovering that the man she
loves is preparing to leave her). Kate Croy's sister, Mrs. Condrip,
proves to be "the literal church" in *The Wings of the Dove*. Mrs.
Assingham "may be called 'the church' " of *The Golden Bowl*. (Indeed
she may: but it is much more interesting to call her an Assingham.)

One learns from Mr. Anderson that the elder James's "taste for the
unconditioned which led to an explicit denial of the reality of sexuality
and death, is present in the novelist, is, in fact, the very ground of his
marvellous capacity for creating aesthetic order." What can be meant
by "an explicit denial of the reality of sexuality and death"—or whether
denials of the two can be aligned so readily—is a problem. But if such a
phrase does mean anything, where in James are we to find the evidence for it? In Catherine Sloper as an example of life as "unconditioned"? In the fate of Roderick Hudson as an instance of the unreality of death? In the radiating power of Kate Croy as "emblematic" of
the unreality of sex? Reading Mr. Anderson's emblematic version of
The Wings of the Dove, one sees poor Milly Theale, the red-haired

American girl with the fatal illness and the yearning to live and the pathetic desire to forgive, being cast as a God. With relief one turns to F. W. Dupee's book on James, to read there that Milly conveys "the essential pathos of all mortality by being under special sentence."

The critic driven by an urge to schematization can become ruthless with his materials. What Mr. Anderson succeeds in doing is to replace James's natural sympathy for his characters with a fanatic rigor: it might be called the wages of monism. In *The Portrait of a Lady*, he tells us, "the aim of being 'exquisite' which the black Osmond quite honestly [Quite honestly indeed!—ask Madame Merle.] proffers is completely congruent with Isabel's own aim as a young woman. The point is that only the self-absorbed person can be trapped by the self-absorbed person. . . ." Mr. Anderson's needs may be served by seeing the aims of Osmond and Isabel as "completely congruent"; but how violent a wrenching of the structure of the novel is required to say this, how deep a disregard for the tone of ironic affection that James preserves toward Isabel throughout the book. And how utterly without affection is Mr. Anderson in writing this. For is it really true, and can we suppose Henry James to have thought, that "only the self-absorbed person can be trapped by the self-absorbed person"? One wonders whether, in Mr. Anderson's universe, inexperience—an inexperience that has its pathos as nothing in Osmond can have—figures at all; whether amid the emblems and the churches and the new Jerusalems young girls can't make mistakes through their very moral idealism.

The American Henry James must finally be judged by the standard Mr. Anderson himself has proposed in discussing the novelist's father. Not moral system but moral "style" seems to have been the elder James's passion; and Mr. Anderson, in his passion for abstract system, has betrayed the son by transforming his work into a Swedenborgian "church" in which the father's insights lie entombed.

Yet the book itself provides us with an "emblematic theme." We have been taught in recent years—and we have profited greatly from the lesson—that in the apparent madness of much modern criticism there can lie hidden a brilliant and enlightening method. May it not be time to stand that lesson on its head?

[1]Not hard for everyone. Mr. Anderson's approach is essentially fanatical, but he is careful to avoid the manner of fanaticism. Only once, to my knowledge, does he slip into the amusing sort of self-congratulation, the claim to unique revelation, which is the rationale for writing criticism to prove that an author has been engaged in some form of secret speech: "He [James the novelist] was of course shrewd enough to know that what was so carefully concealed would be perceived only by an able reader, but he was clearly unaware that his sense of humanity was emotionally so private and historically so special that this scheme would not be apprehensible unless the reader used his father as a guide."

And since of course no one before Mr. Anderson has systematically used the father as a guide. . . .

[2]Novels which, in passing, he violently mishandles, as if they were somehow culpable for being "non-emblematic." Thus, his extraordinary statement that *The Bostonians* is not written from James's usual assumption of "our accountability for our experience." Or his even more extraordinary statement that *The Awkward Age*—a brilliant but very difficult novel—depends on "a spectrum of moral judgments and presumptions about the social scene which the reader possesses before he begins to read." I should think myself that the problem in regard to *The Awkward Age* is to be able to possess its "moral judgments and presumptions about the social scene" *after* one has read it.

[3]Yet we read, concerning this novelist fortunate (and unique) enough to be "exempted . . '. from the tyranny of conditions," that "as a thinker, Henry James is an exquisitely ordered version of the most general manifestations of the culture of his origins." One might suppose that any writer who can be described as a "version" of the manifestations of his culture is not entirely free from the tyranny of conditions.

[4]Here is Mr. Anderson at his most high-powered: "James [in *The Golden Bowl*] seems to have had a great deal of fun in detailing emblematically the marriage of the second or universal Adam, the Grand Man or *Maximus Homo*, to the Eve, or *minimus homo* (also called vir by the elder James). He first named her Charlotte, the emblematic significance being 'little man' or *minimus homo* (Charlotte is a *diminutive* of Carl, which originally meant man, or male). He then imagines the courtship as recapitulating the relation God had to Israel, since Charlotte is spiritually Jewish, that is, is publicly represented by the 'church' and 'state,' the Assinghams." I assure the reader that in context this passage is comprehensible. But could anything be more unfortunate?

GOD, MAN AND STALIN

That Whittaker Chambers told the truth and Alger Hiss did not, seems to me highly probable. Personal tragedy though their confrontation was, it had another, almost abstract quality: the political course of the thirties made it inevitable that, quite apart from this well-groomed man and that unkempt one, there be a clash between two men, one a "liberal" recruited from the idealistic wing of public service, the other a former Communist who repudiated his past and then, as *Witness* testifies, swung to the politics of the far right. If not these two, then two others; if not their shapes and accents, other shapes and accents. And that is why most of the journalistic speculation on their personalities proved so ephemeral: for what did it finally matter whether Hiss was a likable man or Chambers an overwrought one? what did it matter when at stake was the commitment of those popular-front liberals who had persisted in treating Stalinism as an accepted part of "the Left"? and why should serious people have puzzled for long over the private motives of Chambers or Hiss when Stalinism itself remained to be studied and analyzed?

Chambers has told his story and put down his ideas. *Witness* is a fascinating grab-bag: autobiography, account of underground work, religious tract, attempt at an explanation of Stalinism. As confession, it has an almost classical stature: whatever opinions Chambers may now superimpose on his memory, the narrative itself demands the attention of anyone interested in modern politics. As autobiography, the book is embarrassing: Chambers' memoir of his family seems a needless act of masochism while the portrait of his adult self suggests a man whose total sincerity is uncomplicated by humor, irony, or persuasive humility.

The most remarkable fact about *Witness* is that as a work of ideas it should be so ragged and patchy. In all its 800 pages there is hardly a sustained passage of, say, five thousand words devoted to a serious development of thought; everything breaks down into sermon, reminiscence, self-mortification, and self-justification. Service in the G.P.U. is not, to be sure, the best training for the life of the mind; but there is something in Chambers' flair for intellectual melodrama that seems particular to our time and to the kind of personality always hungry for absolutes of faith. Writes Chambers: "I was not seeking ethics; I was seeking God. My need was to be a practising Christian in the same sense that I had been a practising Communist." A little time spent in "seeking ethics" or even a breather from "seeking" anything, might seem to have been in order.

The world, as Chamber sees it, is split between those who acknowledge the primacy of God and those who assert the primacy of man; from this fundamental division follows a struggle between morality and murder, with Communism merely the final version of the rationalist heresy; and the one hope for the world is a return to Christian virtue, the ethic of mercy. These views Chambers announces with an air of abject righteousness. Indifferent to the caution that the sin of pride takes no more extreme form than a belief in God as one's personal *deus ex machina*, he several times acknowledges a Mover at his elbow and declares the appointment of Thomas Murphy as government prosecutor in the Hiss case to be evidence that "It pleased God to have in readiness a man." From *Witness* an unsympathetic reader might, in fact, conclude that God spent several years as a special aid to the House Committee on Un-American Activities.

In reading this book one is nonplussed by the way its polemics violate its declared values. A few illustrations may suggest the quality of Chambers' thought:

Again and again he declares himself interested in presenting the facts. Without questioning his personal story, I must doubt his capacity as historian and social observer. It is not true that Trotsky "led in person" the Bolshevik troops that suppressed the Kronstadt rebellion. It is not true that "Lenin gave up listening to music because of the emotional havoc it played with him"; the man merely said, if Gorky's report of a casual remark be credited, that music made him want to stroke heads at a time when he felt it necessary to make revolutions. It is not true that "Communists are *invariably* as prurient as gutter urchins." It is an exaggeration to say that in the 1927 faction fight in the United States Communist Party, dirty as it was, each side "prompted scandalous whispering campaigns, in which embezzlement of party money, homosexuality, and stool pigeon were the preferred whispers." And it is a wild exaggeration to assert that the Communist agents in Washington, dangerous as they were, "if only in prompting the triumph of Communism in China, have *decisively* changed the history of Asia, of the United States, and therefore, of *the entire world*" (italics mine—I.H.). Mao recruited his armies in the valley of Yenan, not the bars of Washington.

Chambers' extreme political turn has dizzied his historical sense. By noting that Alger Hiss was counsel for the Nye committee during the thirties, he tries to discredit its exposure of the munitions industry. "The penetration of the United States government by the Communist Party," adds Chambers, "coincided with a mood in the nation which lightheartedly baited the men who manufactured the armaments indispensable to its defense as 'Merchants of Death.' " But surely more was involved: the Nye committee revealed that some arms manufacturers had not hesitated to sell in bulk to Hitler, that their profits had been unconscionably high, that some had pressured both sides in the Chaco to buy their products and thus to prolong a war. The truth of these disclosures does not depend on whether Hiss was counsel for the committee that made them.

Chambers complains bitterly, and with justice, about the smears he has suffered from many Hiss supporters. Unfortunately, he is not himself above the use of similar methods. One of Hiss's attorneys was Harold Rosenwald, about whose face Chambers darkly pronounces: "I had seen dozens much like it in my time." The notion that people can be "placed" politically by the shape of their faces, is both preposterous and, at least in this century, sinister.

In the course of breaking away from Stalinism, Chambers came to feel that "it is just as evil to kill the Czar and his family . . . as it is to starve two million peasants or slave laborers to death." What, if anything, does this highly charged statement mean? Coming from a pacifist, it would be perfectly clear, for it would suggest that killing is forbidden under any circumstances. We might then hope to hear as a sequel that "It is just as evil to kill 60,000 civilians in Hiroshima as it was to kill the Czar and his family." But Chambers is not a pacifist, he is willing to "struggle against [Communism] by all means, including arms." So the evil of killing the Czar cannot for him be simply that it was a killing, but must be that it was an unjustified killing—which leaves him with the moral enormity: "Several unjustified killings are just as evil as two million unjustified killings."

Throughout the book Chambers praises the Christian virtues of humility and meekness. Unfortunately, this credo does not prevent him from declaring "the left-wing intellectuals of almost every feather" to have been Hiss supporters and then from calling them "puffins, skimmers, skuas, and boobies." These delicate designations prompt one to remind Chambers that a good many "left-wing intellectuals" of one or another feather fought a minority battle against Stalinism at a time when *both* he and Hiss were at the service of Messrs. Yagoda and Yezhov.

Stalinism is evil, declares Chambers; a proposition neither disputable nor enlightening. Nowhere in his 800 pages does he attempt sustained definition or description, nowhere does he bound the shape of the evil. He seems unconcerned to examine the workings of Russian society, the social role of the Western Stalinist parties, the relation of the Asian parties to native nationalism. And with good reason. If you believe that the two great camps of the world prepare for battle under the banners, Faith in Man and Faith in God, what is the point of close study and fine distinctions? You need only sound the trumpets.

Almost unwittingly, Chambers moves toward the view that the source of our troubles is the Enlightenment: "The crisis of the Western world exists to the degree in which it is indifferent to God." The French Revolution becomes the villain of history, its progeny every godless society of our time. Chambers accepts, of course, the common, crude identification of Stalin's totalitarianism with Lenin's revolutionary state; both seem to him forms of fascism; the New Deal was a social revolution which crippled "the power of business"; and the motto of "the welfare state" is best expressed by his former associate, Colonel Bykov: "Who pays is boss, and who takes money must also give something." Everyone might thus be lumped together: Voltaire, Jefferson, Lenin, Roosevelt, Hitler, Stalin; not all equally evil, but all, apparently, "indifferent to God." A man who thinks in such patterns can hardly be expected to notice—or have much reason to care—that Stalinism and fascism, while symmetrical in their political devices, have different historical origins, class structures, political ideologies, and social rationales. Or that the Keynesian measures of the New Deal, far from constituting a revolution, proved a crutch for a stumbling capitalism.

Chambers' approach to history rests, finally, on no social theory at all; it is a return to Manichean demonology. Since for him everything depends on whether one takes God or man to be primary, he can write that "as Communists, Stalin and the Stalinists were absolutely justified in making the Purge. From a Communist point of view, Stalin could have taken no other course. . . . In that fact lay the evidence that Communism is absolutely evil. The human horror was not evil, it was the sad consequence of evil." The first two of these sentences are historically false; various Communists opposed the purge and proposed other courses of action, among them the removal of Stalin from power. The last sentence is shocking in its moral callousness. In effect, Chambers is saying that those of us who attack Stalinism for its inhumanity are sentimental, lacking in his austere disdain for what he calls "formless good will." Is it, however, more important to attack Stalin for disbelieving in the primacy of God than for killing millions of men? If the killing is to be regarded as a mere "consequence" of first principles, specific moral criticism of it can only seem superficial. But, in fact, the purges were the result of a decision by men in power, a decision for which they must be held responsible. A society is to be judged less by its philosophical premise about God and man, if it has any, than by its actual treatment of men; "the human horror of the purge" was evil, not merely "sad." What matters is not the devil's metaphysics, but his morals.

Chambers' major insight into the problem of Stalinism is his insistence that in this era of permanent crisis it provides a faith, a challenge, even an ideal. Feeding on crisis, Stalinism offers a vision. "The vision inspires. The crisis impels. The workingman is chiefly moved by the crisis. The educated man is chiefly moved by the vision." This is an important observation and a necessary corrective to vulgar theories which make of Stalinism mainly an atavistic drive for power. But Chambers, ignoring the fact that the vision of Stalinism is corrupt, treats it as if it were a legitimate form of socialism, and pays slight attention to the counterrevolution that occurred in Russia during the very years he was its underground agent.

Is this an academic matter? Not at all; for the essence of Stalinism, in its Russian form, is that it rests on a new kind of bureaucratic ruling class which engaged in "primitive accumulation" by destroying the revolutionary generation and appropriating to itself total economic and political power. Outside of Russia, Stalinism utilizes the socialist tradition of Europe and the nationalist sentiment of Asia for its domestic class needs and international power maneuvers. Drawing on a unique blend of reactionary and pseudo-revolutionary appeals, Stalinism attracts, in this age of crisis, all those who feel the world must be changed but lack the understanding or energy to change it in a libertarian direction. Anti-capitalist but not socialist, Stalinism causes, in the words of Marx, all the old crap to rise to the top; under its domination, the best impulses of modern man are directed toward the worst consequences. And the problem for the historian is to determine precisely the blend of seemingly contradictory elements that Stalinism comprises.

Chambers himself provides an anecdote which dramatically confirms these remarks. His boss in the underground, Colonel Bykov, was a perfect specimen of the new Stalinist man: coarse, obedient, unintellectual, brutal. To Bykov "the generation that had made the Revolution . . . seemed as alien and preposterous . . . as foreigners. They belonged to another species and he talked about them the way people talk about the beastly or amusing habits of cows or pigs." So disgusting was Bykov that Chambers felt, before introducing him to Hiss, that he would have to apologize for the Russian. Yet, after a brief conversation, Hiss found Bykov "impressive." Why? I would guess that it was the attraction of an extreme bureaucratic personality for a mild bureaucratic personality, of one man who instinctively scorned the masses of people for another who had been trained to think of them as objects for benevolent manipulation. If Hiss had possessed a trace of either revolutionary or liberal spirit, he would have been contemptuous of Bykov, he would have seen on Bykov's hands the blood of Bukharin and Tomsky and thousands upon thousands of others.

Where will Chambers go? His strength lies in a recognition that we live in an extreme situation; he agrees that "it is necessary to change the world." No longer a radical, scornful of liberals, convinced that "in the struggle against Communism the conservative is all but helpless," he accepts, formally, the position of those reactionaries *manqués* who edit William Buckley's *National Review*. But only formally; for unlike them, he is drenched with the consciousness of crisis, he has none of their complacence, he continues a disturbed and dissatisfied man. What remains? Only the fact that estranged personality and reactionary opinion form an explosive mixture.

In his final sentence Chambers hints that he believes a third world war both inevitable and necessary. Yet he yearns for some spiritual reformation, a turn to God. What likelihood there is that spiritual or any other desired values would survive in a world-wide atomic war, he does not discuss. Would there, in any case, be much point in reminding him that religious faith has rarely prevented despots from being despotic? that many of our most precious concepts of liberty are the work of skeptics? that Stalinism thrives in pious Rome as in worldly Paris? that it wins supporters in an Orient which has not known a loss of religious faith comparable to that of the West? that if Stalin is an atheist, Franco is a believer? that the priests in Russia pray for Stalin as in Germany they prayed for Hitler?

Very little point, I fear; little more than to have told him during the 'thirties that Stalinism was betraying the German workers to Hitler or by its trials and purges murdering thousands of innocent people. Those who abandon a father below are all too ready for a father above. But this shift of faith does not remove the gnawing problems which, if left unsolved, will drive still more people to Stalinism; it gives the opponents of the totalitarian state no strategy, no program with which to remake the world; it makes our situation appear even more desperate than it already is. For if Chambers is right in believing the major bulwark against Stalin to be faith in God, then it is time for men of conviction and courage to take to the hills.

THE SIXTIES

RICHARD WRIGHT:A WORD OF FAREWELL

When Wright's first novel *Native Son* appeared in the thirties, it seemed important both as an example of literary naturalism and an outcry of Negro protest. A few years later came *Black Boy*, the story of Wright's boyhood and youth in the deep South and perhaps his single best piece of work. Here, one felt, was the American Negro novelist who would speak without hesitation, who for the first time would tell the truth not only about the familiar sufferings of his people but about their buried responses, those inner feelings of anger and hatred which no white man could reach. And this, I think, Wright did succeed in doing. He told us the one thing even the most liberal and well-disposed whites preferred not to hear: that Negroes were far from patient or forgiving, that they were scarred by fear, that they hated every moment of their humiliation even when seeming most acquiescent, and that often enough they hated *us*, the decent and cultivated white men who, from complicity or neglect, shared in the responsibility for their plight. No Negro writer had ever quite said this before, certainly not with so much force or bluntness, and if such younger Negro novelists as James Baldwin and Ralph Ellison were to move beyond Wright's harsh naturalism and toward more subtle modes of fiction, that was possible only because Wright had been there first, courageous enough to release the full weight of his anger.

Before the implications of this fact, it seemed not very important that his image of Negro life in America was becoming historically dated (which is true) or that he occasionally succumbed to black nationalism (also true) or that he wrote badly (sometimes true). The bitterness and rage that poured out of Wright's books form one of the great American testaments, a crushing necessity to our moral life.

And now, after fourteen years of voluntary exile in Paris, chosen, as he once told me, because he could no longer bear to live in the United States and see his children suffer the blows of race hatred, Richard Wright is dead. His life was incomplete, as it had to be, and at the end his work as tentative and fumbling as at the beginning. His later years were difficult, for he neither made a true home in Paris nor kept in imaginative touch with the changing life of the United States. He was a writer in limbo, and his best fiction, such as the novelette "The Man Who Lived Underground," is a projection of that condition.

Eight Men is a collection of stories written over the last 25 years. Though they fail to yield any clear line of chronological development, these stories do give evidence of Wright's literary restlessness, his wish to keep learning and experimenting, his often clumsy efforts to break out of the naturalism which was his first and, I think, necessary mode of expression. The unevenness of his writing is extremely disturbing: one finds it hard to understand how the same man, from paragraph to paragraph, can be at once so brilliant and inept—though the student of American literature soon learns to measure the price which the talented autodidact pays for getting his education too late. Time after time the narrative texture of the stories is broken by a passage of jargon borrowed from sociology or psychology: perhaps the later Wright read too much, tried too hard, failed to remain sufficiently loyal to the limits of his talent.

The best stories are marked by a strong feeling for the compactness of the story as a form, so that even when the language is scraggly or leaden there is a sharply articulated pattern of event. Some of the stories, such as "Big Black Good Man," are enlivened by Wright's sardonic humor, the humor of a man who has known and released the full measure of his despair but finds that neither knowledge nor release matters in a world of despair. In "The Man Who Lived Underground" Wright shows a sense of narrative rhythm, a gift for shaping the links between sentences so as to create a chain of expectation, which is superior to anything in his full-length novels and evidence of the seriousness with which he kept working.

The main literary problem that troubled Wright in recent years was that of rendering his naturalism a more supple and terse instrument. I think he went astray whenever he abandoned naturalism entirely;

there are a few embarrassingly bad experiments with stories written entirely in dialogue or self-consciously employing Freudian symbolism. Wright needed the accumulated material of circumstance which naturalistic detail provided his fiction; it was as essential to his ultimate effect of shock and bruise as dialogue to Hemingway's ultimate effect of irony and loss. But Wright was correct in thinking that the problem of detail is the most vexing technical problem the naturalist writer must face, since the accumulation of detail that makes for depth and solidity can also create a pall of tedium. In "The Man Who Lived Underground" Wright came close to solving this problem, for here the naturalistic detail is put at the service of a radical projective image—a Negro trapped in a sewer—and despite some flaws, the story is satisfying both for its tense surface and its elasticity of suggestion.

The reality pressing upon all of Wright's work is a nightmare of remembrance, and without the terror of that nightmare it would be impossible to render the truth of the reality—not the only, perhaps not even the deepest truth about American Negroes, but a primary and inescapable one. Both truth and terror depend upon a gross fact which Wright faced more courageously than any American writer: that for the Negro violence forms an inescapable part of his existence.

In a sense, then, Wright was justified in not paying attention to the changes that have been occurring in the South these past few decades. When Negro liberals write that despite the prevalence of bias there has been an improvement in the life of their people down South, such statements are reasonable and necessary. But what have they to do with the way Negroes feel, with the power of the memories they must surely retain? About this we know very little and would be well advised not to nourish preconceptions, for it may well be that their feelings are quite close to Wright's rasping outbursts. *Wright remembered,* and what he remembered other Negroes must also have remembered. Perhaps by now the terror and humiliation that fill his pages are things of the past, even in Mississippi; but men whose lives have been torn by suffering must live with their past, so that it too becomes part of the present reality. And by remembering Wright kept faith with the experience of the boy who had fought his way out of the depths to speak for those who remained there.

The present moment is not a good one for attempting a judicious estimate of Wright's achievement as a novelist. It is hard to suppose that he will ever be regarded as a writer of the first rank, for his faults are grave and obvious. Together with Farrell and Dos Passos, he has suffered from the changes of literary taste which occurred during his lifetime: the naturalist novel is little read these days, though often mocked, and the very idea of a "protest novel" has become a target for graduate students to demolish.

I too find the murk and awkwardness of most naturalist fiction hard to bear. But I believe that any view of 20th Century American literature which surmounts critical sectarianism will have to give Wright an honored place, and that any estimate of his role in our cultural life will have to stress his importance as the pioneer Negro writer who in the fullness of his anger made it less possible for American society to continue deceiving itself.

Anger and violence may be present in his work, but the Richard Wright I knew, slightly in person and somewhat more through letters, was a singularly good-hearted and sweet man. When I met him in Paris, he was open, vigorous and animated, full of shrewd if not always just estimates of the younger writers, actively concerned with the intellectual life of the African students who clustered about him, and, at a time when it was far from fashionable, still interested in the politics of the democratic left.

Richard Wright died at 52, full of hopes and projects. Like many of us, he had somewhat lost his intellectual way during recent years, but he kept struggling toward a comprehension of the strange and unexpected world coming into birth. In the most fundamental sense, however, he had done his work: he had told his contemporaries a truth so bitter that they paid him the tribute of striving to forget it.

THE SALINGER CULT

Among contemporary novelists Saul Bellow commands literary influence, Norman Mailer an intellectual following and James Baldwin an intense audience. Only J. D. Salinger can be described as the priest of an underground cult.

It is a cult that flourishes mainly among the academic young: those well-scrubbed boys and girls who have inherited the material good of this world and find themselves stirred neither to conquest nor rebellion, but instead remain bright, "cool" and estranged. The holy texts of this cult are *The Catcher in the Rye,* that touching little novel about a boy too frail to cope with his perceptions of the world's evil and too honest to evade them, and a group of stories about the large and talkative Glass family. The two long stories in the present volume, *Raise High the Roof Beam, Carpenters* and *Seymour An Introduction,* focus upon Seymour Glass, the eldest son, a family wiseman who has committed suicide in his early thirties, and left his example as burden and guide to his brothers and sisters.

Salinger has a keen, often vindictive ear for mimicking urban speech. He has developed a style—highly self-conscious, insinuatingly familiar, kittenishly erudite—that is all his own. He can squeeze more suspense out of a fragile anecdote than most living writers. And he is finely attuned to the vibrations of the American *Zeitgeist,* so that one thinks of him as both innovator and recorder of a new mode of feeling, a new style of expression, characteristic of the postwar years.

Salinger speaks for what might be called the "inner emigration" among our sensitive young. I borrow the term from recent Russian history, where it has been used to describe those intellectuals who, because they felt contempt for the Communist dictatorship and help-less before its power, tried to create for themselves a compensating inner life—as if their consciousness were to be a substitute for the physical emigration denied them. Allowing for obvious differences be-tween Russia and the United States, one could say that many of Saling-er's characters and readers also regard themselves as citizens of an "inner emigration."

In his writing this attitude comes through as distaste for the "phonies" Salinger's characters and young readers see cluttering the social landscape, by which they mean the sententious moralists, often their own parents, who do not even try to practise what they preach; as disgust before the world of commercial success together with an in-capacity even to imagine remaking it; and as an urge to withdraw from the clamor of public life in order to build a secret moral enclave of the pure, the fine, perhaps the sacred.

Raise High the Roof Beam, Carpenters and *Seymour an Introduc-tion,* both of which first appeared in *The New Yorker* during the fifties, diverge very sharply from the tense and compact stories with which Salinger won his early reputation. They represent an ambitious effort to unite a narrative mode with contemplative matter, the dynamism of the short story with prolonged moments of quiet in which the narrator keeps staring, to the point of mystical intuition or neurotic crackup, at the character of Seymour Glass. Instead of the usual assumption that in fiction moral significance can be inferred from precise renderings of conduct, these stories rest upon the premise that knowledge of charac-ter can be gained through a sustained contemplation into the very folds of love.

The narrator is Buddy Glass, another of those impossibly articulate, supersensitive Glasses—a family which, under the infatuated guidance of Salinger, is largely devoted to exercises in collective narcissism. An English teacher at a girls' college and a disciple of Seymour's mixture of Zen Buddhist quietism and a sentimentalized version of Christian love, Buddy tries to summon not merely the physical image of Seymour but also the very essence of his being. From Seymour he has learned that "the Fat Lady"—the ordinary varicose-veined creature who clogs our streets, unblessed with the grace or wisdom of the Glasses—is really Jesus Christ and hence to be loved. From Seymour he has also learned that "all we do our whole lives is go from one little piece of Holy Ground to the next. Is he *never* wrong?"

In *Carpenters* Buddy recalls Seymour's marriage, for which at first the bridegroom does not show. The bewildered guests disperse and Buddy has to share a long, stifling taxi-ride with the matron of honor, a woman embodying all the fashionable wordliness that Buddy, and behind him Salinger, dislikes. The matron of honor assaults Seymour with the cliches of psychoanalysis, but her wisdom turns to dust when Seymour does finally appear and elopes with his waiting bride. The story ends with selections from Seymour's journals revealing that his delay was caused by the sheer magnitude of his rapture, but also pointing toward another story, *A Perfect Day for Bananafish*, set a few years later, in which he commits suicide. Apparently, the mid-Manhattan philistinism to which Seymour links himself in *Carpenters* can lead only to the disaster of *Bananafish*.

Seymour an Introduction is an effort on Buddy's part to summon, at times through recollected images of childhood play, the beatitude of Seymour's character. The story is eventless and conflictless: it squats in Buddy's troubled brain and serves mainly to envisage those qualities of Seymour which make him too pure for survival in this world yet for that very reason the only true model for the Glass family.

Hopelessly prolix, both of these stories are marred by the self-indulgence of a writer flirting with depths of wisdom, yet coy and embarrassed in his advances. With their cozy parentheses and clumsy footnotes, their careening mixture of Jewish vaudeville humor and Buddhist prescription, they betray a surrender to cherished mannerisms.

And as the world of Salinger comes more fully into view, it seems increasingly open to critical attack. It is hard to believe in Seymour's saintliness, hard even to credit him as a fictional character, for we are barely able to see him at all behind the palpitations of Buddy's memory. The Salinger world is coated with the sentimentalism of a "love" that, in refusing to distinguish among objects and qualities, ends by obliterating their distinctive life.

There is "love" in this world, but no sex and little of those social contingencies through which men and women must realize their love. There is religiosity, but little of precise religious thought or that struggle with the demons of disbelief which all serious believers know. There is a recurrent display of chic erudition, Asian branch, but very little clear or formulated intellectual content: the Glasses have learned to talk, not yet to think.

There is, moreover, a premature readiness to dismiss the familiar social world without either a hard struggle against it or a true retreat from it, so that Salinger's stories turn out to be guides for those who would comfort themselves with the idea of inner emigration while in public conduct remaining largely compliant.

Postscript

Once, during the mid-sixties, I chanced to say a few mildly critical words about the fiction of J.D. Salinger in a college classroom; the response was astonishing—a rise of indignation, as if I'd assaulted some of the students' most precious values. Perhaps I had. A decade or so later it isn't clear whether the young still read Salinger. I suspect they do, but not with the cultish ostentation of the early sixties. I'm convinced, however, that this minor but interesting writer has had a lasting impact on American culture. His style of "inner emigration", as I've called it, has been picked up by many people, some of them not so young, who may no longer know that it derives most immediately from his fiction.

As my piece suggests, I'm not entirely sympathetic to this worldview. But there is one aspect of Salinger's career that I admire, and that is the complete determination with which he has guarded his privacy and refused all the junk, the vulgarities, the betrayals of our publicity-culture.

FLANNERY O'CONNOR'S STORIES

On and off I have been fussing in my mind with Flannery O'Connor's stories, unable to reach that certainty of judgment which, we all know, is the established trade mark of the modern critic. The skill and ambition of these stories are not lost upon me, yet I hesitate fully to join in the kind of praise they have won from respected critics.

At first I feared my distance from Miss O'Connor's religious beliefs might be corrupting my judgment, but while one cannot, in the nature of things, offer guarantees, the trouble does not seem to reside in the famous "problem of belief." Miss O'Connor was a serious Catholic, and what she called "the Catholic sacramental view of life" is certainly a controlling force in her stories. But it is not the only nor always the dominant one, since she could bring into play resources of worldliness such as one might find in the work of a good many modern writers. Miss O'Connor's religious convictions certainly operate throughout most of her stories, but at so deep a level, as so much more than mere subject matter or fixed point of view, that the skeptical reader is spared the problem of an explicit confrontation with "the Catholic sacramental view of life." Except for an occasional phrase, which serves partly as a rhetorical signal that more than ordinary verisimilitude is at stake, there are no unavoidable pressures to consider these stories in a religious context. They stand securely on their own, as renderings of human experience.

The writing is firm, economical, complex: we are engaged with an intelligence, not merely a talent. Miss O'Connor has a precise ear for rural colloquialism and lower-class mangling of speech; she can be slyly amusing in regard to the genteel segments of the Southern middle class, partly because she knows them with an assurance beyond sentiment or hatred. She has brought under control that addiction to Gothic hi-jinks which marred her early work (though it won her the applause of critics for whom any mode of representation they take to be "anti-realistic" is a token of daring and virtue). Touches of Gothic survive in these late stories, but no longer in a programmatic or obsessional way, and no longer on the assumption that to proclaim the wonders of the strange is to escape the determined limits of familiar life. What these touches of Gothic now do is to provide a shock in the otherwise even flow of narrative, thereby raising its pitch and tensing its movement.

What then is wrong? For most of Miss O'Connor's readers, nothing at all. For me, a tricky problem in method and tone, about which there is no need to pretend certainty.

Miss O'Connor's story "Everything That Rises Must Converge," has been much admired. An aging Confederate lady, fat, stupid and crazed with fantasies of status, keeps battling with her emancipated son Julian, an idle would-be writer. Julian expends ingenuities and nastiness in assaulting his mother, but most of his attacks fall harmlessly upon the walls of her genteel incomprehension. Unavoidably their personal conflict becomes entangled with "the Negro problem": polite racism against a blocked and untested fury for Justice.

Mother and son encounter a "cute" Negro child, upon whom the woman decides to bestow a coin. But there is another mother, an infuriated black giantess who hates such gestures of condescension. The Negro woman strikes the white one, and Julian, as his mother lies sprawling on the sidewalk, gloats: "You got exactly what you deserved." But then, while mother and son start for home, she bewildered and he delighted, the mother collapses, this time from a stroke, and Julian must shed the convenient mask of "emancipation" to recognize his fright, his dependence, and his loss. "The tide of darkness seemed to sweep him back to her, postponing from moment to moment his entry into the world of guilt and horror."

The story is unquestionably effective. We grasp the ways in which the son's intellectual superiority rests upon his emotional dependence, and the mother's social stupidity coexists with a maternal selflessness. Their quarrels are symptoms of a soured family romance, but the romance cuts deeper than the quarrels. As true motives are revealed and protective beliefs dissolved, ironies and complexities fall into place:

which is precisely what, in a good sophisticated modern story, they are supposed to do.

Yet that is all this story is: good sophisticated modern, but lacking in that resonance Miss O'Connor clearly hoped it might have. Why? One clue is a recurrent insecurity of tone, jarring sentences in which Miss O'Connor slips from the poise of irony to the smallness of sarcasm, thereby betraying an unresolved hostility to whatever it is she takes Julian to represent. Repeated several times in these stories, this pattern of feeling seems quite in excess of what the theme might require or the characters plausibly evoke. One can only suppose that it is a hostility rooted in Miss O'Connor's own experience and the kind of literary education she received (intellectuality admired but intellectuals distrusted).

In thus shaping her materials Miss O'Connor clearly intends us to savor a cluster of ironies; her sensibility as a writer of fiction was formed in a milieu where irony took on an almost totemic value. But there can be, as in much contemporary writing there is, a deep failure of ironic perception in a writer's uneqivocal commitment to irony. Mustered with the regularity of battalions on parade, complex ironies have a way of crystallizing into simple and even smug conclusions. Everything becomes subject to ironic discount except the principle of irony itself.

Let me try to be more concrete. Reading the title story, one quickly begins to see the end toward which it moves and indeed must move. The climax is then realized effectively enough—except for the serious flaw that it is a climax which has largely been anticipated a number of pages earlier, where it seems already present, visible and complete, in the preparatory action. One doesn't, to be sure, know that the Negro woman will strike the white woman; but more important, one does know that some kind of ironic reversal will occur in the relationship between mother and son. There is pleasure to be had in watching Miss O'Connor work it all out, but no surprise, for there has been no significant turning upon the premises from which the action has emerged. The story is entirely harmonious with the writer's intent, characterized by what might be called the clarity of limitation. Miss O'Connor is in control of the narrative line from beginning to end, and by the standards of many critics, that is the consummation of her art.

But is it? When I think of stories by contemporary writers which live in my mind—Delmore Schwartz's "In Dreams Begin Responsibilities," Norman Mailer's "The Man Who Studied Yoga," Bernard Malamud's "The Magic Barrel"—I find myself moved by something more than control. In such stories there comes a moment when the unexpected happens, a perception, an insight, a confrontation which may not be in accord with the writer's original intention and may not be strictly required by the logic of the action, but which nevertheless caps the entire story. This moment of revelation gains part of its power from a sharp and sudden brush against the writer's evident plan of meaning; it calls into question all "structural analysis"; the writer seems to be shaken by the demands of his own imagination, so that the material of the story "acts back" upon him.

This final release beyond craft and control, and sometimes, to be honest, beyond clarity, is what I find missing in most of Miss O'Connor's stories. And the reason, I would surmise, is that only toward the end of her career had she fully discovered the possibilities of craft, possibilities she exercised with a scrupulous enjoyment but limited effect. She reached that mastery of means which allows a writer to seek a more elusive and perilous kind of mastery, and in two of these stories, "Revelation" and "Parker's Back," she began to break past the fences of her skill and her ideas.

Like "Everything That Rises Must Converge," "Revelation" starts as a clash between generations, old against new South. The setting is a doctor's office, where gradations of social rank are brilliantly located through inflections of speech. Mr. and Mrs. Turpin, an elderly and hopelessly respectable farm couple, encounter a Southern lady, also waiting for the doctor; the lady has with her an acne-poked and ill-tempered daughter who goes to "Wellesley College," the one "in Massachusetts." Mrs. Turpin trades fatuous pleasantries with the lady about the recent cussedness of the Negroes (though the lady adds, "I couldn't do without my good colored friends"). Meanwhile a poor-white slattern tries to break into the conversation and transform genteel racism into open hatred, but she is coolly pushed aside. Mrs. Turpin, straining her imagination, decides to place the slattern even lower than Negroes on her private scale of virtue. The talk continues, the comedy heightens, but to the "emancipated" daughter from Wellesley College it becomes intolerable. Enraged by every word she hears, the girl bites Mrs. Turpin and then curses her with the magnificent words, "Go back to hell where you came from, you old wart hog." The girl is dragged off to a hospital; Mrs. Turpin staggers home.

Now, thus far the story has followed a pattern close to that of "Everything That Rises Must Converge," But in "Revelation" Miss O'Connor is not content with easy triumphs: she follows Mrs. Turpin home to the farm, to the bed on which she uneasily rests and the pigpen she angrily hoses down. For Mrs. Turpin has been shaken by the girl's curse, as if indeed it were a kind of "revelation." In an astonishing passage, Mrs. Turpin cries out to God: "What do you send me a message like that for?

. . . How am I a hog and me both? How am I saved and from hell too?"
Her rank is broken, her righteousness undone, and a terrible prospect
unfolds itself of a heavenly injustice beyond propriety or comprehension:

"A visionary light settled in her eyes. She saw the streak as a vast swinging
bridge extending upward from the earth through a field of living fire. Upon it a
vast horde of souls were rumbling toward heaven. There were whole com-
panies of white-trash, clean for the first time in their lives, and bands of black
niggers in white robes, and battalions of freaks and lunatics shouting and
leaping like frogs. And bringing up the end of the procession was a tribe of
people whom she recognized at once as those who, like herself . . . had always
had a little of everything and the God-given wit to use it right . . . They were
marching behind the others with great dignity, accountable as they had always
been for good order and common sense and respectable behavior. They alone
were on key. Yet she could see by their shocked and altered faces that even
their virtues were being burned away."

This is not the kind of last-minute acquisition of understanding with
which literature has so often tried to get around life. It is a vision of
irremediable disorder, of God's ingratitude: the white trash, the niggers, the leaping lunatics will all march to heaven ahead of Mrs. Turpin. Something remarkable has happened here, beyond the cautions of
planning and schemes of irony: "How am I a hog and me both?"

It is intolerable that a woman who could write such a story should
have died at the age of thirty-nine.

TREACHERIES OF FAITH

In the caves of Egypt, during the glory of primitive Christianity, desert monks would stand erect through nights of prayer, curbing their vanity and malice with bodily mortification. Had Father Thomas Cawder lived in that era of ecstasy, he would surely have stood among them, blistering his feet on hot sands and freezing them on cold rocks, as he tightened chains of iron around his fleshless body. But it is the misfortune of Father Cawder to have been born in a later age, our age of indifference and skepticism, when the faith is weak and, even in its occasional strength, corrupted by comfort. It is further his misfortune to be moldering as the pastor of Lulworth, a mild and sleepy town in Maryland, where the ethic of martyrdom is not so much denied as unrecognized.

Father Cawder, whom I believe to be one of the most powerful characterizations in American fiction, is the central figure of *The Encounter*. First published in 1950 by a new but not young writer, this novel was neglected by public and critics alike. It sold meagerly; it was barely reviewed even in the serious journals; and only among a few literary people, the kind who enjoy making and sharing discoveries on their own, did it gain an "underground" reputation. Its fate was the fate of too large a portion of serious American writing: to be buried beneath the flood of books, most of them trivial and not worth an hour of attention, that comes pouring off the presses each year. As for the author of *The Encounter*, all one could learn about Mr. Crawford Power was that he is an architect by profession, lives in Virginia and, to his credit, has no interest in literary publicity.

The Encounter evades familiar description. It is too harsh and violent to be called a novel of sensibility, too delicate and reflective to be called a naturalistic novel, and so free from parochial concerns as to be something more and better than what we usually take to be a religious novel. Its hero is a Catholic priest, his *agon* a crisis in conscience, his antagonists members of his own faith; but the book does not smell of the tract nor speak merely to a parochial community. Though starkly plotted in its external action, the true life of the novel is an inner one: the broken rhythms of thought and self-examination which move through the consciousness of Father Cawder.

He is a man of complete dedication. He believes in the truth of God's word, scorns the paltriness of mundane affairs, acknowledges the worm in man's soul. His own dry worm thrives in the stale atmosphere of righteous self-abasement. First seen in a teatime conversation with a parishioner, the comfortable and comfort-loving Mrs. Girard, Father Cawder appears to be following "some fast of his own invention, a private prohibition of cucumbers." When the sensitive Mrs. Girard offers to donate pew cushions to his church (God, she supposes, gains no satisfaction from bruised knees), Father Cawder clumsily declines her gift: "It seems to me the Church ought to be kept clear of this cult of comfort. Christians are getting to be very soft."

Mr. Power's touch in this opening scene is beautifully right. Father Cawder speaks the truth, or part of it, yet he is also the "ridiculous priest" Mrs. Girard hastily judges him to be; Mrs. Girard is correct in assuming that significant good is possible this side of martyrdom, yet she does represent the adulteration of the faith Father Cawder harshly judges her to be. The clash between the two figures, while foreshadowing the serious concerns of the novel, is done with a gritty humor and that potential of the ridiculous which always lurks behind an excess of seriousness. Mr. Power's humor is somber, dry, a measure of his ironic distance from a character with whom a damaging involvement would, for most writers, seem almost inevitable. And Mr. Power's humor is contained by a strong intelligence: he follows Father Cawder into every moral trap which the priest's mixture of Puritan sensibility and Catholic faith can devise, yet he is appropriately respectful of this "ridiculous priest" and his bouts of self-assault.

Bony and graceless, his mouth slit wide like a shark's, and his body recalling "the violated ugliness of a headless fowl," Father Cawder has eaten no meat for twelve years, and feels no difficulty in supposing that "a strict moralist could find occasion of sin in a daily hot bath." Each of the opening chapters establishes Father Cawder through a precise contrast: first with Mrs. Girard, the agent of ease and cultivation; then with his assistant, Father Moran, a Catholic radical keen to the uses of credit unions but dull to the spirit of Calvary; and then with his house-keeper, Mrs. McGovern, a sly mixture of personal sloth and familiar Mariolatry, neither of which Father Cawder can abide.

In the abstract he is right against all three, for each of them repre-sents some deviation from the faith into worldliness and sentimen-talism; but in the immediacy of his voice, his gestures and his bearing, he sins against them through judgment and impatience. And his sins against these people seem as large as theirs against the faith, for by an unmodulated insistence on his single truth he subtly violates their spirits. He cannot see that there may be use, or even goodness, in niceties of custom, or in Father Moran's eagerness to root out poverty, or in Mrs. McGovern's acceptance of her own trivial substance. Strain-ing toward an exalted faith, he yields to the heresy of supposing that the world is merely a burden to be endured, rather than the natural residence of the soul.

Is there a sin that consists in nothing but a constant concern with God? If so, that is Father Cawder's sin. As a seminary student in his youth, he had been tempted by his friend, the Reverend Edmund Owen—"Ned" the Devil in stately ecclesiastic black—to "learn the degree of his favor with God." In later years, even while grasping the enormity of this temptation, he continues to measure his faith: *he needs always to know where he stands with God.* Not for a moment can he lift from his consciousness the thought of God as a factor of self or forget the shamefulness of the pride that keeps it there. He commands all the forms of piety except that "natural piety," a reverent ease before the objects of human life, without which no man can safely make his way through the small, lacerating troubles of daily existence.

Steadily, layer by layer, Mr. Power examines the moral and psychological life of Father Cawder; and perhaps the most notable fact about this life is that the priest, entangled though he may be with his intellectual vanity, never lacks in self-awareness. He knows the truth of all that can be said against him, and a good deal more; and because he believes that, even if denial is enjoined upon saints, his own denial masks stubbornness of will, he continues to mortify himself all the more. He thereby compounds the very sin from which he struggles earnestly to break loose: that overdeveloped keenness of self-per-ception which, as it reveals cause for humility, goads him into further presumption.

The result, for this intensely religious figure, is a crushing load of guilt: the guilt of being unable to live with one's guilt and of realizing

that in some perverse way one enjoys this dilemma; the guilt of knowing that the greatest impertinence for him is to assume that, by himself, he can sustain the weight of guilt. Father Cawder tries to compete
with God by taking upon himself an autonomy that, in the religious
scheme, no man should venture. His sinfulness he quickly grants; his
unworthiness too; but the fact of limitation and the need to accept it as
a step toward love of God while, at the same time, neither glorifying
nor even acquiescing in it—that is terribly hard.

Father Cawder's crisis, which forms the outer action of the novel, is
provoked by a dream in which there is revealed to him the possibility
that a circus acrobat named Diamond, visiting Lulworth with a carnival, is his worldly double, an invisible brother in spirit. But can one
trust a dream? Is it a signal from God, or a trick of mania?

It was not impossible to God. If it was presumptuous to think the finger of God
might point out a circus performer as in a parable, an unknowable portentous
gesture—on the other hand, it was not permitted to limit God. Forbidding
Him intervention, if such was His will. He could make use of a priest in a
country town, allying him in some not unimaginable way with a carnival acrobat. If He wished He could make His will known in intelligible form, projecting analogies on a man inert in sleep, inclining a human will to His mysteries.
If it was the will of God! Before he slept, once and for all, it must be dealt
with—plaguing doubt, ridiculously possessing him like an ache, like a bodily
constriction.

Pride tempts Father Cawder to dismiss the dream as absurd: what
link can there be between him and a petty acrobat? Pride leads him to
search out Diamond and slowly burrow into the man's life: for could
not this circus performer "conceal under the disguise of a buffoon an
experience of grace?" Nothing about Diamond seems promising,
neither a spark of spirit nor a sign of grace: "he was merely mediocre,
suspicious and lustful. He existed, according to the custom of the
world, for the brief sensations of each day, the pleasures to be had in a
woman's body, a soft bed, food and drink and pocket money. Like all
the millions of the earth, a creature moved like a puppet by his appetites."

Like all the millions of the earth—the phrase brands Father Cawder.
But in a restrained symbolism, the affinity between the two men is
gradually displayed. At the carnival where Father Cawder and Mrs.
Girard wait for Diamond to perform his stunt of diving from a high
platform into a narrow pool of water, he remarks to her that he is
"waiting for the dive."

"You like that sort of thing?"
"I prefer it to the rest of this."

"Really? It seems so crazy, jumping all that distance. They always break their necks sooner or later, don't they?"

Preferring "the dive," Father Cawder links himself to Diamond: they share a readiness to "break their necks," as Mrs. Girard prudently remarks, "sooner or later." So there begins a slow interweaving of two lives: priest and diver, consecrated man of God and drifting acrobat. Though a mere "paltry foxlike tout of a man," Diamond soon discovers Father Cawder's weakness, as Smerdyakov sensed the weakness of Ivan Karamazov: that is the traditional role of the double in literature, to embody qualities hidden or dormant in the central figure. If Diamond thus brings to brazen light the element of mediocrity shared by all men—(but that is what Father Cawder cannot bear: to be like all men!)—he also personifies a willingness to live in the world as it is, which Father Cawder scorns and lacks and needs. Between the two characters Mr. Power builds an extremely complex relationship, the full meaning of which I do not find at all easy to grasp; it is a relationship, in any case, which controls the plot and prepares for the climax of the novel.

Father Cawder's passion is God; Diamond's a former prostitute named Stella. For both men, love signifies possession: they cannot adore without wishing to appropriate. "I guess he's got his good points," says the tough- and sometimes mean-spirited Stella about Diamond, "but he's always at me. I'm getting good and sick of the way he is. He won't leave me be for a minute." The nagging jealousy with which Diamond harasses the girl is an equivalent to the tormented exaltation with which Father Cawder seeks his God. At first Father Cawder does not see this parallel—it is one of the few things he does not see immediately—but he is nonetheless driven to enter Diamond's life more and more deeply, helping to find a home for the child Stella has left in a New Jersey brothel and becoming their worldly rather than strictly spiritual advisor.

In some subtle way Father Cawder betrays all of his friends: Mrs. Girard, by refusing her gestures of amiability; Father Moran, by discussing him ironically with their bishop; Stella, by lecturing her on morals; and Diamond too. At the climax of *The Encounter* Diamond comes to Father Cawder's new church—a run-down parish in Philadelphia—seeking protection. He has murdered Stella in an outburst of rage, and now the police are closing in upon him.

Here Mr. Power, through the discipline of craft, escapes the dual temptations of sentimentality and routine piety. Father Cawder does admit Diamond to sanctuary, for as a spiritually disheveled priest he at least commands the imagination to see the grandeur of an act rehearsing the humane gesture of the medieval church. But it is an act which leads neither to a reconciliation of love nor a liberation of spirit; on the contrary, it sharpens the conflict between the two men. Refusing to accept Diamond's shabby denial that he has committed a crime, Father Cawder tells him: "I'm not compelled to believe what you say. Do you think only a man who speaks the truth can come into this house?"

Ringing with the glory of traditional Christendom, this statement represents the most serious moment in Father Cawder's aspiration toward grace. Yet it is Diamond, wretched murderer though he is, who takes the last word. "I can just about figure out what you're thinking," he tells the priest. "If you'd been on hand . . . if you'd done something you forgot to do, said a little prayer, she'd be alive yet . . . At first you had me fooled. But you can't stand to lose a trick, can you? You just can't stand to lose out, can you?" To this harsh judgment, stripping his sacred office to a scrap of egoism, Father Cawder makes no reply. He has none to make. Neither through works nor faith can Father Cawder escape what he is: that much the "foxlike tout of a man" has taught him.

All he can now do is to draw up a balance sheet with himself: he does not love God, he does not fear God, he believes in nothing but the existence of God. "I can envy the joy of those who love God, I who cannot even love another man." With God his struggle must continue; with man it is done. To have lived among other men and yet not with them, was a betrayal; and in his failure with Diamond and Stella he sees a reflection of his failure with God. He is still cut off, this anguished and "ridiculous priest"; but he knows where he stands and who he is. How shall we name his affliction? That "acedia," which Joseph Pieper describes as "the refusal to acquiesce in one's being"? That dismay we all experience at learning how much less we feel than we feel we should? Or perhaps something more terrible: a dryness of soul which neither prayer nor intelligence nor decision can begin to moisten?

Yet at the end of The Encounter one wonders—as one might wonder about someone intimately known in life—what final estimate we are to make of Father Cawder. That even in his concluding laceration he still suffers from pride, seems clear enough. But perhaps there is also a kind of bleak grandeur in his knowledge that what he is, so must he remain; his awareness that the utmost discovery of self offers no relief from its torment.

The Encounter is the work of a mature and undeluded artist with a seemingly instinctive—which is probably to say, a hard-won and deeply-considered—mastery of form. Perhaps the surest sign of Mr. Power's skill is that he enforces his own pace—slow, "thick" and reflective—upon the reader, demanding strict attention not because of complications in plot or syntax but because of the density of his material. Mr. Power shuttles between two vastly different environments, the bare room in which Father Cawder struggles with himself, and the tawdry streets of Trenton and Philadelphia in which Diamond and Stella squander their lives. The prose of the novel is tense, dark, close-grained, at times so packed and nervous as to create friction with the narrative. Here are a few sentences describing the trip to the New Jersey brothel:

The car began to move faster, skirting a pasture where a flock of ragged sheep was grazing. It took the incline of a concrete ramp. Raised now on stilts, the road lay across a marsh. Pools and shaggy grass wavered away out of sight toward a belt of clouds. The marsh at first was rank and green; further along it turned gray, heaped up in scaly folds. A yellow smoke rose from a crack in the shelving earth. . . .

The most remarkable achievement in this novel is that Mr. Power succeeds in making dramatic the long passages of Father Cawder's reflections, so that one may say of his writing, as Eliot says of Donne's, that his intellect seems at the tip of his senses. Mr. Power portrays a mind in motion, realizing its tangled impulses in a dialectic of clash and conversion; he shows not merely a thoughtful man but a man in the act of thought; and at every moment one is aware of the numerous ways in which his effort to think is preyed upon by unconscious emotion and the demands of the will.

Crawford Power sees the faith in its glory and its squalor, yet the perilous mixture of the two never betrays him into the sensationalism of a Graham Greene or the snobbery of an Evelyn Waugh. His moral seriousness and something of his tone warrant comparison with François Mauriac, though simply as a novelist he seems to me considerably more pliant and sympathetic than Mauriac. The unbeliever can respond to *The Encounter* with quite as much intensity, if not perhaps the same kind of involvement, as the religious person. For in the end, the language of art is always the same, and that is the language Mr. Power speaks.

A FINE NOVEL OF ACADEMIC LIFE

The style, assumptions and matter of John Williams' *Stoner* are at variance with those dominating current American fiction. If I add that *Stoner* is set in a remote province called Missouri; that it assumes human existence in Missouri to be open to drama, variety and significance; that it follows the career of an English professor from a barren youth to a bleak death; and that it takes as a central theme the vocation of teaching, which it treats with the kind of seriousness usually reserved these days for black humor, boredom, collapse and murder—then the difficulty of persuading anyone to read *Stoner* multiplies. But let me try.

Mr. Williams, author of several books of fiction and verse, begins with a few chapters that seem almost "mythlike." He places his central figure in a milieu so harsh and deprived, it thwarts most impulses to personality. William Stoner is born on a Missouri farm, to poor and speechless parents. The amenities of life are few here; not much of Western culture has settled onto the stark dirt of this place. Sent off in 1910 to the state university's agricultural school, the awkward boy seems at the beginning without individuality, deliberately resembling the kind of figure that has appeared again and again in American fiction between 1890 and 1940: the young man from the Midwest struggling to break into consciousness, as if to recapitulate in his own few years the history of the race.

At the university Stoner attends the class of a sardonic professor who teaches English "as if he perceived between his knowledge and what he could say a gulf so profound that he would make no effort to close it." The professor reads aloud Shakespeare's seventy-third sonnet ("That time of year thou mayst in me behold") and, with the dry impassioned hostility which often seems a necessary part of teaching, turns to ask the farm boy: "Mr. Shakespeare speaks to you across three hundred years, Mr. Stoner; do you hear him?" The boy cannot answer; no one could. But overcome with shame and anger, and made suddenly to thirst for the power of speech, he comes to realize that his life is being transformed.

Stoner is seized by a hunger for learning, a need to assimilate and ponder upon his knowledge with a private completeness, alone in his attic room where for a moment he has "a vision of denseness into which he was compacted and from which he could not escape, and had no wish to escape. Tristan, Iseult the fair, walked before him; Paolo and Francesca whirled in the glowing dark. . . ."

At this point the novel reaches its controlling rhythm: a narrative movement that is tense and summary, only now and again broken by a section of detail. Mr. Williams is more concerned with the curve of experience than its local segments, since the life of a man like Stoner can acquire value only when regarded from some distance and with a sense of how incorrigibly wasteful all human existence is. Stoner is realized as a character not through an accumulation of incident but through a kind of novelistic rumination, a firm grasp of what is significant, perhaps exemplary, in his life. He thereby becomes a persuasive and moving figure, in part because he is an agent of the failure we see in ourselves, but more important, because Williams, with the severe objectivity that is the mind's ultimate kindness, reaches toward the fragment of integrity that survives in Stoner's years.

By every familiar sign, Stoner is a failure. A bad marriage; a daughter helplessly loved, who drifts into drunkenness; a middle-aged affair, poignant and hopeless; aspirations to scholarship frustrated and an academic career not especially notable—all these form his lot. Yet something virtuous survives in him, resembling what Conrad called the "job sense" but here more positive and thrusting, an inner stubbornness which redeems Stoner to the history of his culture, if not to his immediate fellows or himself.

Stoner does his work with a fierce integrity; he does not fake; he is a witness in behalf of values he would hesitate to name. He forms part of the fabric of civilization, as it weaves, ungloriously, through the generations. For years he struggles against a colleague, flashier than he but badly flawed as a teacher. A climax occurs when Stoner and the colleague battle one another during a qualifying examination for a graduate student, with Stoner ruthlessly, yet in complete and necessary justice, exposing the flimsiness of a "brilliant" student. I would not have supposed that an occasion so routine to academic life could be used with such effectiveness to embody the tensions of the moral life. Perhaps the lesson is that the occasions for drama, if not everywhere in commonplace existence, are still more frequent than most recent novelists have cared to suppose.

What makes *Stoner* an impressive novel is the contained intensity author and character share, not so much in behalf of teaching as a vocation, but in regard to the idea—the sacramental character—of work. By the end of his life Stoner has done little as a scholar: a single book, unread and by no means a neglected masterpiece. But if the idea of tradition is more than a consoling fancy, it is men like Stoner who in their very failure and waste form the substance from which tradition is composed.

The book has faults. A few secondary figures are unclear; some of the action is stock. Mr. Williams employs a tone of unrelieved gravity which can slip into sententiousness, just as his unrelieved stress upon the ethic of stoicism can become a life-constricting sentimentality. And perhaps most important: Mr. Williams firmly establishes a critical distance from Stoner the character, but does not keep himself sufficiently clear from Stoner's intellectual position. The novel thereby declines, at several points, from a vivid portrait of a man to a sectarian brief for a wintery kind of academic conservatism.

Even when this happens, however, Mr. Williams writes with discipline and strength: he is devoted to the sentence as a form, and free from the allure of imagery. He disobeys Ford Madox Ford's dictum that the novelist should show rather than tell, on the assumption that to tell with enough force and intelligence is to create a mode of drama. I think there should be a few thousand people in this country who will find pleasure in this book.

DORIS LESSING:
NO COMPROMISE, NO HAPPINESS

In our time the life of cultivated people is marked by a fierce attachment to "personal values." I put the phrase in quote marks to point toward something more problematic than the usual web of involvements that appear when human beings live together in society. The condition I have in mind—perhaps new for us, though hardly unprecedented—can be observed in the cosmopolitan centers of the West and increasingly in the more advanced totalitarian countries.

"Personal relations" as the very substance and sufficient end of our existence; "personal relations" as a surrogate for transcendence through religion, fulfillment through work, satisfaction through community; "personal relations" as a fragile shelter for sensitive men, a bulwark against the nihilist void, an ideology of privacy to replace the lapsed ideologies of public action—all this has become a style of life in New York and Moscow, London and Warsaw, accepted by some intellectuals with a tiresome literalness and by others with a skeptical grin. Among ourselves the devotion to "personal relations" seems at times like a malaise eating away at personal life; in the Communist countries it can serve as a rallying call for marginal freedoms. But in both parts of the world, psychological man begins to replace social man.

It is a particular distinction of *The Golden Notebook,* a long and ambitious novel by the gifted English writer Doris Lessing, that while dealing with some of the materials favored by the novelists of sensibility, it escapes their constrictions of tone and outlook. Both Miss Lessing and her characters are deeply caught up with the cult of "personal relations," yet she is able to keep some critical distance from her material and to look upon it as merely the latest turn in the confusion of modern history. She yields her sympathies to those of her characters who fall back upon "personal relations" in order to get through their days, but she tries not to settle for the limitations of experience they must accept. She understands that the idea of "personal relations" has been shaped by the catastrophes of our time and, in the form we know it, is not to be taken as an absolute or uncontaminated value.

It is a further distinction of Miss Lessing's novel that its action is mainly carried by that rarity in modern fiction: a heroine, Anna Wulf, who is a mature intellectual woman. A writer with a sophisticated mind, sharp tongue and an abundance of emotional troubles, Anna Wulf is sufficiently representative of a certain kind of modern woman to persuade us that her troubles have a relevance beyond their immediate setting; she is also an intelligence keen enough to support the public combativeness and personal introspectiveness that Miss Lessing has given her. At the very least, Anna Wulf is someone who has measured the price for being what she chooses to be—"a free woman," she would say with pride and irony—and who is prepared, no matter how much she groans, to pay it.

Miss Lessing is radically different from other women writers who have dealt with the problems of their sex, first in that she grasps the connection between Anna Wulf's neuroses and the public disorders of the day, and second in that she has no use either for the quaverings of the feminist writers or the aggressions of those female novelists whose every sentence leads a charge in the war of the sexes. The feminine element in *The Golden Notebook* does not become a self-contained universe of being as in some of Virginia Woolf's novels, nor is the narrative voice established through minute gradations of the writer's sensibility, as in some of Elizabeth Bowen's.

Anna Wulf and her old friend Molly understand perfectly well that modern women do face crippling difficulties when they choose one or another role of freedom. But they do not fall back upon their charm, wit or headaches; they take their beatings, they ask no quarter, they spin and bear it. They are tough-minded, generous and battered—descriptives one is tempted to apply to the author herself, formerly close to the English Communist movement, a woman whose youth in southern Africa had shaken her into a sense of how brutal human beings can become, a novelist who has published extensively and taken the risks of her craft. One feels about Miss Lessing that she works from so complex and copious a fund of experience that among women writers her English predecessors seem pale and her American contemporaries parochial.

At the center of *The Golden Notebook* is a series of remarkable conversations between Anna Wulf and Molly. Meeting in one another's London homes, they talk again and again about "personal relations," but always with a muted irony, an impatience with the very topics they know to concern them most. They are alternately open and guarded, sometimes wounding but usually honest. Simply as precise and nuanced dialogue, this is the best writing in a novel that never stoops to verbal display and is always directed toward establishing a visible world.

When they discuss their failures in love, their problems as divorced women with children to raise, their disillusionments as former Communists who would still like to needle the Establishment, their inability to talk with the passionless and apolitical young, their contempt for the new gentility of intellectual London, their difficulties in reconciling the image they hold of a self-sufficient human being with the needs they feel as anything but self-sufficient women—when these conversations between Anna and Molly recur throughout the book, one turns to them with the delight of encountering something real and fresh. My own curiosity, as a masculine outsider, was enormous, for here, I felt, was the way intellectual women really talk to one another when they feel free and unobserved.

Though their interest in politics has lessened, both Anna and Molly feel themselves to be voices of a baffled generation, those people who gave their youth to radicalism and ended not knowing how to live. This could be, it so often has been, a sticky self-pitying kind of subject; but not in *The Golden Notebook*, for it is a virtue of these deeply interesting women that even while suffering neurotic torments they can still regard themselves as objects of laughter. And also, as figures of hope. History, they feel, has left them stranded, but on the beaches of disillusion there must still be other stranded ones, there must be men of strength, to help them.

For both women remain interested in men with a curiosity that is almost archaeological: as if there were so few good ones left that it is necessary to hunt for them amid the ruins. Both Anna and Molly, in a wry and pleasing way, are frank about their sexuality; both are ready to have affairs when their emotions are stirred. Yet, as they feel it, men somehow "fail" them. Their men do not "come through," and the more pliant they seem, the less dependable they prove. All this serves as a subject for jokes between Anna and Molly, jokes with an edge of desperation.

In temperament the two women are sharply different: Anna morose and burrowing, Molly cheerful and extrovert; but they share problems, needs, failures. Both try hard to preserve their independence, which means not a refusal of relationships but a hard decision not to delude themselves when they do take up with second-raters and even more, a strict watch, mostly within themselves, against the mediocre, the resigned, the merely comfortable. At the end Molly does give in to a marriage of convenience, though with a characteristic quip: "There's nothing like knowing the exact dimensions of the bed you're going to fit yourself into." Anna, reduced to hysteria by a disastrous affair with an American writer, still keeps pushing ahead, deciding to go into Labour Party work and—a nice touch of irony—to take a job as a marriage counsellor ("I'm very good at other people's marriages"). She remains loyal to that refusal to compromise which had bound the two women in friendship.

Refusal to compromise with what? It is not easy to say, since the answer depends at least as much upon Anna's visceral reactions as her conscious ideas. Miss Lessing, with the patience of a true novelist, keeps returning to the problem, not explicitly but through a series of narrative variations. Sick as Anna is, trapped as she often finds herself in a pit of anxiety, she still commands a burning sense of the possibilities of life. That this very restlessness of hers may itself be a function of neurosis, she also knows; for she has undergone the inevitable analytic bout, with a spiderish lady doctor she calls "Mother Sugar."

Yet she clings to her saving difference. She demands from her men the completion of her being. She demands that they provide those elements of strength and assurance which she, as a woman, cannot. She wants in her men both intimacy and power, closeness and self-sufficiency, hereness and thereness. Modernist in sensibility, she is traditional in her desires. And no matter what she must settle for at a given moment, she does not delude herself; she will not compromise with the idea of compromise.

Anna is the kind of woman who would send D. H. Lawrence into a sputter of rage: so much the worse for him. To be sure, many of the complaints he might make of her would be accurate. She whines, she is a bit of a drag, she often drives her men crazy. She does not inquire closely enough as to why she seems so gifted at picking losers. In her steady groaning about her writer's block, she does not ask herself whether it is caused by a deep contempt for the whole idea of the intellectual life—like many women of her sort, she has fitful passions for cooking and domesticity—or whether it is caused by overweening ambition—at times one suspects her of wanting to write a novel as good as *The Golden Notebook*. She is open to almost every judgment except that of having died before her death.

In its structure *The Golden Notebook* is original but not entirely successful. Miss Lessing has wanted to show the relation between Anna's past and her present, as well as between both of these and her fantasies, but she has wanted to show them not simply through the usual juxtaposition of narrative strands which might, for her purposes, lack tension and the effect of simultaneity. She therefore hit upon the ingenious device of carrying her narrative line forward in the present while inserting long excerpts from several notebooks Anna keeps, each a different color and representing a distinct part of her life. The advantage of this scheme is that Miss Lessing can isolate the main elements of Anna's experience with a sharpness that might not be possible in a traditional kind of novel; the disadvantage, that she has had to force large chunks of narrative into a discursive context.

In a black notebook Anna returns to her youth, sketching a group of English radicals astray in a provisional African town and preying on each other's nerves. In a red notebook Anna looks back upon her political life, drawing a number of amusing vignettes of left-wing intellectual circles in the London of the fifties. In a yellow notebook she writes a fictional version of her own experience, focusing on a love affair which has, in the narrative present, already reached its end. And in a blue notebook she keeps an objective record of her daily life, which comes to a brilliant climax in a detailed account of a single day. Bit by bit she builds up the mosaic of anxiety: how she must face early in the morning the conflicting needs of her lively child and sleepy lover; how she copes with the irritations of work in a fellow-travelling publishing house; how she gives way to the compulsion of repeatedly washing her body for fear that her period causes her to have a bad smell; how she returns home at night to the nagging of her thoughts.

Finally there comes the golden notebook which is to record the reintegration of the various Annas who appear in the other notebooks. But as the love affair on which she stakes her hopes begins to crumble, the golden notebook turns into a record of collapse, and in pages of nightmarish power Anna is shown entering a psychotic episode, locking herself into her bedroom where she pastes alarming newspaper items on the walls and slowly tastes the progress from despair, in which she abandons herself to the vividness of remembering what she has lost, to desolation, in which the image of loss becomes dim but the pain, feeding on itself, lives on.

Doris Lessing is a natural writer: she has the prime novelistic gift of involving one so deeply in the desires and frustrations of her characters that one reads with a positive yearning to spend more time with them. Some of her failures, however, I found disturbing. The cumbersome structure of the novel allows for a rich interweaving of complexities but does not fully encourage the free flow of emotion which her story demands. She writes about Americans with the astigmatism peculiar to certain English leftists: she has no ear for American speech nor eye for American manners. More important, at the end of the book she fails to keep a sufficient distance from her heroine, so that Anna's hysteria comes dangerously close to taking over the narrative. Perhaps Miss Lessing faced an insoluble problem at this point: she achieves enormous intensity through surrendering herself to Anna's suffering, but the price she pays is a loss of the critical objectivity she had maintained in earlier pages. It is a feat of evocation, but not matched by steadiness of control. Still, *The Golden Notebook* moves with the beat of our time, and it is true.

Postscript

In the years since *The Golden Notebook* appeared, a number of friends have charged me with having overestimated the book, which they found claustrophobic, humorless, overwrought. Perhaps they are right; I have never reread it. But a reviewer of contemporary writing ought not to have his eye on "the ages;" his job is to respond honestly, immediately, and with an inner awareness that he cannot possibly command the objectivity of judgment which time may enable. I am speaking here not of commercial trash or the obviously meretricious, but of serious books to which one responds with a certain initial gratitude, even if also with an element of excess. What mattered about a novel like *The Golden Notebook* was that it touched a nerve of contemporary life, and that is why, I imagine, it stirred many readers when it first came out. I'm glad I was one of them.

THE STORIES OF PIRANDELLO

Pirandello is one of the honored names of European literature, but few Americans know anything about him. Literate persons are likely to be familiar with one or two of his titles: there is the play *Six Characters in Search of an Author* and then . . . well, there is the fact that he was a highly intellectual dramatist specializing in the interchange of appearance and reality. And usually that is about as far as it goes. For Pirandello has survived in our culture more as a name then a living force; he has not shaped our feeling or bent our thought as Kafka or Lawrence or Proust has. Look hastily into his plays and you may well accept the stock judgment that they are clever theatrically but lacking in range and depth. Pirandello the writer is not warm or lovable or magnetic; he bears no theories of social renovation or psychic rebirth; he is not a culture-hero promising, or threatening, to transform our lives.

Yet Pirandello is a major figure. Like Thomas Hardy, he managed in one lifetime (1867-1936) to complete two fullscale literary careers. He began as a writer of prose fiction, publishing several novels and hundreds of stories, and then he became a dramatist, composing over forty plays, several of them masterpieces. Actually the plays and stories overlap in time of composition, but it is useful to regard them as products of two distinct careers.

Why then has he failed to capture or hold the imagination of American readers and theater audiences? Some reasons are obvious: the early

118

translations frequently muffled his brilliance, there has arisen a false
notion that he is a mere juggler of a very few ideas, and the liberal
intellectuals have been hostile to him because of his membership,
more the result of opportunism than principle, in the Italian Fascist
Party during the twenties.

There are other reasons, more elusive and important. Serious
twentieth-century readers turn to literature not so much for the direct
pleasure of seeing human experience represented fictionally or of
savoring mastery of language and form. We expect more from literature: we expect that it discover norms of conduct, that it yield revelation as well as portray reality. Almost unwittingly we find ourselves
insisting that the great modern writer be not merely a portraitist of life
but also a self-affirmed prophet, a moral revolutionist, an agent of
transcendence. The message of guidance that neither politics nor
philosophy nor religion now seems able to provide, we look for in
modern literature.

That message Pirandello refuses to give. He refuses on principle, for
he does not believe there is such a message, and he does not believe
the writer would have any business offering it even if it did exist.
Pirandello's best work is characterized by doubt, at times by an extreme relativism of perspective that can be said to approach epistemological panic. He searches for approximate truths rather than a
fixed salvation, and meanwhile he offers little hope or solace. This
skepticism, which in the actual course of his writing often serves as an
incitement to humaneness, is the only "salvation"—modest and depressing as it may be—that he would claim to offer. He never yields to,
though he often deals with, rhetoric and apocalypse, vanity and program. The reader who comes to a Pirandello play or story with the
usual complement of anxiety will leave without having been disbur-
dened.

There is more to it. Pirandello is a writer strongly marked by the
tone of his time, the tone of grayness that gradually suffuses the culture
of Europe during the late nineteenth and early twentieth centuries.
The energy of the immediate past, a moment of bourgeois confidence,
has begun to wane; the energy of the immediate future, a moment of
experimental daring, has not yet quite appeared. It is remarkable how
widespread is this mood of twilight sadness, this feeling of psychic
depression. Pirandello, Chekhov, Gissing, Hardy, the early Mann, and
a bit later Martin du Gard—these writers, very different from one
another, all reflect in their work the feeling that a great century of
hope, work, and progress has come to an end and that a littleness of
spirit has overtaken Europe.

Perhaps this feeling is due to the intensified crisis of bourgeois soci-

ety, perhaps to the triumph of scientistic ideologies, perhaps to the
decay of religious conviction, perhaps to the growth of our modern
cities. For the moment it hardly matters. What does matter is that in
writer after writer who comes to maturity at this time there is a weariness of spirit, a shared conviction, as the great German sociologist Max
Weber put it, of being witness to "the disenchantment of the world."
The forms of social existence harden. Energy seems to run down.
Values crumble. The spirit of denial and cold rationalization takes
command. And Freud's dictum that civilization is purchased through
the suppression of instinct and pleasure must be regarded not merely
as a theoretic speculation or even a personal statement but as the
expression of attitudes common to many thoughtful men of the time.

Nowhere is this tone of things more seriously—or austerely—
communicated than in Pirandello's stories and plays. The stories are
filled with glimpses of lonely city streets, barren provincial towns,
sluggish middle-class homes, stuffy Sundays, torn families. Pirandello
is the poet of frustration, the kind that seems inevitable and pervasive
in civilized existence. Few writers have ever dealt more honestly with
the tiresomeness and boredom of daily life, not as the emblem of some
"deeper" metaphysical condition but simply as an irreducible fact in
itself. Finally, the vision of denial that dominates his work is more
frightening than the visions of horror that would later appear in the
work of the great twentieth-century modernists. To stay with a writer
like Pirandello takes strong nerves, a gritted determination to see
things as they are.

Luigi Pirandello was born in Agrigento, Sicily, the son of a moder-
ately well-to-do sulfur dealer. Sicily figured as the setting in a number
of his early stories and one or two plays, mostly as a scene of social
brutishness and provincial deprivation. It also proved important to his
career in another way: the dominant literary influence upon his early
work was the naturalism of the Sicilian novelist, Giovanni Verga.

As a youth Pirandello turned to philological studies, earning a degree at the University of Bonn and translating Goethe's *Roman Elegies*
into Italian. He wrote some conventional verse, but his talent first
came into evidence with *The Outcast*, a novel published in 1893. During this phase of his career Pirandello found life extremely difficult, at
times insupportable. Because his family had lost its money in a mining
disaster, he had to turn to the drudgery of teaching at a girl's school in
Rome. His wife, an extremely jealous woman, finally collapsed into
insanity, and Pirandello, with his characteristic muted stoicism, nursed
her at home, a virtual prisoner of her whims and delusions. In the
twenty years between *The Outcast* and the First World War he

nevertheless managed to publish a great many stories and four full-length novels, including the very fine one entitled *The Late Mattia Pascal* (1904).

Only in 1916 did Pirandello begin to devote his major energy to writing plays. He had written one or two before, but there now occurred an astonishing outburst of creative speed: brilliant work composed in a few days or a week. In 1921 his famous play, *Six Characters in Search of an Author*, was produced, and the following year perhaps his greatest play, *Henry IV*. Pirandello now became an international literary figure, his work being performed in theaters throughout the world and the catchphrase "Pirandellian" applied, not always carefully, to a kind of cerebral drama that released the philosophical skepticism and the concern with social and personal identity that had been troubling serious minds in the West for some time. In 1925, partly through a subsidy from the Mussolini government, Pirandello started an art theater in Rome; later he took it on tour through the major capitals of Europe. Though now relieved of financial worries and the burden of his deranged wife, Pirandello himself seems to have found little pleasure in his fame: he had suffered too intensely in the earlier years, his personality had, it seems, become too dry, and he had too keen a sense of the ridiculousness of success to remain anything but the isolated spectator he had always been. There is an amusing late play of his translated into English as *When Someone Is Somebody*, which portrays a great Italian writer, clearly a version of Pirandello himself, who has become so thoroughly a national institution he is not even named but merely designated as XXX. The great writer tries, through a clever trick, to establish for himself a new public identity, but the pressures upon him, not least of all the pressures from his decaying body, are too great. In a final scene XXX slowly turns into his own statue, a mere stone. Shortly before this happens he explains to his young admirers the reason for his loss of nerve:

You don't know what an atrocious thing happens to an old man, to see himself all of a sudden in a mirror, when the sorrow of seeing himself is greater than the astonishment of no longer remembering. You don't know the almost obscene shame of feeling a young and hot-blooded heart within an old body
. . .

Here is the true Pirandello note, and the man who struck it could not yield himself very easily to transient vanities.

This is not to say that he was at all heroic. During the twenties Pirandello joined the Italian Fascist Party, not, so far as one can tell, out of enthusiasm for its chauvinist braggadocio, but simply because he preferred not to make difficulties for himself. Like most people, Pirandello seems to have had no strong political convictions; he took the easy way out, partly from indifference and partly for advantage; I suppose that his support of the Fascist regime in Italy had about the same sort of ritual expediency as the support certain Russian writers give to the Communist regime. In any case there is no close or direct relationship between this Fascist membership and the content of his plays. Not only are the plays quite nonpolitical, but the very style of thought they display is at odds with the anti-intellectualism and nationalist demagogy of the Fascists. In much of Pirandello's work there is a devotion to cerebral intensities, an anxious concern with reflection as a value in life, and this is in no way lessened by his having to conclude that human thought seems to him hopelessly rutted in subjectivity. Whatever the practical or personal reasons for his support of the Mussolini regime—and they are to be seen as reasons, not justifications—Pirandello's major plays are the work of a *European* writer, a "good European."

"Under Fascism," writes Eric Bentley, "Pirandello's playwriting entered a third and more problematic phase. . . . Pirandello withdraws into a strange, subjective world of his own . . . or, as he would probably prefer to say, tries to create myths." At the end of his career Pirandello was still an unsettled writer; he abandoned the philosophical comedy that marks his greatest achievement and turned to a semi-allegorical, almost dream-like mode of composition. Some of his late plays, such as *The Mountain Giants* and *The New Colony*—difficult but impressive—indicate that, far from yielding to the chiliastic vulgarities of totalitarianism, he remained a skeptic to the end. In *The New Colony* the skepticism is tempered by a strong humaneness, as Pirandello shows the effort of a group of smugglers and toughs to start a utopian community and its subsequent disintegration in petty disputes and human failings. He writes with considerable sympathy for these colonists, and his critique of their utopian impulse is anything but scornful: there is nothing here, so far as I can make out, that can be described as fascist either in tone or outlook.

In the concluding gesture of his life Pirandello clearly dissociated himself from the secular and religious institutions of his world. "When I am dead," he gave instructions, "do not clothe me." (The Fascists would come to bury him in a black shirt, but be denied by his will.) "Wrap me naked in a sheet. No flowers on the bed and no lighted candle. A pauper's cart. Naked. And let no one accompany me, neither relatives nor friends. The cart, the horse, the coachman, *e basta.* Burn me . . ."

Pirandello's stories are in the main tradition of nineteenth-century European realism. Except for those set in Sicily, which have a distinctive regional flavor and something of the pained intensity that can be found in the work of a writer returning to the miseries of his homeland, they are stories that often seem close in manner and spirit to the writings of the French realists and naturalists. Ordinary social life forms their main setting. The weariness of middle-class routine, the sourings of domesticity, the familiar cruelty of city life provide their characteristic subjects. Like Flaubert, though with less fanatic insistence, Pirandello cuts himself out of his picture. He does not speak directly in his own voice; he allows the action to unfold according to its inner necessities. His prose is neither elevated nor familiar, for he cares very little about "fine" writing, and when he does engage in a rhetorical flight, it is usually for ironic effect or in behalf of the elliptical characterization required by the short story. He composes in a middle style, denotative, austere, and transparent, the style of an observer who achieves sympathy from a distance rather than through demonstration.

Far more than we have come to expect in the modern short story, Pirandello's stories depend upon their action, which sometimes contains enough matter to allow a great deal of expansion. It is not hard to see why some of the stories would later become the basis for plays: they read like compressed scenarios, full of quick notation. It is also characteristic of Pirandello's stories that while one remembers the general tone and atmosphere of his "world," one rarely keeps in mind the features or voice of a particular character. In so masterful a story as "Such Is Life," it is the ambience of frustration and disappointment, the final sense of human entanglement, that stays in one's mind far more than the characters themselves.

There are rarely Joycean epiphanies of insight or Chekhovian revelations through a massing of atmosphere. Pirandello is more somber and subdued, more committed to the necessities of the ordinary. The function of his style is to serve as a glass with a minimum of refraction or distortion; and whatever we may conclude about his ultimate literary purpose must come, not from a fussing with details of metaphor, but from a response to the line of the action. In this respect Pirandello the story writer is not quite a "modern" writer.

There is still another way in which he is not quite a "modern" writer. Though in his plays he breaks with the psychology of nineteenth-century literary realism, abandoning the premises of a fixed individual character and of the knowability of human relationships, his stories do not go that far. The stories remained accessible to educated persons of his generation who had been brought up on rationalist assumptions. Such readers may have found them excessively bleak—one does not leave Pirandello in a mood to embrace the universe—but they had no difficulty in grasping their import, as later they would with the plays.

Pirandello himself has provided a valuable summary of his major themes:

> . . . the deceit of mutual understanding, irremediably founded on the empty abstraction of words, the multiple personality of everyone (corresponding to the possibilities of being to be found in each of us), and finally the inherent tragic conflict between life (which is always moving and changing) and form (which fixes it, immutable.)

Most of these are already visible in the stories, though the theme of "multiple personality" is fully realized only in the plays. But Pirandello's treatment in the stories is by and large a conventional one—he would save his experimentalism for the plays. The stories, that is, deal with the difficulties of communication among human beings, the radical isolation of the self as it confronts its public guises, the tragic absurdity of trying to fix the flow of existence in perceptual and behavioral schemes. Yet even as they deal with these matters, the stories do not threaten the reader with a vision of the human lot as beyond comprehension or as open to so many meanings that there must follow a paralysis of relativism.

Pirandello has a sharp eye for absurdities, but this is still far from the view that life is inherently absurd. There may be anticipations of existentialism in his stories, as there may be in many writers of his day who were oppressed by the loss of nineteenth-century convictions; but precisely the writers, like Pirandello, who do seem to have anticipated the existentialist stress upon the utter insecurity of life prove in the end to be the ones who resist its full display. And this, in turn, has some relation to the fact that they were raised in a culture where Christianity retained a portion of its historic power: for if the faith no longer survived in full radiance, men still responded to its call to duties, burdens, and limits.

Pirandello's stories are controlled by his sense of middle-class life. Fantasy, playfulness, sexual abandon, religious emotion, any sort of imaginative transcendence—these seldom break through in the stories. A full tragic release is rare. Much more characteristic are stories in which the final sadness arises from an acceptance by the characters that they will have to live on, performing their tasks without hope or joy. In a five-page masterpiece, "The Soft Touch of Grass," a bereaved and aging man is mistakenly suspected by a girl of having lewd intentions. Overcome by the hopeless confusion of things, he goes back to his room and turns "his face to the wall." The phrase could serve as Pirandello's literary signature.

In "Such Is Life," a work that would do honor to Chekhov, a hopeless marriage, long broken, is hopelessly resumed. This story, written with a hard austerity and unrelieved by a single rebellious gesture, stays painfully close to experience. Its power depends upon Pirandello's decision not to allow his sympathies to interfere with what he sees. At the end the central figure is left with "an ever-present torment . . . for all things, all earthly creatures as she saw them in the infinite anguish of her love and pity, in that constant painful awareness— assuaged only by fleeting peaceful moments which brought relief and consolation—of the futility of living like this. . . ."

Reading these somber stories, one is struck by the accuracy of Eric Bentley's description of Pirandello's motifs.

His characters are effective not in direct relation to [his] conceptions, but because these conceptions enable him to suggest beneath the Mask of the physical presence the steady ache of suffering humanity.

There are some humorous stories, too, such as "The Examination," in which a good-tempered glutton is diverted from his studies by friends tempting him with shares of pleasure. One smiles at the end, for Pirandello manages it with suavity and tact. But it is a humor of sadness, and it brings little gaiety or relief. About the pleasure of simply being alive Pirandello has little to say in his stories, certainly nothing to compare with his one marvelously lighthearted play Liolà, in which youthful energies bubble without restraint or theory.

What I have been saying may seem to be contradicted by the brilliant long story, "The Merry-Go-Round of Love." Traditional Italian humor, which delights in the undoing of a miserly schemer and in the longevity of an old man whose death everyone desires, seems to come alive once again in Pirandello's pages. (It is a humor somewhat similar to that of recent Italian films: a ridicule, both merciless and tender, of those who would live beyond their physical and psychic means.) Yet as the action unfolds there is a gradual darkening of tone, and the earlier comic absurdities give way to grotesque obsessions, so that finally the story comes to seem a revelation of the way energy itself, the very life-principle, can become a malicious affront to human life.

Only the stories set in Sicily have a certain buoyancy, not because Pirandello glosses over the misery of his homeland or indulges in peasant romanticism, but simply because here the human drama plays itself out with quick violence. Men rise, men fall; but they do not know the dribbling monotonies of an overrationalized mode of existence, as do so many characters in Pirandello's urban stories.

Behind Pirandello stands his master, the Sicilian novelist Giovanni Verga, from whom he learned to disdain Italianate grandeur and rhetoric. Reading Verga's great stories one feels they are not so much "made-up" fictions as communal fables, the record of a people born to catastrophe. Reading Pirandello's stories one feels they have been wrought by a man increasingly estranged from a world he knows intimately. Pirandello does not achieve the virile spareness of Verga; no one does. In Verga everything is subordinated to the decisiveness of the event; in Pirandello one must always be aware of psychological motives, even if these seldom appear on the surface of the story, and then mainly as a film of melancholy. Verga's happenings are more terrible than Pirandello's, yet are easier to take, since in Verga men howl as they suffer. Only a few decades separate the two writers, but the distance between them reflects a deep change in spiritual temper, a loss of zest and will.

Writers, like the rest of us, do not choose their moment of birth, and it would be absurd to "blame" Pirandello for the depressing atmosphere of his fiction. So quick an intelligence must have been awre of the difference in the literary possibilities open to Verga and himself, and he must have realized that most of the advantages lay with the older man. But no serious writer chooses his subject he can only choose whether to face it.

GEORGE ELIOT IN HER LETTERS

Regarded in her own time as one of the greatest English novelists, George Eliot came to suffer a strange loss of critical esteem during the earlier decades of our century. Didactic, moralizing, heavy-handed— these were among the standard accusations against her books. Today this estimate of our elders seems incredible, and Lord David Cecil's remark that he shrank from reading her novels, their very titles sounding "like the names in a graveyard," strikes one as a prize critical boner. (Besides, names in graveyards sound exactly like those of living people.)

Among serious critics George Eliot is again honored as a master of the novel, partly because recent shifts in intellectual climate have made her seem close to us and partly because a number of critics, notably F. R. Leavis, have championed her work and taught us to appreciate its meanings. And George Eliot herself has become for many of us a kind of literary heroine, representing the highest intellectual seriousness, the finest literary commitment and purity. We admire her for very great achievements, but even more, for a capacity to unite harmoniously the intellectual and creative sides of her personality, the writer who struggled with every leading idea of her time and the writer who brought to the English countryside a sweetness of affection it had seldom known before. And if ever it is recognized that *Middlemarch* is also one of the wittiest books in English, her triumph will be complete.

Except perhaps for Dr. Leavis' excellent study, George Eliot has received no tribute in our time equal to that now paid her by the publication of three immense volumes of her letters, totalling 1500 pages, and two-thirds of them in print for the first time. Three more volumes are to come, and when the project is completed, it will surely rank as one of the most significant among modern achievements in literary scholarship. Professor Gordon Haight has spent 20 years collecting and editing these letters; the result, unlike a good deal of literary scholarship in America, justifies the labor.

In any obvious sense George Eliot was not a great letter writer. One seldom finds in her letters that brilliance of phrase which makes Keats' letters so unforgettable, nor the psychological melodrama of Cowper's, nor the historical dramatics of Byron's. She wrote with no eye to publication or posterity: she wrote to her friends. In the main her letters are impersonal, though we do get a few glimpses of her neurotic dispositions, her insatiable need for reassurance (she wryly chastises "that traitor within, the love of human praise"), her prostrating migraines and, more happily, the enviable solidity of her marriage with G. H. Lewes. Once we move past the sticky—yet oddly impressive, as any strong faith is impressive—young evangelist of 19 who does not hesitate to compare herself with St. Paul, the writing becomes firm and supple, excellent in a wholly unliterary way: these are letters, not compositions. And precisely for this reason they provide us with an unexcelled portrait of the intellectual life of a century ago, which in its tones and tensions, if not in the specific problems that agitated it, bears an astonishing resemblance to our own time.

The disintegration of orthodox Christian belief as the unquestioned heritage of educated Englishmen had reached a point of crisis during Eliot's youth. The assaults of the "higher criticism," rudimentary by comparison with the German but still damaging enough; the corrosions of agnosticism, which as Engels remarks was often in England but a timid form of atheism; the lures and rivalries of science; the thrusting weight of a new industrial society—all these, and far more, were slowly grinding down and crushing the very bones of religious orthodoxy. For Eliot, nonetheless, it was a very great advantage to have been raised in an atmosphere of evangelical piety, for it gave her the moral courage to engage in a conscientious and fully-considered repudiation.

Coming under the influence of the Brays and the Hennells, two families of advanced religious and social views, her mind began to ferment with bold heterodox opinions, just as her style grew more fluid, precise and humane. There is a remarkable, previously unpublished letter which she wrote at 23 to her father, trying to explain why she would no longer go to church. Even those to whom her struggles of belief involve matters by now settled or irrelevant must feel a tremor of historical recognition as they read her sentence about the Scriptures: "I regard these writings as histories consisting of mingled truth and fictions. . . ." It is a sentence which, in its numerous mutations, is to rock the century. And the firmness with which she announces her break from the church, when compared with the anguished self-torment of another letter to a father, the letter by Kafka—this is the stuff of high intellectual drama.

It is customary these days to yearn for the advantages a writer gains when he can receive in full-force and at the level of implicit communication the traditional values and beliefs of his forebears; but there may be at least as great advantage for a writer to mature at a time when a faith has begun to decay yet is still a powerful shaper of the collective imagination. For a struggle against a revered faith requires a kind of *critical piety*, a capacity to face its claims, as to acknowledge its deficiencies, with the fullest resources of consciousness; and it is precisely this balance of acceptance and rejection, loyalty and criticism, which makes George Eliot's work so valuable. As a girl she writes a sentence that seems a key to her intellectual biography: "I was considerably shaken by the impression that religion was not a requisite to moral excellence." This "impression" once registered, everything else, the whole plunge into modern skepticism, inevitably follows.

It is too well known to need further description here. The letters themselves do it with unparalleled detail and richness: the pious little missy, stiff as a board, becomes a sharp, almost terrifying intellectual, revelling in polemics and disputes, meeting on equal terms Herbert Spencer, Harriet Martineau and Charles Dickens, sending the editor of the *Westminster Review* a deserved rebuke for his violation of the laws of syntax, translating Strauss, Feuerbach and Spinoza, and writing articles so thoughtful and well-grounded that they could still be profitably reprinted. The common image of George Eliot as a rather forbidding blue-stocking is sheer misconception, largely the result of the carefully twisted biography written by her second husband, John Cross. Actually the George Eliot of these earlier letters is a woman of almost bewildering emotional readiness, waiting to be impressed, like the heroine of *Middlemarch*, by men of intellect; she is all eager warmth and receptivity, hungering for affection and struggling to contain her pride; and she is a woman of rare wit, able to say of her meeting with Strauss, "my deficient German prevented us from learning more of each other than our exteriors, which in the case of both would have been better left to imagination." Finally, she is a woman of great personal power and massive integrity, who writes that great sentence in defense of her "irregular union" (as the literary historians call it) with G. H. Lewes, a sentence which seems a germ of the style of *Middlemarch*:

Light and easily broken ties are what I neither desire theoretically nor could live for practically. Women who are satisfied with such ties do *not* act as I have done—they obtain what they desire and are still invited to dinner.

The general impression one gains of her intellectual development is quite close to the careful summary provided by Basil Willey in his *Nineteenth Century Studies*—except in one important respect. Willey treats her shift from evangelical Christianity to a softened form of the "religion of humanity" in purely religious terms, which seems to me not so much mistaken as one-sided. He fails to recognize that in the nineteenth century social and political issues were often fought out in the guise of theological controversy, and one does not therefore get from his study a sufficient sense of the George Eliot—not the major George Eliot, but an important one nonetheless—who said that it was worth learning French simply to read Rousseau's *Confessions* or who wrote in 1848 a letter in which she analyzes the French Revolution in terms that recall both Stendhal's letters about the revolution of 1830 and Marx's little book *Class Struggles in France*. She speaks of her "sanscullotish" sympathies, she summons the picture of "the men of the barricade bowing to the image of Christ 'who first taught fraternity to men'," she declares that "our decayed monarchs should be pensioned off: we should have a hospital for them, or a sort of Zoological Garden, where these wornout humbugs may be preserved." Then she proceeds to an extremely shrewd analysis of the differences between the French and the English workers, and a little later she identifies herself with those who have "a presentiment, a yearning, or a clear vision of the time when this miserable reign of Mammon shall end . . . I feel that society is training men and women for hell." None of this, of course, is to deny the deeply conservative bent of her temperament; it is only to emphasize the conflicting bent of her early opinions.

The third volume of the letters takes us to the point where Eliot, after orgies of self-doubt, becomes a writer of proven success, though her best work is still before her. She keeps returning to her views on literature, in which she makes the kinds of discriminations that modern criticism labors to impress. She refuses to tell her publisher the story of *Adam Bede* before he sees the manuscript, "on the ground that I would not have it judged apart from my *treatment*, which alone determines the moral quality of art." She withdraws from ideological contention ("opinions are a poor cement between human souls") and refines her sense of the "religion of the heart," which is the enemy of all dogma and revelation. And at the age of 41 she writes the great passage which is the negative side of her commitment to the life of "sympathy," the passage that ends, "The highest 'calling and election' is to do *without opium* and live through all our pain with conscious, clear-eyed endurance."

The figure of George Eliot, as it slowly builds into shape from these letters, is not god-like nor even grand; we see her in all her vulnerability, her debilitating enthusiasms and her irremovable weakness. But I cannot recall having read any letters or diaries in which the idea of intellectual devotion is realized with such a blend of common humanity and selfless austerity. To read these letters is to learn that the life of the mind can be a thing of glory.

THE COUNTRY OF THE POINTED FIRS

Sarah Orne Jewett was a writer of deep pure feeling and a limited capacity for emotional expression: there is always, one senses, more behind the language than actually comes through it. In her best work she employed—it was an instinctive and inevitable choice—a tone of muted nostalgia. She knew that the Maine country she loved so well was slowly being pushed into a social impasse: it could not compete in the jungle warfare that was American life in the late nineteenth century. But even as this knowledge formed and limited her vision of things, she did not let it become the dominant content of her work, for she understood, or felt, that the obsolete also has its claim upon us. She was honest and tactful enough not to inflate her sense of passing and nostalgia with the urgencies of a heroism that could only have been willed; in her bare, linear stories about country people struggling to keep their farms alive, she made no false claims, for she saw that even when one or another figure in her Maine country might be heroic there was nothing distinctively heroic in the spectacle of a community in decline, a way of life gradually dying. But she knew—it was an enviable knowledge—that admiration and love can be extended to those who have neither the vocation nor the possibility for heroism. She paid a price, of course. In a country where literature has so often been given over to roaring and proclaiming and "promulging" it was nearly impossible for so exquisite an artist—exquisite precisely because she was, and knew she was, a minor figure—to be properly valued.

At first glance *The Country of the Pointed Firs* bears a certain structural resemblance to Mrs. Gaskell's *Cranford*. In both books a young woman who has tasted urban knowledge returns to a quaint, outmoded village which represents pre-industrial society, and there observes the manners of its inhabitants with a mixture of fondness and amusement. But charming as *Cranford* obviously is, it does not seem to me nearly so good as Miss Jewett's book. Too often Mrs. Gaskell is content to bask in the soft glow of eccentricity and oddity, so that her narrator leaves Cranford pretty much the person she was. But Miss Jewett's "I" registers the meaning of Deephaven with an increase of force and insight that is beautifully arranged: for her the experience of arriving and leaving becomes an education in mortality.

The people in *The Country of the Pointed Firs* are eccentrics, a little gnarled by the American weather and twisted by American loneliness; but it is not for a display of these deformities that Miss Jewett presents them. She is interested in reaching some human core beneath the crusted surface and like so many other American writers, like Anderson and Frost and Robinson, she knows the value and pathos of the buried life. That is why it is harmful, despite the fact that her stories are set in the same locale, to speak of her as a regional writer; for regional literature, by its very premise, implies a certain slackening of the human measure, a complacent readiness to accept the merely accidental and quaint.

Miss Jewett moves her light from one figure to another: the shy fisherman William who late in life returns to the interior country to claim his love; the jilted Miss Joanna Todd who in the immensity of her grief cuts herself off from humanity and lives alone on a coastal island; the touched sea captain who remembers journeys to places that never were; and most of all, Mrs. Almiry Todd, the central figure of the book, sharp-tongued. wise, witty, a somewhat greyed version of George Eliot's Mrs. Poyser. (As Mrs. Todd recalls her dead husband, "She might have been Antigone alone on the Theban plain. . . . An absolute, archaic grief possessed this countrywoman; she seemed like a renewal of some historic soul, with her sorrows and the remoteness of a daily life busied with rustic simplicities and the scents of primeval herbs.") The book is set in a dramatic present that is necessarily somewhat fragile, but it resounds with full echoes of the past: tradition lives as an element of experience, not a proposition of ideology. ("Conversation's got to have some root in the past," says an old lady, "or else you've got to explain every remark you make, and it wears a person out.")

The Country of the Pointed Firs gains organic structure from its relaxed loyalty to the rhythms of natural life. The world it memorializes is small and shrinking, and the dominant images of the book serve only to bound this world more stringently: images of the ranked firs and the water, which together suggest the enclosing force of everything beyond the social perimeter. But meanwhile a community survives, endowed with rare powers of implicit communication: to say in this world that someone has "real feelins" is to say everything.

Finally the book is a triumph of style, a precise and delicate style such as we seldom find in nineteenth century American prose. The breakdown of distinctions between prose and verse which occurs under the sponsorship of romanticism and for a variety of reasons is particularly extreme in America, where it produces two such ambiguous figures of genius as Melville and Whitman—this breakdown hardly affected Miss Jewett. Very probably this is one reason she remained a minor figure while Melville and Whitman were, occasionally, major ones. But at the moment there is much to be gained from a study of her finely modulated prose, which never strains for effects beyond its reach and always achieves a secure pattern of rhythm. Listen to this sentence with its sly abrupt climax: "There was something quite charming in his appearance: it was a face thin and delicate with refinement, but worn into appealing lines, as if he had suffered from loneliness and misapprehension." Or to the lucid gravity of this sentence: "There was in the eyes a look of anticipation and joy, a far-off look that sought the horizon; one often sees it in seafaring families, inherited by girls and boys alike from men who spend their lives at sea, and are always watching for distant sails or the first loom of the land." Or to the wit of Mrs. Todd as she places her minister: "He seemed to know no remedies, but he had a great use of words."

The Country of the Pointed Firs is not a "great" book; it isn't *Moby Dick* or *Sister Carrie* or even *The Great Gatsby*. It cannot sustain profound exegesis or symbol hunting. But living as we do in a country where minor works are underrated because major ones are overrated, it is good to remember that we have writers like Miss Jewett calmly waiting for us to remember them.

ROBERT FROST: A MOMENTARY STAY

The best of Robert Frost, like the best of most writers, is small in quantity and narrow in scope. There are a few dozen of his lyrics which register a completely personal voice, both as to subject and tone, and which it would be impossible to mistake for the work of anyone else. These lyrics mark Frost as a severe and unaccommodating writer: they are ironic, troubled and ambiguous in some of the ways modernist poems are. Despite a lamentable gift for public impersonations, Frost has remained faithful to what Yeats calls "the modern mind in search of its own meanings."

This Frost seldom ventures upon major experiments in meter or diction, nor is he as difficult in reference and complex in structure as are the great poets of the 20th Century. But as he contemplates the thinning landscape of his world and repeatedly finds himself before closures of outlook and experience, he ends, almost against his will, in the company of the moderns. With their temperament and technique he has little in common; he shares with them only a vision of disturbance. This Frost is problematic in his style of thought, quite unlike the twinkling Sage who in his last years became the darling of the nation.

Frost has also written a small number of memorable poems in another vein: dramatic monologues and dialogues set in northern New England which present realistic vignettes of social exhaustion. While neither as original or distinguished as the best of his lyrics, they often live in one's mind, somewhat as a harshly monochromatic picture might.

In his long poems, most of them uniting satire and didacticism, Frost is at his worst. An early long poem, "New Hampshire," foreshadows the sly folksiness that would later endear him to native moralists, lady schoolteachers, and miscellaneous middlebrows. The verse is limp; the manner coy; the thought a display of provincialism. In the least happy sense of the word, the poem is *mannered:* Frost catering to his own idiosyncracies and minor virtuosities. Even when he is clever ("Lately in converse with a New York alec / About the new school of pseudo-phallic"), it is with the cleverness of a man holding fast to his limitations.

Some years ago Malcolm Cowley compared Frost to Hawthorne, Emerson and Thoreau and shrewdly noticed the narrowing of sensibility Frost had come, at his worst, to represent:

Height, breadth and strength: he falls short in all these qualities of the great New Englanders. And the other quality for which he is often praised, his utter faithfulness to the New England spirit, is not one of the virtues they knowingly cultivated. They realized that the New England spirit, when it stands alone, is inclined to be narrow and arithmetical. It has reached its finest growth only when cross-fertilized with alien philosophies.

Much of Frost's later work—"A Masque of Reason," "Build Soil," "A Masque of Mercy" and the bulk of "Steeple Bush"—illustrates the hardening of his public pose. It is a pose of crustiness and sometimes even heartlessness, and it reflects the feeling of a writer that he need not engage with the problems of his time. In such writing he is the dealer in packaged whimsies, the homespun Horace scrutinizing man, God and liberalism. Because political fashions changed during the last decades of his life, the aged Frost found himself being applauded for precisely the sententia which had previously, and with good reason, been attacked. But now his hard-shelled individualism won the admiration of readers who in their own experience had increasingly to acknowledge that it would no longer do: perhaps that is why they wished to admire it in poetry.

In these poems conversational tone slips into garrulousness, conservatism declines into smallness of mind, public declamation ends as mere vanity of pronouncement. If this were all we had of Frost, there would be no choice but to accept the attack launched upon him some years ago by Yvor Winters. Frost, wrote Winters, had a way of "mistaking whimsical impulse for moral choice," a kind of irrational romanti-

cism that left him a "spiritual drifter." Reading such passages as the one
in "A Masque of Reason" where God declares—

> I'm going to tell Job why I tortured him
> And trust it won't be adding to the torture.
> I was just showing off to the Devil, Job.

—one is tempted to go along with Winters. Frost permits himself such
mindless flippancies because he knows that by now his audience has
been trained to admire his faults at the very point where they become
magnified by cleverness. The writer who does not struggle to overcome his limitations ends by parodying them.

Frost the national favorite is a somewhat different figure. He is a
writer of lyrics that often achieve a flawed distinction: the language
clear, the picture sharp, the rhythm ingratiating. "Birches," "Mending
Wall," "The Death of the Hired Man," "The Pasture"—such poems are
not contemptible but neither are they first-rate. They lack the urge to
move past easy facilities. They depend too much on the unconsidered
respect good Americans feel obliged to show for "nature." They yield
too readily to the common notion of poetic genius as an unaccountable
afflatus:

> At least don't use your mind too hard,
> But trust my instinct—I'm a bard.

And they create a music too winsome and soothing:

> This saying good-by on the edge of the dark
> And the cold to an orchard so young in the bark
> Reminds me of all that can happen to harm
> An orchard away at the end of the farm.

The appeal of such poems rests upon Frost's use of what might be called
false pastoral. Traditionally, pastoral poetry employs an idyllic setting
with apparently simple characters in order to advance complex ideas
and sentiments, often implying a serious criticism of the society in
which the poet lives. The pastoral seems to turn away in disgust from
urban or sophisticated life and to celebrate the virtues of bucolic retreat; but it does not propose that we rest with either simple characters
or simple virtues. It accepts the convention of simplicity in order to
demonstrate the complexity of the real; and only in an inferior kind of
poetry is the pretense of the pastoral taken at face value.

In his lesser poems, however, Frost comes very close to doing precisely that. He falls back upon the rural setting as a means of endorsing

the common American notion that a special wisdom is to be found, and found only, among tight-lipped farmers, village whittlers and small-town eccentrics. Overwhelmingly urban, our society displays an un-flagging nostaliga for the assumed benefits and beauties of country life. Millions of Americans who live in cities and suburbs preen themselves on homely virtues they neither possess nor could profitably employ if they did. They like to fancy themselves as good rugged country folk, or suppose they would have a better and happier life if they were. And the second-rank Frost is their poet.

He *becomes* his audience, mirroring and justifying its need for pastoral fancies. The more a magazine like *The New Yorker* influences the quality of sophisticated middle-class life, the more will many Americans feel a desire for some assuaging counter-image—woodsy, wholesome, a bit melancholic—such as Frost can provide. As a writer who bends his gift to the sincere misapprehensions of his readers, he has become a figure deeply integral to our culture; and the middlebrows who adore him must in fairness be granted some right to claim him as their own. All that can be said by way of qualification is that not the whole or best of Frost is theirs.

Matters are more complicated still. Frost is so skillful a performer that some of his most popular poems, like "Acquainted With the Night," "After Apple-Picking," and "Stopping by Woods on a Snowy Evening" are also among his finest. It might be convenient, but is also a dangerous simplification, to draw a sharp line between his popular and superior poems. The two have a way of shading into one another, as has always been the case with those major writers of the past two centuries, like Dickens, Mark Twain and Sholom Aleichem, who managed to speak both to cultivated persons and to the mass audience. And part of what Frost's ordinary readers admire or look for in his poetry they are, I think, right in wanting: a renewal of primary experience, a relatedness to the physical world, a wisdom resting on moral health.

In his dramatic poems Frost seldom falls back upon ready-made pastoral. These are poems of rural realism: New England as a depressed landscape, country people who are poor and deprived, families torn apart by derangement. The best of this group, such as "Home Burial" and "Servant to Servants," are studies in frustration, often the frustration of women who can no longer bear the weight of suffering. There is no "community" behind these figures, no sustaining world in which they can move, no Tilbury Town or Winesburg Ohio to define social boundaries. The men and women of Frost's poems are isolated; they are figures left over by a dead or dying culture; and the world they live in has begun turning into stone.

Powerful as some of these dramatic pieces are, they share a number of faults. Frost lacks the patience, the involvement, and the deep concern with moral nuance that are essential to a writer wishing to evoke human character. He tries to conform to the hard outlines of economical portraiture and to avoid the kind of detail that would be appropriate only to a novel, but the result is often that the poems rely too much on photographic anecdote. The events they depict are supposed to speak for themselves; but events seldom do.

Precisely the shading and implication one misses in Frost's dramatic poems are what distinguish the dramatic poems of his immediate New England predecessor, Edwin Arlington Robinson. Though not nearly so brilliant a virtuoso as Frost, Robinson writes from a fullness of experience and a tragic awareness that Frost cannot equal. No other American poet commands so rich a sense of moral life as does Robinson in "Eros Turranos," "The Wandering Jew," "Rembrandt to Rembrandt" and "The Three Taverns"—poems beside which Frost's work in the same genres seems stiff in portrayal and crude in psychology. Frost has a strong grasp on melodramatic extremes of behavior, usually extremes of loneliness and psychic exhaustion, but he lacks almost entirely Robinson's command of the middle range of experience. The life of Frost's poems is post-social, and the perspective from which it is seen a desperate one. Frost achieves a cleaner verbal surface and a purer diction, but Robinson is more abundant in moral detail and insight. Compared strictly on their performances as dramatic poets, Robinson seems a major poet and Frost a minor one. For while Frost can be a master of nuance, it is only, or almost only, when he speaks in his own voice.

And that he does when he bears down with full seriousness in his small number of distinguished lyrics. Here the archness and sentimentalism have been ruthlessly purged; he is writing for sheer life. To read these poems, as they confront basic human troubles and obliquely notice the special dislocations of our time, can be unnerving—they offer neither security nor solace. They are the work of a poet who, without the mediation of formal thought or religious sentiments, gives close and hard battle to his own experience. They seek to capture those moments when we confront experience in its bareness, observing some natural event or place with a pure sense of the dynamics of reception. They set out to record such tremors of being in their purity and isolation: as if through a critical encounter with the physical world one could move beyond the weariness of selfhood and into the repose of matter. But Frost, now supremely hard on himself, also knows that the very intensity with which these moments are felt makes certain their rapid dissolution, and that what then remains is the familiar self, once

again its own prisoner. Approaching a condition in which the narrator
strains to achieve a sense of oneness with the universe and thereby lose
himself in the delight of merger, these lyrics return, chastened, with
the necessity of shaped meaning. And in their somewhat rueful turning
back to the discipline of consciousness, the effect is both painful and
final. They conclude with the reflection that the central quandary of
selfhood—that it must forever spiral back to its own starting point—
cannot be dissolved. That Frost sees and struggles with this dilemma
seems to me one reason for saying he inhabits the same intellectual
climate as those modern writers whose presumed disorder is often
compared unfavorably to his supposed health.

Frost's superior lyrics include: "Storm Fear," "An Old Man's Winter
Night," "The Oven Bird," "Dust of Snow," "Stopping by Woods on a
Snowy Evening," "Spring Pools," "Acquainted With the Night," "The
Lovely Shall be Choosers," "Neither Out Far Nor in Deep," "Provide,
Provide," "Design," "Happiness Makes Up in Height for What It
Lacks in Length," "The Most of It," "Never Again Would Bird's Song
Be the Same," "The Silken Tent," and a few others.

These poems demand from the reader a sharp recognition of their
brevity. They focus upon a moment of intense realization, a lighting-up
of hope and a dimming-down to wisdom. They attempt not a full seizure of an event, but an attack upon it from the oblique. They present a
scene in the natural world, sometimes one that is "purely" natural and
apparently unmarred by a human observer, but more often one that
brings the "I" of the poem starkly against a natural process, so that the
stress falls upon a drama of encounter and withdrawal. The event or
situation—how spring pools will be sucked dry by the absorptive
power of trees, in "Spring Pools"; how an albino spider perched on a
"white heal-all" forms a dumb-show of purposeless terror, in "Design";
how the loneliness of a winter moment encompasses an observer unawares, in "Desert Places"; how a family caught in a fearful storm may
not, unaided, be able to rescue itself, in "Storm Fear"—is rendered
with a desire to make a picture that will seem complete in itself, but
that will also, through the very perfection of completeness, carry an
aura of suggestion beyond itself. Frost allows for the sensuous pleasure
of apprehending a moment in nature, but he soon cuts it short, since
the point is not to linger over scene or pleasure but to move beyond
them, along a line of speculation. Perhaps that is what Frost meant
when he said that poetry "begins in delight and ends in wisdom."

These lyrics can be placed on a spectrum ranging from a few that
seem entirely focussed upon a natural event to those which move past
the event toward explicit statement. Despite the critical dogma which
looks down upon statement in poetry, there is nothing inherently

superior about the first of these kinds; Frost's greatest poems, as it
happens, are those which end with a coda of reflection. "Spring Pools"
is an example of a poem that seems, at first, merely a snapshot of the
external world:

> These pools that, though in forests, still reflect
> The total sky almost without defect,
> nd like the flowers beside them, chill and shiver,
> Will like the flowers beside them soon be gone,
> And yet not out by any brook or river,
> But up by roots to bring dark foliage on.
>
> The trees that have it in their pentup buds
> To darken nature and be summer woods—
> Let them think twice before they use their powers
> To blot out and drink up and sweep away
> These flowery waters and these watery flowers
> From snow that melted only yesterday.

As a rendering of a natural event, the poem is precise, expert and
complete. Exactness of description can be very moving, and so it is in
"Spring Pools"; but beyond that, the poem—partly through a skillful
play with prepositions in the tenth line—suggests how hard yet necessary it is that the brief loveliness of youth be sucked dry to form the
strength of our prime. Where the poem moves beyond description and
implication is in its problematic use of a parallelism between natural
event and human experience. An implied equivalence between nature
and man quickly brings a writer to the edge of the sentimental; but
Frost does not cross it, for the poem, in its descriptive self-sufficiency,
leaves to the reader the problem of what symbolic import to infer and
how much tact he can muster in defending the poem against his own
inference. It is a poem about spring pools, the poignancy of youth, and
problems of thinking, not in any hierarchy of value which dissolves
everything into the "spiritual," but in a poised equality of perceiving.

Most of Frost's superior lyrics end with direct statement, and one
measure of their success is his ability to make the statement seem an
adequate climax to the remarkable descriptive writing that has pre-
ceded it. The problem is not one to be approached with *a priori* notions
about the relationship between imagery and statement in verse. When
Cleanth Brooks writes that "Frost does not *think* through his images;
he requires statements," he is guilty of a modernist dogma to the
extent that he means his remarks as an adverse criticism. Poetry has
always been full of statement, even the poetry of many modernist
writers who are supposed to confine themselves to symbolic indirec-

tion; and the critical problem in regard to Frost, or any other writer, hinges on the extent to which the concluding statement is related, through logical fulfillment or irony, to the texture of the poem, and the extent to which the statement is in its own right serious in thought and notable in diction.

In "Desert Places" Frost starts with a description of a natural scene and then, in a very moving way, brings in the human observer:

> Snow falling and night falling fast, oh, fast
> In a field I looked into going past,
> And the ground almost covered smooth in snow,
> But a few weeds and stubble showing last.
>
> The woods around it have it—it is theirs.
> All animals are smothered in their lairs.
> I am too absent-spirited to count;
> The loneliness includes me unawares.
>
> And lonely as it is that loneliness
> Will be more lonely ere it will be less—
> A blanker whiteness of benighted snow
> With no expression, nothing to express.

Thus far the poem is very fine, but there follows the concluding stanza—

> They cannot scare me with their empty spaces
> Between stars—on stars where no human race is.
> I have it in me so much nearer home
> To scare myself with my own desert places.

—in which Frost collapses into the kind of coyness one has come to associate with his second-rank poems. Cut out the final stanza and "Desert Places" is a perfect small lyric; as it stands, the poem is a neat illustration of Frost's characteristic strengths and weaknesses; but the weakness of the last four lines is due not to the fact that Frost ventures a statement, but to the quality of the statement he ventures.

In most of the lyrics I have named Frost handles this problem with assurance. "The Oven Bird" presents a picture of a bird which in mid-summer sings loudly, as if in celebration of the lapsed spring:

> He says the early petal-fall is past
> When pear and cherry bloom went down in showers
> On sunny days a moment overcast;
> And comes that other fall we name the fall.

The writing here, both vivid and witty, is satisfying enough, and the

theme, though treated with greater toughness, resembles that of
"Spring Pools." The bird is assigned, as a pleasing conceit and not a
sentimental indulgence, something of the poet's stoical resilience:

> The bird would cease and be as other birds
> But that he knows in singing not to sing.

Then come the concluding lines, in which Frost achieves a triumph of
modulated rhetoric, a statement that can be regarded as an epitaph of
his whole career:

> The question that he frames in all but words
> Is what to make of a diminished thing.

Many of Frost's first-rate lyrics unite with similar success a rapid passage of description and a powerful concluding statement. The familiar
"Acquainted With the Night" owes a good part of its haunting quality
not merely to Ford's evocation of a man walking the streets alone at
night—

> I have stood still and stopped the sound of feet
> When far away an interrupted cry
> Came over houses from another street
>
> But not to call me back or say goodbye;

—but also to the lines that immediately follow, lines of enigmatic
statement indicating an ultimate dissociation between the natural
world and human desire:

> And further still at an unearthly height,
> One luminary clock against the sky
>
> Proclaimed the time was neither wrong nor right.
> I have been one acquainted with the night.

In discussing such poems it has become a commonplace to say, as W.
H. Auden does, that Frost's style "approximates to ordinary speech"
and that "the music is always that of the speaking voice, quiet and
sensible." This does not seem an adequate way of describing Frost's
lyrics. Try reading "Spring Pools" or "The Most of It" in a voice ap-
proximating to ordinary speech: it cannot be done, short of violating
the rhythm of the poem. Quiet these lyrics may be, "sensible" they are
not. They demand a rhythm of enticement and immersion, a hastening
surrender to unreflective nature—which means a rising and tensing of

the voice; and then a somewhat broken or subdued return to reflec-
tiveness. They are poems that must be read with a restrained intoning,
quite different from "ordinary speech," though milder than declamation.

It is a way of reading enforced by their structure and purpose: the
structure and purpose of wisdom-poems. Frost's best lyrics aim at the
kind of wisdom that is struck aslant and not to be settled into the
comforts of an intellectual system. It is the wisdom of a mind confessing
its nakedness. Frost writes as a modern poet who shares in the loss of
firm assumptions and seeks, through a disciplined observation of the
natural world and a related sequel of reflection, to provide some tentative basis for existence, some "momentary stay," as he once remarked,
"against confusion." The best of his poems are antipathetic to the notion that the universe is inherently good or delightful or hospitable to
our needs. The symbols they establish in relation to the natural world
are not, as in transcendentalist poetry, tokens of benevolence. These
lyrics speak of the hardness and recalcitrance of the natural world; of its
absolute indifference to our needs and its refusal to lend itself to an
allegory of affection; of the certainty of physical dissolution; but also of
the refreshment that can be found through a brief submission to the
alienness of nature, always provided one recognizes the need to move
on, not stopping for rest but remaining locked, alone, in consciousness.
The lyric that best illustrates these themes is "The Most of It," which
dramatizes our desire for cosmic solace and the consequence of discovering we cannot have it.

> He thought he kept the universe alone;
> For all the voice in answer he could wake
> Was but the mocking echo of his own
> From some tree-hidden cliff across the lake.
> Some morning from the boulder-broken beach
> He would cry out on life, that what it wants
> Is not its own love back in copy speech,
> But counter-love, original response.
> And nothing ever came of what he cried
> Unless it was the embodiment that crashed
> In the cliff's talus on the other side,
> And then in the far distant water splashed,
> But after a time allowed for it to swim,
> Instead of proving human when it neared
> And someone else additional to him,
> As a great buck it powerfully appeared,
> Pushing the crumpled water up ahead,
> And landed pouring like a waterfall,
> And stumbled through the rocks with horny tread,
> And forced the underbrush—and that was all.

A NEGLECTED AMERICAN POET

Frederick Tuckerman, almost forgotten and certainly neglected, was a nineteenth-century New England poet, contemporary with the Transcendentalists but sharply different from them in outlook and style. During his lifetime he published a single volume, *Poems*, in 1860, which went through three further printings with minor textual changes; he won a very modest recognition, mostly through private letters from Hawthorne, Emerson and Longfellow. Living in near-isolation in the Berkshires, Tuckerman seems not to have cared about getting into print the work he composed after 1860; he was genuinely the kind of poet who writes to himself; and once he died, in 1873 at the age of fifty-two, he passed into obscurity.

Some thirty-five years later an American critic, Walter Eaton, published an essay calling attention to Tuckerman's verse, an incomplete selection of which he had seen and admired; this article, in turn, came to the notice of the poet Witter Bynner, who in 1931 issued a volume bringing together the five series of sonnets written by Tuckerman (only the first two series had appeared in the 1860 *Poems*) and providing a fine introductory appreciation. In the main, however, criticism of Tuckerman has been sparse and unsatisfactory.

For the first time, all of Tuckerman's work has now been brought together in a single and decidedly impressive volume, *The Complete Poems of Frederick Tuckerman*. N. Scott Momaday, who has edited the texts with care, has also provided a biographical-critical Introduction.

I offer this little chronicle because it seems, unnervingly, to retrace the pattern of neglect and discovery that has characterized too much of American literary history. That so unspectacular a poet as Tuckerman could become the subject of strong popular interest, is unlikely; but this would not preclude a boom in the academic world, where the need for "subjects" grows omniverously. One can only hope that the appearance of Mr. Momaday's edition will end the injustice of neglect without provoking the vulgarity of "revival."

About Tuckerman himself not much is or needs to be known. Son of a wealthy merchant, he was graduated from Harvard with a law degree but chose not to practice. He retired to western Massachusetts, where, equipped with telescope and herbarium, he lived as a country gentleman distinguished by a semi-professional interest in science. In 1847 he married, and happily; ten years later his wife died, after childbirth; and from this blow Tuckerman seems never to have recovered— indeed, he seems, in some deeply serious way, to have *chosen* not to recover.

A good part of Tuckerman's work consists of narrative and reflective pieces, some of them derivative from the Romantic poets, most of them too long and limp, and few of them memorable. Emerson liked "Rhotruda," an amusing verse tale set in Charlemagne's court, and Hawthorne praised "The Stranger," a sketch of country character; both judgments were sound. There are passages in which Tuckerman, writing about New England life, somewhat anticipates E. A. Robinson, though without Robinson's genius for psychological penetration:

> Where silence brooded, I longed to look within
> On the completed story of his life;
> So easy still it seemed to lift the hand,
> And open it, as I would a disused door
> Locked with a dusty web: but he passed out;
> And if he had a grief it went with him,
> And all the treasure of his untold love.

Tuckerman's distinguished work is to be found in the sonnets and "The Cricket," and these are strikingly different from most American poetry of his time. He had no interest in blending the roles of poet and prophet, no temptation to employ his writing as a platform from which to rise to a condition of transport, whether traditionally Christian or romantically pantheistic. He had no taste for the soaring line, the vatic pronouncement, the inflammation of selfhood which Emerson was drawn to and Whitman practised; he was incapable of the mystical exaltation of Jones Very or the gnomic compression of Emily Dickinson. All of these poets, whatever their differences, were linked by a

desire somehow to achieve union—or at least enter intimate
relation—with a transcendent principle. And they tried to achieve this
through a variety of spiritual exercises and exposures.

Tuckerman wrote from a sharper endowment of common-sense
realism. Like anyone raised in nineteenth-century New England, he
felt the gradual slipping-away of God as a personal trouble; but he
never tried to force his way into belief or bludgeon his soul into ecstasy
("Still craves the spirit: never Nature solves/That yearning which with
her first breath began"). If he fails to reach Very's sublimities or Dickinson's intensities, neither is he guilty of forcing his emotions or
pumping up his self. And he abstains from the characteristic temptation of nineteenth-century writers, which is to spiritualize the natural
world as a way of relocating a displaced and diminished God.

In the sonnets and "The Cricket" Tuckerman writes out of a hard
awareness of human limitation: he does not confuse himself with the
cosmos, the trees, or the spiritual aether. He is not a soul on the
lookout for mergers, he knows himself as a discrete and particular
being. Just as he does not wish to spiritualize the outer world, so he
does not try to mythicize himself. Perhaps all writers create a *persona*
for their work that is distinct from their actual selves, but in the case of
Tuckerman the distinction between the two is minimal. One feels that
the poems contain the direct reflections of a serious and thoughtful
man: not very hopeful in regard to himself but strongly alive toward the
world about him. And in the nineteenth-century American context,
where poets too often are straining to inflate the self into a universal
presence or to roll it into a neat capsule of wisdom, this even-voiced
meditation—it is by no means conversational speech—comes as something of a relief.

Though marred by an occasional breakdown of syntax and archaism
of diction, Tuckerman's poems are realistic in psychology and moral
tone. His characteristic topics—the burden and value of grief, the way
in which distance enables a proper inspection of the world, the pressures of *ennui* tempting one to sink back into insentience—are all
treated as elements of common experience. Nothing in his work
reaches the exalted power of Very's "Thy Brother's Blood," but one can
feel about Tuckerman, as not about Very, that he is a recognizable
contemporary.

Tuckerman's descriptions of the natural world are sharp and clean, as
one might suppose the descriptions of an imaginative scientist would
be:

> Dank fens of cedar, hemlock branches gray,
> With trees and trail of mosses, wringing-wet,

> Beds of the black pitchpine in dead leaves set
> Whose wasted red has wasted to white away,
> Remnants of rain and droppings of decay . . .

This is very fine, especially the fourth line in which an aura of implication like that in Frost's "Spring Pools" is achieved through striking exactness of detail. Emerson courted the essence of Nature, Tuckerman observed the local phenomena of nature. Distinguished poetry can be written from both outlooks, but to most modern tastes Tuckerman's control of particulars will seem the more congenial. In another sonnet he reflects upon the settling of his countryside:

> Here, but a lifetime back, where falls tonight
> Behind the curtained pane a shelterered light
> On buds of rose or vase of violet
> Aloft upon the marble mantle set,
> Here in the forest-heart, hung blackening
> The wolfbait on the bush beside the spring.

Perhaps there is a slight drop into flatness in the third and fourth of these lines, but the opening ("but a lifetime back") and the concluding lines are of a high order.

Respecting the integrity, the "thereness," of the natural world, Tuckerman refused to assimilate it into any metaphysical improvisation. In a way that makes him seem a modern sensibility even though no one would suppose him a modern poet, Tuckerman keeps returning to the experience of duality between the perceiving self and the perceived world—an experience that seemed to him basic to the human situation, so that no theory can undo it or sophistication dismiss it.

A poetry of observation, dwelling mainly on the pleasures and qualities of appearances, gives way in Tuckerman's work to a poetry of meditation, dwelling mainly on the sensibility of the bereft. The first is usually more successful than the second, for the poet's anguish, insufficiently grounded in precise situations and lacking variety of pitch, comes to sound like a minor chord struck over and over again. But when Tuckerman fuses the meditative and descriptive modes, when he brings together the ruminative speaker and a setting of brilliantly observed phenomena, he usually avoids that emotional droop which Mr. Winters describes as the "romantic . . . divorce of feeling from motive." There follows a compressed drama in which the self rallies almost against its will, responding to a sky "blue with white tails of cloud" and noticing that even as graves remain stirless "Creation moveth, and the farmboy sleeps/A still strong sleep till but the east is red."

The sonnets, read systematically, reveal frequent lapses into stock filler and mannerism; they have a way of not completing themselves;

they betray a lack of emotional energy and will. The problem with depletion as a subject is that too often it ends up as the condition of poetry. Precisely the sorrow one recognizes as utterly authentic gets to be dulling, soporific, clotting. Tuckerman's voice becomes predictable, like that of a friend in mourning whose sorrow one credits but concerning which one becomes guiltily impatient.

Let me quote, however, one of the lovelier sonnets, which also has its soft lines and Romantic commonplaces, but which nevertheless illustrates Tuckerman's high meditative eloquence:

> An upper chamber in a darkened house,
> Where, ere his footsteps reached ripe manhood's brink,
> Terror and anguish were his lot to drink;
> I cannot rid the thought nor hold it close
> But dimly dream upon that man alone:
> Now through autumn clouds most softly pass,
> The cricket chides beneath the doorstep stone
> And greener than the season grows the grass.
> Nor can I drop my lids nor shade my brows,
> But there he stands beside the lifted sash;
> And with a swooning of the heart, I think
> Where the black shingles slope to meet the boughs
> And, shattered on the roof like smallest snows,
> The tiny petals of the mountain ash.

LITERATURE ON THE COUCH

In American literary life, the crank is by now a familiar figure. He is a man who believes he has found a total and thereby solacing explanation for the chaos and multiplicity of existence. Usually we think of him as a Midwesterner, a jarring voice from the plains to be contrasted with the smoother accents of the sophisticated Easterner. But in recent years, as part of the flattening-out of American culture, the two types have sometimes come to blend, so that writers like Ezra Pound and William Carlos Williams are both suave and simple-minded, sophisticated and crankish.

There has been a similar development in literary criticism. Reputable scholars turn out studies to show that Kafka's novels are cabalistic notations concerning homosexuality, that Melville was engaged in an elaborate mystification to conceal his venom against God, that Henry James wrote his major novels as allegorical tracings of Swedenborgian philosophy. What can one say about such books except that they are sincere, often ingenious, and quite batty?

Leslie Fiedler, a man of learning and intelligence, has composed another of those fascinating catastrophes with which our literary scholarship is strewn. *Love and Death in the American Novel* seems to me destined to become a classical instance of sophisticated crankiness; it rides a one-track thesis through 600 pages of assertion, never relenting into doubt or qualification, and simply ignoring those writers and books that might call the thesis into question.

"Our great novelists," writes Fiedler, "though experts on indignity and assault, on loneliness and terror, tend to avoid treating the passionate encounter of a man and a woman . . . they rather shy away from permitting in their fictions the presence of any full-fledged, mature woman, giving us instead monsters of virtue and bitchery, symbols of the rejection or fear of sexuality." The "failure of the American novelist to deal with adult heterosexual love" leads to, or is evidenced in, an "obsession with violence" and helps explain the growth of "a gothic fiction, nonrealistic and negative, sadistic and melodramatic." Most American fiction, suggests Fiedler, falls either into the gothic or sentimental category, neither of which allows a confrontation with the needs of maturity.

To support this view Fiedler goes back to the European novel, to Richardson, Rousseau and others, tracing the effects of their romanticism (at once inhibited and exhibitionist) upon the earlier American writers. He then launches a full-scale examination of our major literary figures to show how the grip of repression has affected their work. Unable to deal with the central experiences of adult life, they turned either toward gothic projections of sexual fantasy or toward sentimental evocations of an asexual fraternity.

Now there is a fraction of truth in all this, as anyone who has read D. H. Lawrence's *Studies in Classic American Literature* surely knows. It is a way of looking at the American novel which serves in relation to some 19th-Century writers: Cooper, Melville, Twain, none of whom is notable for his treatment of the relations between the sexes. But even here Fiedler's psychosexual approach points only to one aspect of, say, Melville's work and hardly exhausts what is valuable in it. When pressed with Fiedler's monomania, this approach requires us to ignore and—what is worse—to dissolve Melville's feelings about American society, the metaphysical concerns he inherited from Calvinism, the quasi-anarchist revulsion from civilized life which dominates some of his books.

What Fiedler discards meanwhile is awesome. Literature is removed from any fluid relation to the development of ideas; it becomes an eternally recurrent psychodrama, dissociated from history, in which bloodless and abstracted Presences (the Dark Lady, the Good Good Girl, the Good Bad Girl, the Handsome Sailor, the Great Mother, the Avenging Seducer) monotonously rehearse a charade of frustration; it has nothing to do with, and does not even credit the reality of, socioeconomic problems (". . . the unemployed libido," remarks Feidler, "enjoys marching on the picket lines"); and its apparent concern with

moral problems can usually be exposed as evasion or disguise. Like a
mass-culture imitation of a psychoanalyst, Fiedler refuses on principle
to honor the "surface" events, characters, statements and meanings of a
novel. He will never allow himself to be deluded by what an author
says; he invariably knows better. For him the manifest content of a
work signifies only insofar as he can penetrate it, and then plunge into
the depths of latent content. Otherwise, he seems to feel, what use
would there be for a critic?

Indeed, his strategy is not that of a literary man at all. He engages
not in formal description or historical placement or critical evaluation,
but in a relentless and joyless exposure. The work of literature comes
before him as if it were a defendant without defense, or an enemy
intent upon deceiving him so that he will not see through its moral
claims and coverings. And the duty of the critic then becomes to strip
the American novel to a pitiful bareness and reveal it in all its genital
inadequacy.

Now this is a method which works at least as well with tenth-rate
books as with masterpieces, and Fielder is no less illuminating on
Charlotte Temple than on *Huckleberry Finn*. It is a method that disre-
gards the work of literature as something "made," a construct of mind
and imagination through the medium of language, requiring attention
on its own terms and according to its own structure. A Twain or Melville or Hawthorne becomes a "case" at the mercy of his repressions
while he, Leslie Fiedler, speaks with the assurance of maturity.

That some of the evidence, even from 19th-Century American writing, does not support his thesis, seems hardly to trouble him. Is it true,
for example, that there is an absence of "full-fledged, mature women"
in American fiction? One thinks of Hawthorne's Hester, Zenobia, and
Miriam; of Twain's Roxanna; of James' Chrstina Light, Mme. de Vionnet, Kate Croy, Charlotte Stant and the later Maggie Verver; of Edith
Wharton's Lily Bart and Ellen Olenska; of Dreiser's Carrie. Not
perhaps the most impressive list of women in literature, and some of
them, like other mortals, certainly had their troubles; but enough, one
would think, to give pause to a thesis-ridden critic and perhaps even
some comforts to his masculine imagination.

For that matter, when you come to look at modern European literature, you realize that it too can easily be given Mr. Fiedler's treatment.
Where do we find these exemplars of "adult sexuality" which *Love and
Death* tacitly poses against American immaturity? Stendhal, connoisseur
of the fiasco, whose greatest novel shows a grown-up woman pining
after an undersexed boy? Flaubert, who said of his sickly heroine,
"Emma Bovary c'est moi?" Dostoevsky, with his fantasies of child viola-

tion and fluttery neurasthenic heroines? Dickens and his sugar-plum ladies? Or Conrad? Or Proust and Kafka?

But Fielder is not a man easily rattled, even when the evidence goes against him. Since *The Scarlet Letter* is posited on illicit relations between Hester and Dimmesdale and since this would threaten his thesis, he simply asserts that "it is finally hard for us to believe *on a literal level* in the original adultery. . . ." Or he describes Maggie Verver in *The Golden Bowl* as another Nice American Girl, partly because James says early in the book that "she wasn't born to evil"—though the whole, one would think the inescapable point of the novel is that, suffering greatly and paying heavily, Maggie comes to know evil and to know it in sexual terms.

Here is a little anthology of Fiedler's offerings: "the fear of not seeming manly enough haunts [the English novelist Henry Fielding] everywhere, inhibiting reflection and delicacy and subtlety alike"; Henry James' "real subject" is "necrophilia" and Cooper's Leatherstocking Tales are "really" concerned with miscegenation: *The Scarlet Letter* is no less than "the supreme example of the "gothic tale" in American fiction and *Huckleberry Finn*, far from being a river idyll, is also "gothic in theme and atmosphere"; Hawthorne's Dimmesdale, that timid New England minister, is "a descendant of [Richardson's aristocratic rake] Lovelace via [Rousseau's] Saint-Preux"; Faulkner's Flem Snopes, the money-grubbing redneck, is "a comic Faust" and the scene in *Sanctuary* where the impotent Popeye watches Temple Drake make love "is projecting a brutal travesty of the American artist, helpless and fascinated before the fact of genital love"; Mark Twain "quite deliberately denied . . . all sexual impulses in Huck Finn and Nigger Jim" (the father of a family); Lambert Strether in James' *The Ambassadors* "represents the supreme effort to make of the voyeur a hero and a moral guide" and in this novel James "is reluctant to make explicit the genital facts of the case or, indeed, incapable of revealing them . . ."

What matters about such statements is not merely that they are inaccurate, absurd and sensational, but that they have little to do with literature and even less with that scrupulous loyalty to a work of art which is the critic's primary obligation. Mr. Fiedler cares not about books and writers, but about archetypes, myths, trends, depths and sensations. He tells us, for example, that "to understand the Leatherstocking series . . . is to understand the most deeply underlying image of ourselves"—which seems a very considerable claim for Cooper's novels. A few pages later we read, however, that "Cooper, alas, had all the qualifications for a great American writer except the simple ability to write." But if he lacked this ability, then a fig for the archetypes, the miscegenation, the "most deeply underlying image" and all the rest!

Mr. Fiedler lacks the one gift—I think it a gift of character—which is essential to the critic: the willingness to subordinate his own schemes and preconceptions to the actualities of a particular novel or poem, the love or generosity which persuades a critic to see the work in its own terms and not to bend it to his personal or ideological needs. Another way of saying this is that the critic needs a conscience.

THE WOUNDS OF ALL GENERATIONS

For those Americans to whom fishing and hunting are the substance of life, Professor Carlos Baker has written the perfect biography of Ernest Hemingway. No one could be more faithful to Hemingway's sporting enterprise, no one more keenly generous in reporting his prowess with rod and gun.

Over the side Ernest [our biographer establishes his intimacy at the cradle and maintains it to the grave] could watch the silver tarpon feeding and rolling in the slip. Each day there were dozens of small boats bottom fishing for red snapper or jigging for mackerel. Farther out were the commercial marlin fishermen, drifting for the fish that were traveling deep, with heavy handlines baited to them at forty to seventy fathoms. . . .

Such passages recur throughout Mr. Baker's book, quite as if the obsession with detail characteristic of yesterday's New Criticism were now being transferred from metrics to fish. A similar sort of positivist scrupulosity is to be found in the hunting scenes:

At the sound of the rifles, the huge bulls broke into a heavy gallop. Then two were down and there was only the third, bleeding from four wounds yet still galloping steadily through the dry scrub. . . . As with the lions, Ernest had expected a charge. . . .

Yet I should not want anyone to suppose that only the outdoor public

155

will enjoy this book. Mr. Baker takes notable pains in charting Hemingway's comings and goings; he will not allow that some of these were merely part of the flat business which fills up all our lives. For Mr. Baker facts are facts; a journey is *real*, and everything else mere phantom, the smoke of the mind. Among our recent literary biographers Mr. Baker is the Great Dispatcher, and all those Americans who enjoy pouring over timetables will find in him a sympathetic spirit.

What has been happening to the art of biography? During the past few decades, when our professors have been composing a large number of Definitive Lives, we have had only one major work in this genre, Richard Ellmann's *James Joyce*, a book pleasing for its ability to evoke the spiritual history of a great novelist without slipping into pedantry or sentimentalism.

A good many of our professors write badly: it is beyond imagining that we should live in a culture where as many people were able to write English as read it. A good many of our professors have fairly modest intellectual interests and powers. And almost all of them lack the artistry required by the biographical form: that gift for bringing together accurate information with a significant idea, or for endowing a narrative with spiritual coherence.

As it happens, Mr. Baker commands genuine talents. His prose, if rarely glowing, is never clotted. He is seldom the victim of political or psychological preconceptions—indeed, as if to drive virtue into vice, he seems rather innocent of ideas altogether. He doesn't gossip about Hemingway's habits in bed or with booze, nor does he succumb to the Hemingway who devoted a good portion of his later life to self-burlesque. Mr. Baker writes out of entirely decent motives, and these days, when writers can win fame and money by declaring themselves to be morally worse than they are, decency isn't to be sneered at.

Mr. Baker also displays certain skills as a biographer. He likes "action" in the old-fashioned, Western-movie sense. He can turn out a lively set piece, as in his vivid pages about the World War II years, in which Hemingway first makes a fool of himself prowling around the Caribbean to search for German submarines, and then sets himself up on the Western front as a latter-day Jeb Stuart commanding a band of French and American irregulars with skill, courage, and good sense. As long as the matter in hand is external event dealing with that sequel of excitements which formed *part* of Hemingway's life, Mr. Baker can perform creditably. But as soon as he approaches Hemingway the writer Mr. Baker collapses.

Through accumulation of detail, Mr. Baker gives us a colorful yet finally commonplace man—at once soft-hearted and tough, finely sensitive and a hopeless braggart, superbly generous and a wretched bully—who had more than his share of adventures, troubles, accidents, and wives. Now, if this "Ernest" were to appear as a character in a story by Hemingway we'd immediately believe in his reality, for behind the character there'd be the authority of his creator. But Mr. Baker fails to provide a convincing portrait of the man who might have *written* the story in which "Ernest" appears, and this for at least two reasons: first, he wishes not to be mistaken for one of those literary "highbrows" whom Hemingway liked to snarl at, and second, he has been misled by the Hemingway who masked himself as a tight-lipped regular guy, devoted to sensations of wine, fishing, and bed, and quite without intellectual depths or difficulties. Mr. Baker reports, for example, that Hemingway both subscribed to *Partisan Review* and kept denying he ever saw the magazine; but what this piquant detail might signify, or how it might fit into Hemingway's complex shuffle of public faces, he does not stop to investigate.

To some details he is endlessly attentive. Back from the first world war "Ernest" dates a pretty girl named Irene Goldstein. Since Mr. Baker sees fit to mention this matter several times, my curiosity was aroused. I was disturbed by Hemingway's nastiness about Jewish friends ("kikes" and "smart jews") and wondered whether Irene's second name might have some special significance; and I suspected that Mr. Baker must be planting some clues for a future drama. Was Irene a secret love of Hemingway's late sad years whom Mr. Baker alone had tracked down? Or had she, in the abandon of old age, revealed some fascinating secrets about "Ernest?"

Well, waiting for Irene came to be about as profitable as waiting for Godot. After her few dates with "Ernest," she never turns up again; she had been an utterly casual presence in his life and is thereby an utterly pointless datum in Mr. Baker's book. Why then did he include her? Only, I imagine, because somewhere in his research (it took him seven years and just as Jacob ended with Leah, so Mr. Baker ended with Irene . . .) he found some reference to her and thought she would help "fill out" the story.

So there is Irene Goldstein with three entries in the index, while Ivan Turgenev has only two. Yet Turgenev was a major presence in Hemingway's imaginative career, one of the few writers whom Hemingway acknowledged as a literary influence, and to a biographer who understands that nothing a writer does is more important than his writing, the idea of Turgenev as master and model should have seemed endlessly absorbing.

Hemingway was often a disagreeable man, and it is to Mr. Baker's credit that he neither avoids nor makes too much of this fact. The only reason for bothering with the messiness of the middle-aged "Ernest" is that he retained some connection to the Hemingway who had been and now and again could still be a marvelous writer. This means that he had—*it means he must have had*—a sustained if not always coherent or visible inner life. Let's even say he had a spiritual life, and, despite all the swagger, an intellectual life. But you'd be hard put to know this, or at least to know it with the necessary fullness and depth, from Mr. Baker's book. Brush aside the heroics: the hunter in Africa, the drinker in Cuba, the reporter in Spain, the fighter in Germany. Brush aside the bathos: the champ who flattened Max Eastman for doubting his virility, the sage who exchanged recipes for wisdom with Marlene Dietrich. What meanwhile was going on in Hemingway's mind? What changes of feeling toward the word, and what modulations of attitude toward the world? If Hemingway's mind was simple, as critics too readily said, or his art confined, as they too expansively said, how did he nevertheless manage to produce some unforgettable stories?

Now it isn't as if Mr. Baker lacks the materials for such a spiritual-intellectual account, if only even as the subdued line of a double plot in which the dominant line will be hunting, fishing, and boxing. Here, for instance, is an exchange between a Soviet critic, Ivan Kashkeen, who wrote well about Hemingway, and Hemingway himself, who responded to the Russian, one suspects, because he recognized the voice of a real critic:

Kashkeen: You read the joyless tales of Hemingway's favorite hero, ever the same under his changing names, and you begin to realize that what had seemed the writer's face is but a mask. . . . You imagine the man, morbidly reticent, always restrained and discreet, very intent, very tired, driven to utter despair, painfully bearing the too heavy burden of life's intricacies.

Hemingway: Everyone tries to frighten you now by saying . . . that if one does not become a Communist or have a Marxian viewpoint one will have no friends and will be alone. They seem to think that to be alone is something dreadful; or that to not have friends is to be feared. . . . I cannot be a Communist now because I believe in only one thing: liberty. First, I would look after myself and do my work. Then I would care for my family. Then I would help my neighbor. But the state I care nothing for. All the state has ever meant to me is unjust taxation. . . . I believe in the absolute minimum of government. . . .

A writer is an outlyer like a Gypsy. . . . If he is a good writer he will never like the government he lives under. His hand should be against it. . . . He can be class-conscious only if his talent is limited. If he has enough talent, all classes are his province. He takes from them all and what he gives is everybody's property. . . . A true work of art endures forever; no matter what its politics.

Though it occurred in 1934, a short time before Hemingway went to Spain as a Loyalist supporter and adopted a rather unpersuasive stance of collective solidarity, this exchange is valuable for the serious and quite moving way in which Hemingway articulates his bedrock, stoical individualism. The sentence about standing alone is stirring, and as true today as when Hemingway wrote it. The concluding passage about the writer and society, though in my judgment somewhat confused, is valuable for anyone who cares about modern writing. Imagine what a critic like Edmund Wilson or a biographer like Richard Ellmann would make of this material, how they would weave it into an account of Hemingway as a man shaken to the roots by the blood he had seen in the first world war and later a man who had so disciplined his will that his very fright became the source of courage. (Mr. Baker repeats, very nicely, the famous story of Hemingway sitting at a table in a barn during the second world war: a sudden artillery barrage, all lights out, everyone dives for cover, and when the lights go on again, there is Hemingway sitting alone at the table, composed and quietly drinking.) But Mr. Baker makes nothing of the Kashkeen-Hemingway exchange; it remains in his book a raw lump of fascinating data.

There are other failures. In 1950 Lillian Ross published in *The New Yorker* a profile of Hemingway that was widely regarded as exposing Hemingway's less attractive side. As I remember the profile, Hemingway spoke with a mixture, by now entirely characteristic, of silliness and shrewdness about his relations to the great writers of the past. Victim of his own anti-intellectual posture, he saw himself getting into the ring—all the world, at least all literature, is a prizefight—with Rimbaud and Stendhal and Tolstoi, holding his own with some but not with others. Now you'd think this would completely fascinate a biographer; but all Mr. Baker does is to mention briefly the public reception of Miss Ross's profile, he does not even trouble to discuss Hemingway's implied self-estimate as a light-heavyweight in the "ring" of literature.

This was not the only occasion in which the aging Hemingway treated himself to self-parody. He watched the fat collect on his soul, as it would collect on his style; and most of the time he knew exactly what was happening. In his stories he transformed these personal troubles into the materials of esthetic detachment, and in his great story "The Snows of Kilimanjaro" he described a writer slowly dying of gangrene in Africa who speaks to himself about his wife and his talent:

She shot very well this good, this rich bitch, this kindly caretaker and destroyer of his talent. Nonsense. He had destroyed his talent himself. Why should he blame this woman because she kept him well? He had destroyed his talent by not using it, by betrayals of himself and what he believed in, by drinking so much that he blunted the edge of his perceptions, by laziness, by sloth, and by snobbery, by pride and by prejudice, by hook and by crook. What was this? A catalogue of old books? What was his talent anyway? It was a talent all right but instead of using it, he had traded on it.

Simply to identify this character with Hemingway would be foolish, but it would be still more foolish to suppose there is no connection. Projecting his fears that he would die before getting his work done— and "gangrene" was a valid image of the state in which he found himself as a famous writer—Hemingway was here cleansing himself of his self-contempt and trying to salvage something from the years of sterility and exhibitionism. "The Snows of Kilimanjaro" is a picture of every writer entangled with the humiliations of success, but in some oblique way it is also a self-portrait. For not many modern writers have charted their spiritual condition as accurately as Hemingway did in his fiction, all the way from the early stories about Nick Adams, the young man back from the war who tries to calm his nerves at the big two-hearted river, and Jake Barnes, the somewhat older man also back from the war and unable to sleep without a light on, down to the blowsy Colonel Cantwell of *Across the River and Into the Trees*, who systematically despoils his own memories. All this you'd hardly know from Mr. Baker.

There was a time, only a few decades ago, when Hemingway was the most influential figure in Western literature. Everyone seemed to be imitating him, from students in Iowa to novelists in Japan. Stylization, tightness of narrative line, clipped understatement, restrained bravado, manliness regained, sensuous purity, "grace under pressure"—those tokens of the Hemingway code stirred the imagination of a great many readers and writers. And Hemingway himself, at once very proud and uneasy, had a keen sense of how far his cultural influence extended.

Now to say this isn't merely to notice a fact of interest for students of modern literature, a class into which a literary biographer ought to fall; it is also to notice a fact of interest for anyone writing a life of Hemingway. Yet this is never discussed by Mr. Baker in any serious or comprehensive way, perhaps because he supposes that the Hemingway approach to such matters is to avoid seeming "literary." If so, he has been tricked again.

SOUTHERN AGRARIANS
AND AMERICAN CULTURE

All through the 19th and deep into the 20th century, American culture has been significantly regional in character. The idea of a unified national culture kept recurring as both wish and program, but the reality was a series of regional outbursts from what might be called the sub-countries of the imagination. First and most powerfully in New England, where the claims of place were exalted through the authority of religion; then in the 'old Southwest," where folk humor reached an apotheosis in Mark Twain; and then in the Midwest, where the revolt against the village signified a larger striving toward personal freedom—it was from such geographically and intellectually bounded areas that American literature made its fitful appearances. Just as the harsh distinctions of social class set workable limits for European culture, so the fluid movements of regional sensibility affected the shape—perhaps the shapelessness—of American culture.

Paradoxically, the American region which had been the most willfully self-contained was also the last to make itself felt in our writing. The Old South may have had some mild esthetic graces to adorn its dismal social structure, but not until the third decade of our century did Southern poets and novelists of the first rank appear. Only at the point where the South began to abandon its fantasies of a glorious homeland defeated by commercial invaders, to examine slightly its appalling heritage of slavery and to enter, kicking, into the modern world of urban industrialism—only then, as a reward for the pain of self-examination, did we get the alloyed genius of Faulkner, the craft of Katherine Anne Porter, the wild humor of the early Erskine Caldwell. And on a more intellectual plane there cohered in Nashville during the early twenties a group of young poets who called themselves the Fugitives and whose most distinguished members were John Crowe Ransom, Allen Tate and Robert Penn Warren. In the years 1922-25 they published 19 issues of their magazine, *The Fugitive*, then little read and less regarded but now commonly accepted as a major source of contemporary American writing.

Fugitives from what? From the claims of worldly success, from bourgeois indifference, from Southern torpor and nostalgia. (*The Fugitive*, wrote Ransom in an early issue of the magazine, fled "from nothing faster than from the high-caste Brahmins of the Old South.") Ransom, Tate and Warren began as student writers at Vanderbilt University. Their first verses were little more than watery imitations of Swinburne and the pre-Raphaelites, for they knew almost nothing about the modernist experimentation then sweeping across American poetry.

But soon they revolted against their own beginnings and started to struggle toward their later, mature styles. In a few decades Ransom, Tate and Warren would gain distinction as poets; Ransom and Tate as critics; and Warren as a novelist.

Now, in an act of qualified celebration, John L. Stewart, a professor of English at the University of California, has written a history of this literary group. Urbane in tone, refined in method, strict in criticism, *The Burden of Time* is one of those undertakings that does credit to American literary scholarship (while also raising the problem as to why our professors take two pages to say what could better be said in one).

The Fugitives started from a difficult intellectual position. They were contemptuous of magnolia romanticism, yet shared the hostility of their people toward Northern urbanism. The image they projected, writes Stewart, "is stoutly anti-progressive, anti-rationalist, anti-humanist, for it insists on the irreducible mystery in life, the all-pervasiveness of evil in human affairs, and the limitations of man's capacity to understand and control his environment and his own nature." Overcome by a "nostalgia for ceremony"—a nostalgia which, to their credit, they refused glibly to attach to the Old South—they found themselves trapped between two worlds, aliens in the past and present, in the South and North. Increasingly Ransom and Tate grew hostile to modern science and technology which, this time glibly enough, they held responsible for the deracination and abstractness of modern life.

Their dilemmas as Southern poets drove them (Ransom and Tate much more than Warren) to become Southern ideologists, not of the usual ranting sort, but rather as literary men driven to the manufacture of a social theory they called Agrarianism. Neither back to the old plantation nor forward to the new machine, was their battle-cry. They insisted, rather, that men could break away from the tyranny of historical progress and move toward a self-sufficient agrarian economy in which the small farmer, independent and proud as they imagined the early Southern settlers to have been, would serve as both the dominant social type and something of a culture-hero as well. What they desired, in effect, was a version of the Jeffersonian ideal of an independent yeomanry, but under circumstances that made it impossible.

In discussing this social ideology, Mr. Stewart is both analytically caustic and humanly sympathetic. He demonstrates that agrarianism had little basis in reality, that in a market economy the small farmer could seldom preserve either the economic self-sufficiency or personal virtues the Agrarians attached to him. While agreeing with the early Ransom and Tate that the idea of historical progress, uncritically accepted, can become a form of intellectual slavery, he also insists that certain elements of historical change, such as industrialism, must be considered irreversible.

Yet Mr. Stewart grasps the ways in which the Agrarian effort to create a myth or "fictive version" of the South—an idyll reflecting their desire and revealing their desperation—gave Ransom and Tate a vantage point of powerful criticism of American society. It gave them what might be called a perspective from the social rear: whatever else might be true, they could not be trapped in the fatuous self-congratulation which overcame many American intellectuals during the last several decades. In a small and much less profound way, they enjoyed a view of American culture somewhat like that which Dostoevsky, in backward Russia, had of the advanced countries of Western Europe.

Later, with characteristic candor, Ransom delivered the *coup de grâce* to his own ideas. The Agrarians, he admitted, could never cope with the "farmer's wife," for whom the very industrial advances they opposed meant relief from endless toil. And he wrote:

"We must have cities, we shall have them, even if suddenly of late we have become conscious of the squalor, the discomfort, the shoddiness, and the pretentiousness which is in them all. . . . 'Agrarians' may not like cities temperamentally . . . yet they too go to cities and are influenced by cities, and it is a matter of fact that the city focuses all the features of a culture as nothing else does."

In the development of our political thought, agrarianism counted for little, but in our literary life it meant a great deal. For somewhat as with the Marxists of the thirties, it was through the decomposition of their ideology that writers like Ransom and Tate were enabled to do their best work.

Each of the major Fugitive-Agrarians went his own way, though retaining cordial relations with one another through the years. Not surprisingly, most of them ended up living and teaching in the North. Their influence was at its greatest during the forties and fifties when they became the spokesmen for the New Criticism—an effort to locate literary judgment in the study of the particulars of a work, apart from social or ideological reference, and sometimes ripped out of historical context. Having begun their careers with a fierce social passion, these writers gained a following among the literary young as models for pure or formalistic criticism.

Mr. Stewart thinks highly of Ransom's poetry, finding in it "a unique mixture of fastidiousness and daintiness—amounting at times to preciousness—with an irony so harsh as to be almost morbid." Ten or twelve years ago one might have rebelled against the author's prefer- ence for Ransom's wry miniatures over the torment and congestion of Tate's verse, for it then seemed that Ransom was turning out enjoyable trifles while Tate was confronting the basic dilemmas of modern life. Now, in the coolness of distance, it is hard not to agree with Stewart that Ransom's elegant mastery of minor forms seems a permanent achievement, while Tate's fury in coping with "the malady of disbelief" often victimized his poems.

Yet, as a literary man trying to achieve a distinctive style not merely in his work but also in his public presence, and as a serious writer engaged in a quest for the absolute which brought him to the Roman Catholic Church, Tate has been the most vivid figure among the Fugitive--Agrarians. He is a kind of swashbuckling Quixote with a Southern accent, mixing a touch of genteel hauteur, a stronger touch of self-derisive humor and a flair for dramatizing literary issues.

Mr. Stewart observes that Ransom and Tate were the most con- sciously ideological among the literary Agrarians, but that Warren ab- sorbed Agrarian consciousness most profitably into his work. "Of all the Fugitives, he was to have the most profound sense . . . of the inweav- ing of the past within the present." There is truth in this remark, especially with regard to Warren's first and, I think, best novel, *Night Rider*; but it is even more true in regard to Warren's career as a public man.

Like no other Southern writer except perhaps Faulkner, Warren has struggled with the central problems and torments of Southern life. Over the years he has steadily educated himself beyond the bias of his region, until, at the peak of his fame, he has become an admiring and scrupulous chronicler of the Negro revolution. It's been a long journey from Nashville in the twenties, a journey of growth and liberation.

ENDGAME: THE FATE OF MODERNISM

The critical literature on the problem of "literary modernism" keeps growing rapidly, as if to acknowledge a shared impression that we are witnessing the end of a cultural epoch. No one supposes such an end can be dated precisely; it may stretch out over several decades; and as if to demonstrate an attractive perversity, it may even go through a series of convulsions that would bring about a new kind or phase of modernism. Yet anyone attentive to the troubles of serious writers, to say nothing of the revolt against culture which has swept through our culture, must recognize the appropriateness of registering a stop, be it period or semicolon.

In Renato Poggioli's *The Theory of the Avant-Garde*, anxious musings of this kind barely appear. A serious and provocative work, it breathes that confidence in survival which the defenders of literary modernism shared until recently. We may suspect that even this confidence was by then no longer warranted—though to say this is to indulge in the wisdom of hindsight. Poggioli writes, perhaps as a strategy of exposition and perhaps out of his charming enthusiasm, as if modernism were assured of an indefinite future, indeed a future as extensive as that of the social-historical crisis from which it largely stems. But he may be in error here. It is almost impossible to see literary modernism as merely an immanent development within Western culture; even the least socially-oriented critics find themselves having to relate moder-

166

nism to a crisis of historical consciousness. Yet just as effect may survive cause, so cause may survive effect. The persistence of the historical crisis of Western society into the decades to come does not necessarily signify the flourishing or rebirth of the culture of modernism.

The Theory of the Avant-Garde is a perplexing book. Every page bears evidence of a keen mind, a fine sensibility, a wide scholarship; but the writing is so clogged and pulpy that one grows first impatient and then enraged.

If one digs, there are nuggets: a useful distinction between the intelligentsia and the intellectual elite (the first a social-cultural formation likely to be antagonistic toward modernism as a diversion from political tasks, and the second a literary-intellectual group forming the characteristic audience and fierce spokesman for modernism); the deep affinity displayed by modernism for sentiments of anarchism "which is, if only in non-ideological forms, the single political ideal that the avant-garde artist sincerely feels, despite any totalitarian sympathies, left or right"; the close if uneasy kinship between modernism and "the cult of violence"; the mixture of dependence and hostility in the relationship between the avant-garde and the fashions of popular culture; the thrust of modernism to race through the century, as if the present had no intrinsic value but were merely a tract of obsolescence to be left behind; the drive of modernism toward self-consumption, an end to speech and art, the silence of anti-art—which is why its greatest practitioners kept shy of the limits they kept approaching.

Poggioli chooses, rightly I think, to locate the distinctiveness of modernism in a complex of values and responses to life, rather than through formal traits and properties, although he is of course sufficiently sophisticated to underscore the fact that the distinction is primarily an analytic convenience. Like Zamyatin in his great essay on modern literature, Poggioli sees experimentalism as a secondary feature in the development of modernism (the matter would no doubt be different if he were discussing art and music). Among the controlling values Poggioli cites are these:

activism—the characteristic modernist group is a movement not a school;

antagonism—what the Russian futurists called "a whack at public taste" and Poggioli shrewdly notes as leading to "an exaltation of youth," with the consequent dangers of regressing to cultural infantilism;

agonism—"an anguish alien to any metaphysical or mystical redemption . . . a sacrifice to the Moloch of historicism," sometimes reduced to an alienation "almost gratuitous . . . a morbid taste for present suffering";

futurism—the wish, says the Italian critic Massimo Bontempelli, to create "the primitive or, better, primordial condition out of which is then born the creator found at the beginning of a new series."

These categories are serviceable enough, and what I would regard as a central motif in modernist writing—its confrontation with an inner impulse toward nihilist surrender—Poggioli subsumes under his last two categories, though not with a sufficiently strong recognition of how desperately the modern masters, those who truly were masters, struggled against that impulse. Reading Poggioli's exposition on these matters, I have been struck by how ragged they have become: we must now learn to see the idea of the problematic as itself problematic, that is, paradoxically, as having become a mode of complacence. And the more a critic elaborates a synthetic description of modernism as if it were indeed a coherent and self-contained cultural style, the more he must move away from the great texts which can alone give it enduring value. What happens is that in time the abstracted categories are taken to have some independent or suprahistorical value: so that a new fetishism is thrown up and a great literature left behind.

As is proper for a critic with a strong historical sense, Poggioli stresses the continuities between romanticism and modernism, so much so that those literary historians who deny a severe rupture between the two will find solace in his pages. Poggioli, like others before him, has no difficulty in showing that most of the central traits or properties of modernism have their sources in the literature of romanticism. (Or at the least, that there are many similarities with romanticism.) How then could one provide a usable support for the claim that there did occur at some point in the second half of the nineteenth century a break sufficiently sharp to warrant speaking of modernism as a major new cultural style or outlook? My own disposition would be to say that enumerating formal divergences and innovations is not enough; one would have to invoke, as well, the risky notion of a fundamental shift in values and philosophic temper. The modernist writers abandon, once and for all, the wish or effort to see the universe as constituting an order which can be apprehended through transcendent revelations or intuitive flashes; they accept, to an extent the romantics did not, the "deadness" and distance, the beyondness of the world; they have lost, or care little about, what Frye calls "the sense of identity with larger power of creative energy [which] meets us everywhere in Romantic culture." And even as they share with the romantics a worship of the imagination as the central agency of creation, they do not seek a sanction for it in the external world. As a pure type—fortunately no such monster exits—the modernist writer is post-Christian in the sense that he has largely (no one could have entirely) shaken off the traumas which had followed on earlier, nineteenth century improvisations of skepticism.

Poggioli seems to me unsatisfactory in his assumption that modernism will and indeed must remain the dominant culture of the West for the indefinite future. He recognizes that "the avant-garde is condemned to conquer, through the influence of fashion, that very popularity it once disdained—and this is the beginning of its end." Precisely. But then he posits a series of modernist recurrences in which "a new fashion, movement or avant-garde appears." Here I think he succumbs to a certain confusion: a new fashion, yes, as a parody-fulfillment of the modernist impulse, but a new fashion isn't at all the same as a new movement and still less the same as a new avant-garde.

Theorists of modernism often trap themselves in a dubious either/or: either there will occur a phoenixlike renewal of modernist sensibility as the necessary response to unabated historical crisis or there will be a total disintegration leading to a new cultural epoch. But the evidence, I think, points to a third possibility—just as, to indulge in a very loose analogy, the course of Communist society led not toward socialist renewal or bourgeois restoration but a unique bureaucratic deformation. In the realm of culture, the third possibility is that of a slow and triumphantly "successful" degeneration, a modernism popular, fashionable and inauthentic. Rather than remaining the intransigent enemy of mass culture—as Poggioli, with his eye on recent decades, calls it—modernism will now become its swinging partner. Now it is possible to object that this would no longer be modernism as we have known it, and in an obvious sense the objection is valid—except that we must then grapple with one of the most vexing problems of our time, the relationship between original and carbon, master and epigone, authentic and fake.

Poggioli quotes Ortega y Gasset: "All the art of youth is unpopular and not casually or by accident, but by virtue of an essential destiny." A brilliant observation, when directed toward the great years of modernism; but no longer true for the present moment. On the contrary. The "essential destiny" of "all the art of youth" is now a suffocating popularity, a rapid success on the market. Even if we had no other signs, this would be enough to lead us into speculations about the end of modernism.

W.E.B. DuBOIS:GLORY AND SHAME

If the name "Du Bois" means anything at all to most Americans, it is probably linked in their minds with those campus sects—the Du Bois clubs—that speak for Moscow-style Communism. Richard Nixon, with his special gift for parodying native follies, once suggested that the campus Communists were trying to capitalize on the phenotic kinship between the Du Bois clubs *(dew boys)* and the Boys Clubs *(da boys)*. Actually, the Communists were quite within their rights, for in the last decade of his remarkable life—he died in 1963 at the age of ninety-five—William Edward Burghardt Du Bois had become a loyal and, it must be added, a courageous spokesman for Stalinism.

Most of his life Du Bois was something decidedly better. He was the first American Negro in the twentieth century to gain national recognition as intellectual, tribune, and agitator. Prickly, gifted, endlessly articulate, Du Bois was both sufficiently self-aware to see how his unavoidable embattlement had forced him, as he said, into a "twisted life" and sufficiently principled to keep right on battling. He taught, he exhorted, he prodded and shamed American Negroes into their climb from passivity to militancy. He was a scholar of some importance, both as sociologist of urban Negro life and historian of Black Reconstruction. He kept hammering away at the thick hide of American conscience, and by his example made ridiculous the racist nonsense in which Americans indulged themselves. Above all else, he was a formidable antagonist, tough in polemic, fierce with a phrase, impatient toward fools.

Hardly a tendency in Negro politics today, but it owes something to Du Bois. In the course of his long life he tasted the repeated defeats of the American Negroes and, with the energy of despair, kept changing his views, sometimes to place his stress on absolute integration and sometimes to fall back on a kind of segregated nationalism. His experience sums up almost every impulse and opinion among American Negroes. Yet this remarkable man is barely known today—we Americans are not very strong when it comes to historical memory.

Du Bois wrote two incomplete autobiographies, *Darkwater* at fifty and *Dusk of Dawn* when past seventy. The first shows Du Bois at the point in his career, surely the most interesting, when he had fought a hard battle against Booker T. Washington's creed of accommodation; the second shows Du Bois at a point when he had in effect turned his back on American society and accepted a quasi-nationalist view of the Negro struggle, which in some respects was similar to that of Washington himself. The book now issued as his *Autobiography* was completed in 1960, when Du Bois was past ninety, and together with an account of his life in the Negro movement, every page of which is valuable, it includes sections on his travels in Russia and China and his harassment as a political suspect during the McCarthy years, every page of which is predictable.

International Publishers, the Communist house that has issued this book, fails to make clear that the *Autobiography* is by no means an entirely new piece of work; when it comes to commercial caginess, it has little to learn from bourgeois publishers. Nevertheless, the *Autobiography* is a work of considerable importance. Parts of it, dealing with Du Bois's youth and early years, form a classic of American narrative: composed in a lovely if old-fashioned formal prose, rich in portraiture of late nineteenth-century New England, and packed with information and opinion about the early years of Negro protest. Other parts read as if they came from a mimeograph machine.

The classical outcry of Negro autobiography in America is probably Richard Wright's *Black Boy*, a record of suffering so extreme and anger so harsh as to be almost beyond bearing and sometimes beyond belief. Claude Brown's *Manchild in the Promised Land* follows roughly in the same tradition. By way of contrast and correction, Ralph Ellison's scattered memoirs stress the inner strength and occasional joy of American Negro life; Ellison rejects the notion that all has been deprivation and insists upon the capacity of a people to create its own values and improvise its own pleasures. Nothing written by these or other gifted

American Negroes prepares one, however, for the opening autobiographical pages of Du Bois, an account of his youth that seems quintessentially American in its pastoral serenity:

I was born by a golden river and in the shadow of two great hills, five years after the Emancipation Proclamation, which began the freeing of American Negro slaves. The valley was wreathed in grass and trees and crowned to the eastward by the huge bulk of East Mountain, with crag and cave and dark forests. . . . The town of Great Barrington, which lay between these mountains in Berkshire County, Western Massachusetts, had a broad Main Street, lined with maples and elms, with white picket fences before the homes. The climate was to our thought quite perfect.

The black Burghardts had been living in this area since the late eighteenth century, part of a tiny enclave that hardly knew segregation or hostility. When the elder Du Bois, a man of mixed blood, came to Great Barrington, he joined a clan of Negroes who lived by farming, minor crafts, and service jobs: a world relatively comfortable and enjoying the stiff democracy of the New England town. All the traits we associate with New England—the Puritan stress upon work, the inbred life of the family, the personal styles of reticence and rectitude—seem to have been absorbed by these Negroes obscurely nestling in Western Massachusetts. And when Du Bois writes about his boyhood, he presents himself not so much as a Negro but as an American of an older and more virtuous age:

The schools of Great Barrington were simple but good, well-taught; and truant laws were enforced. I started on one school ground, and continued there until I was graduated from high school. I was seldom absent or tardy. . . . We learned the alphabet; we were drilled vigorously on the multiplication tables and we drew accurate maps. We could spell correctly and read with understanding.

This was not, nor could it be, an untarnished idyll. Negroes, even when living in comfort, had an awareness of limited opportunities. Still,

The colored folk were not set aside in the sense that the Irish were, but were a part of the community of long-standing; and in my case as a child, I felt no sense of difference or separation from the main mass of townspeople.

Bright in school, the boy found encouragement among the townspeople; once he bought Macaulay's *History of England* in five volumes, in 25-cent weekly installments; and when the time came for him to go to college, the local whites raised a purse, a sort of community scholarship.

What grips one in reading these pages is the story of a life that on almost every outward level follows the pattern of American industry and ambition yet must carry within itself the certainty of frustration, the doom of rage which American brutality toward the Negro still evokes. Young Du Bois seems to have sensed all this himself: he was class orator when he was graduated from school in 1884, but the address he gave was a celebration of Wendell Phillips, the Abolitionist leader. It is as if that "twisted life" about which decades later he would speak so bitterly had enforced itself upon his consciousness from the very start.

Yet the boy had never moved beyond the protected circle of Negro life in Western Massachusetts. He knew little or nothing, at first hand, about the life of American Negroes in the terrible years when the white South had reestablished itself through terror and the white North had sunk back into indifference. When the idea came up that he should go to Fisk University, a Negro school in Nashville, Du Bois's family objected strongly, for *they* must certainly have understood what their darling would encounter on a journey south. But their darling went, and it changed his life forever.

"Henceforward I was a Negro."

Some of the finest pages in the *Autobiography* describe Du Bois's work as a summer teacher in Eastern Tennessee, where he was greeted by the Negro farmers with a touching and absolute faith:

I travelled not only in space but in time. I touched the very shadow of slavery. I lived and taught school in log cabins built before the Civil War. My first school was the second held in the district since Emancipation. . . .

Despite his difficulties in opening himself to other people—perhaps because of them—Du Bois proved to be a good teacher:

I loved my school, and the fine faith the children had in the wisdom of their teacher was truly marvelous. We read and spelled together, wrote a little, picked flowers, sang, and listened to stories of the world beyond the hill.

Exposure to the post-Reconstruction South brought crucial lessons: "No one but a Negro going into the South without previous experience of color caste can have any conception of its barbarism." After Fisk, Du Bois was lucky enough to get into Harvard for graduate work, and as one of the very few Negroes then to be admitted there, he slipped still more deeply into the schizoid way of life from which, it now seems clear, he really had no escape: half pampered prodigy, half despised nigger. He studied with William James (who was genuinely kind) and Santayana; the years in the South had prepared him psychologically for the mixture of icy correctness and subtle segregation he would find in Cambridge; and he turned, by way of defense, into "a self-centered 'grind' with a chip on my shoulder." But meanwhile he was learning how to shape his life: he was learning to live inwardly, tensely, at a high emotional price but also from the incomparable resources of his pride. "I had my 'island within' and it was a fair country."

Picture him now at twenty-six: a young scholar who had done graduate work at Harvard and spent time in further study abroad; a bit of a dandy flashing a Van Dyke beard, elegant gloves, and a cane; yet stonebroke and glad to take a teaching job at Wilberforce University, a Negro denominational school, for $800 a year. In these years he commanded "a terrible bluntness of speech that was continually getting me into difficulty." Between his grating iconoclasm and the fundamentalist pieties of the Negro college at the turn of the century, there could be no lasting truce.

As Du Bois struggled through academic life—with a happy thirteen-year stay at Atlanta University, one of the few Negro schools that deserved to be taken seriously—he slowly carved out his special role. He would be both scholar and tribune, both a dispassionate student of the socioeconomic situation of Philadelphia Negroes and the leading spirit among those Negro intellectuals who set themselves the goal of the outer liberation and inner regeneration of their people. This was then, as now, an overwhelming task, for it required Du Bois to confront both white domination and black demoralization.

Altanta was poor but hospitable. It gave Du Bois freedom to begin serious sociological studies of Negro life, to build a lively community of Negro scholars and intellectuals, and to hold his annual Conferences where the programmatic bases would be worked out for the Negro movements of tomorrow. The one thing modern history seems to bear out is that every movement for liberation requires first of all a totally committed intelligentsia, a vanguard of visionaries—and this Du Bois helped create. Living now in the Deep South, however, he could not work in isolation or without disturbance. Very soon he had to confront—which meant, unavoidably, to clash with—Booker T. Washington, then the dominant figure in American Negro life and one of the canniest politicians ever to operate in this country. Nothing in Du Bois's life, nothing in the history of twentieth-century American Negroes, is more important than this clash.

The standard "enlightened" view of Washington runs something like this:

When Booker T. Washington made his famous 1895 Address at the

Atlanta Exposition, he offered the white South a *detente* which in effect meant a surrender. According to Washington, the Negroes would cede their claims to equal citizenship and would repress their struggle for political power, civil rights, and higher education. In return for this recognition of the supremacy it had just wrested through terror, the South would call a halt to lynching and wanton brutality, and would help the Negroes gain vocational training, so that they could find employment in crafts and new light industries.

White and Negro labor (I continue to summarize Washington's scheme) would be taken out of competition, by strict segregation in work and by granting the whites a near-monopoly of skilled employment. Negroes would be left with farm and unskilled labor. As a sweetener for this arrangement, Northern white philanthropy would enter the picture by providing financial help, so that the Southern Negroes could establish their craft and industrial training schools. Disfranchised and resigned to second-class status, the Southern Negroes would at least find a peace of sorts and be able to achieve some economic improvements.

For the militant Negro intellectuals led by Du Bois, this strategy seemed little short of a sellout. Du Bois opened the attack:

The black men have a duty to perform . . . a forward movement to oppose a part of the work of their greatest leader. So far as Mr. Washington preaches Thrift, Patience, and Industrial Training for the masses, we must hold up his hands and strive with him. . . . But so far as Mr. Washington apologizes for injustice, North or South, does not rightly value the privilege and duty of voting, belittles the emasculating effects of caste distinctions, and opposes the higher training and ambition of our brighter minds . . . we must unceasingly and firmly oppose him.

Years later an authoritative Negro historian, J. Saunders Redding, would continue in the vein of Du Bois:

Having raised [Washington] to power, it was in white America's interest to keep him there. All race matters could be referred to him, and all decisions affecting the race would seem to come from him. In this there was much pretense and, plainly, not a little cynicism. There was pretense, first, that Washington was leader by sanction of the Negro people; and there was the pretense, second, that speaking in the name of his people, he spoke for them.

But what if, like it or not, Washington *did* speak for them? And still more painful, what if Washington's strategy was the only workable one for Southern Negroes at the turn of the century? These were questions that radicals, liberals, and militant Negroes never thought to ask—and for perfectly understandable reasons. During recent decades it has

been necessary above all to break from the psychology of acquiescence
which Washington had encouraged. But now that time has passed and
some historical perspective is possible, we can see that the Du Bois-
Washington battle was far more complex than we had supposed.

Booker T. Washington was in effect *the leader of a conquered
people,* and a conquered people is never quite free to choose its own
leaders. He was, if you like, the Pétain of the American Negroes, but
far shrewder and far more devoted to his people than Pétain to the
French. The evidence also suggests that Washington was sometimes a
surreptitious de Gaulle, deeply involved in a quasi-underground resistance.

Professor August Meier, a historian whose sympathies are wholly
with the civil-rights militants, has printed in the *Journal of Southern
History,* May 1957, a fascinating account of the Washington-Du Bois
struggle in which he presents a large amount of evidence to show that
the issues between the two men cannot be reduced to acquiescence *vs.*
militancy. Du Bois was an intellectual whose obligation it was to think
in terms of long-range ends; Washington was a leader who had to cope
with immediate problems. The white South had just achieved a
counterrevolution in which Negroes had been reduced to near-slavery;
in fact, as Washington made clear in his still-impressive autobiography
Up from Slavery, the Negroes were in many respects worse off than
before the Civil War. They were frightened, demoralized, and eco-
nomically helpless. Simply to come to them and cry out for militant
struggle in behalf of political enfranchisement or full integration, would
have elicited no response from them, would have been of little help to
them, and would have provoked ghastly retaliation from the white
South.

Washington had therefore to maneuver from day to day, making the
best he could out of an all but total defeat. He spoke deprecatingly of
political rights in order to assuage the whites whose money and tolera-
tion he needed; but in practice, as Professor Meier shows, he covertly
tried to preserve the Negro franchise and kept supplying funds for test
cases in the courts.

Washington was an extremely skillful leader. He built up a network
of semi-visible agents throughout the country, whom he kept under
strict control by means of subsidies and shrewd tactical advice. He
maintained close connections with the Republican party and especially
Theodore Roosevelt, serving as its central agency for dispensing pat-
ronage (such as it was) to Negroes. He was friendly with some of the
richest and most reactionary white industrialists. Professor Meier concludes: "Washington was surreptitiously engaged in undermining the
American race system. . . . The picture that emerges from

Washington's correspondence is distinctly at variance with the in-gratiating mask he presented to the world."

Yet when Du Bois launched his fierce assaults upon Washington, he was clearly speaking to the point. For it was true that in large measure Washington had pledged the Negroes to the humiliations of Jim Crow. It was true that officially he had made peace with the reigning powers. It was true that he felt strong hostility toward the handful of Negro intellectuals who distrusted his political machine, his dictatorial methods, and his wily rhetoric.

Washington was not an attractive figure; he was a remarkable leader who helped sustain the morale of a broken people. And to the extent that he succeeded, he prepared the way for his own removal. Du Bois was a brilliant intellectual who insisted that only a program of uncondi-tional equality could be acceptable to enlightened Negroes and who proposed as a major immediate task the training of a Negro elite, "the Talented Tenth," which might lead the black masses into struggle. In a recent biography of Du Bois, Mr. Francis Broderick provides a vivid sketch of their differences in personality and style:

Washington, thick-set and slow-moving, had the assurance of a self-trained man. A shrewd, calculating judge of people, he had the soft speech and ac-commodating manners that made him equally at home among sharecroppers and at the President's table. A master of equivocation, he made platitudes pass as earthly wisdom. . . . Du Bois, slight, nervous in his movements, never forgot for a moment his educational background. Proud and outspoken, he held aloof from the Negro masses, but felt at home with a small company of his peers. . . . Washington had the appearance of a sturdy farmer in his Sunday best; Du Bois, with his well-trimmed goatee, looked like a Spanish aristoc-rat. . . .

In the short run, there can be no doubt that Washington offered the Southern Negroes more than Du Bois possibly could, if only because Washington had an economic program which might slowly yield visible benefits. But Du Bois, in part because he lacked Washington's deep roots in Southern life and in part because he worked from a truly national perspective, opened the way for the decades of struggle that were inevitable. He might not be able to compete with Washington at the moment—what could he offer an industrious Negro hoping to learn carpentry?—but he was right in saying that even if Washington's entire program were realized it would not begin to solve the problems of the American Negroes. For as the historian Vann Woodward has re-marked, "Washington's individualistic doctrine never took into account the realities of mass production, industrial integration, financial com-bination, and monopoly. . . . His training school . . . taught crafts and attitudes more congenial to the pre-machine age than to the twentieth century. . . ."

We see here one of those utterly tragic situations in which two enormously talented men are pitted against each other in ferocious struggle, each clinging to a portion of the truth, each perceiving a fraction of necessity, but neither able to surmount those objective barriers which the triumphant whites place before all Negroes, acquiescent or rebellious. The more men like Du Bois and Washington were penned in as Negroes, the more they were driven as Negro leaders to fight with one another. Yet from that war, at unmeasured cost, there emerged the Negro movement as we have come to know it. In 1905 Du Bois and a handful of intellectuals started the Niagara Movement, which put forward, with stirring bluntness, a program for unconditional equality. From the Niagara Movement there soon emerged the NAACP, in which Du Bois would spend a large portion of his life, as editor of its journal *Crisis*, as its main spokesman to the world at large, and as a hard battler within its ranks for whatever his ideas happened at a given moment to be.

The final years were somewhat less than glorious. Du Bois, whose whole life had been devoted to a restless experiment in unorthodoxy and rebellion, ended his life by lapsing into Stalinism, that dismal orthodoxy of the once rebellious. His pages about the Soviet Union show not the slightest trace of discomfort, even though they were written after the Khrushchev revelations. On the Hungarian revolution: "I was glad when the Soviet Union intervened and thus served notice on all reactionaries . . ." etc., etc. On China: "envy and class hate are disappearing." On Russia: "the overwhelming power of the working class . . . is always decisive."

What troubles one is not merely that such remarks are inane, but that Du Bois surrendered all those critical attitudes he had spent a lifetime sharpening. And this cannot be explained by senility; he kept his powers to a remarkable extent. I see, then, two ways of grappling with the problem, either of which could form a conclusion:

• W. E. B. Du Bois suffered every defeat and humiliation of his people, and he kept changing his views because none seemed able to gain for American Negroes what should simply have been their birthright. Is it not entire understandable that in his ultimate despair he should have turned to the ideology of Stalinism? That he should have ignored its repressions and murders, so long as it seemed to champion the rights of black men? What is surprising is not that Du Bois turned toward a totalitarian outlook but that so few Negroes joined him. To judge the octogenarian Du Bois is to display a failure in sympathy concerning the emotions of the oppressed.

• To understand is one thing, to justify another. The explanation just offered for Du Bois's acquiescence in totalitarian politics may be quite correct, yet that does not remove the fact that he, so long a victim of injustice at home, became an apologist for injustice abroad. After all, there were other Negro leaders, equally militant, who found it possible to fight against Jim Crow in America without becoming apologists for dictatorship in Europe and Asia.

Which of these conclusions shall we accept? For me, at least, there can be no doubt. To refrain from saying that Du Bois's final commitment was soiled both morally and intellectually is to indulge in precisely the sort of condescension he had always scorned. Better to fight it out than "make allowances" because his skin was black. And besides, he wasn't the kind of man who needed allowances—not from anyone.

THE SEVENTIES

DELMORE SCHWARTZ:
AN APPRECIATION

However we may regard the story of Delmore Schwartz's life—as pathos, melodrama, or an experience both terrible and resisting easy explanation—there is a real danger that his work will be brushed aside as he himself becomes the subject of a lurid cultural legend. I don't want to be righteous about this, since I find Schwartz's life as fascinating (though also frightening) as anyone else does. The image of the artist who follows a brilliant leap to success with a fall into misery and squalor, is deeply credited, even cherished in our culture; it is an image that, despite sentimental exploitation, has a costly share of reality behind it. Nevertheless, we ought to insist that what finally matters is the work that remains, far more so than the life that is gone. What matters is the stories, poems, essays Schwartz wrote, perhaps most of all his stories, five or six of which are lasting contributions to American literature. The rest is pain, gossip, regret, waste.

Schwartz's most famous story, "In Dreams Begin Responsibilities," came out in 1937, as the leading piece of fiction in the first issue of the new *Partisan Review*. Those of us who read it at the time really did experience a shock of recognition. The intellectual heavyweights of the *PR* group had been mobilized for this opening issue, and they performed in high style. Young readers like myself who looked forward to the magazine as a spokesman for "our" views on culture and politics—that is, the views of the anti-Stalinist left—were probably more interested in the polemics than the fiction. Still, we did read Schwartz's story, if only because the editors had put it at the top of their table of contents; and we were stunned. Many people I know have remembered the story long after forgetting everything else in that first issue.

We were charmed by the story's invention, though this could hardly explain the intensity of our response, since you didn't have to be a New Yorker, you could as well live in London or Singapore, in order to admire Schwartz's technical bravura. Still, it was the invention—the sheer cleverness of it—that one noticed first. A movie theatre becomes the site of dreams; the screen, a reflector of old events we know will soon be turning sour. The narrator watches father propose to mother at a Coney Island restaurant. Already, during the delights of courtship, they become entangled in the vanities and deceptions that will embitter their later years. But what can the audience do about it? The past revived must obey its own unfolding, true to the law of mistakes. The reel must run its course: it cannot be cut, it cannot be edited.

When I first read the story, at the age of 17 or 18, I felt my blood rise at the point where the narrator cries out to his parents on the screen: "Don't do it. It's not too late to change your minds, both of you. Nothing good will come of it, only remorse, hatred, scandal, and two children whose characters are monstrous." The hopelessness, and as it seemed then, the rightness of the son's lament appealed to my deepest feelings as another son slipping into estrangement. Naturally, this struck me as the high point of the story, the cry against the mistakes of the past.

Only later, when I would now and again reread the story, did I come to see what I could not yet see in 1937: that its tragic force depends not so much on the impassioned protest of the young narrator as on the moment in the last paragraph when an usher hurries down the aisle of the theatre and says to him: "What are *you* doing? Don't you know that you can't do whatever you want to do?" This voice of remonstrance, as it speaks in Kafka-like accents for inexorability, fulfills the story both on the plane of invention (the business in the movie house) and the plane of implication (how presumptuous yet inevitable that we should want to unwind the reel of our lives!) Once you see that the usher's statement has to be given a central place in the story, then you also realize that the narrator's outcry, whatever our sympathy for it, is not so much a protest against mistakes, but a protest against life itself, inconceivable without mistakes.

There is still one thing more, and it comes in the last line of the story, a phrase that would serve almost as Schwartz's literary signature: the young narrator wakes up on a bleak winter morning from his dream of a movie depicting the past of his parents, and outside, on the window sill, he sees "a lip of snow." It is a lovely, haunting phrase—the plenitude and renewal of nature become through metaphor a human shape, soon to melt, but still, the shape of that part of our body with which we speak and love. Through all the wretchedness of Schwartz's later years as man and writer, he would now and again invoke such images of snow as an enchanting presence, the downpour, as if through God's or nature's generosity, of purity, beauty, evanescence.

The tone of "In Dreams Begin Responsibilities"—flat, grey, a little sluggish, but with sudden spinnings of eloquence and literary self-consciousness—is distinctively urban. It speaks of Brooklyn, Coney Island, and Jewish immigrants fumbling their way into the new world, but also of their son, proudly moving toward the culture of America and finding there a language for his parents' grief. This sense that Schwartz had found both voice and metaphor for our own claustral but intense experience—this, more than any objective judgment of his technical skill—must have been the source of our strong response. We heard a voice that seemed our own, though it had never quite existed until Schwartz invented it: a voice at home with the speech of people not quite at home with English speech.

For a decade there followed story after story in which Schwartz wrote about his characteristic themes: the pathos and comic hopelessness of the conflict between immigrant Jewish families and their intellectual children, the occasional recognition by those children that they had left behind not only a ghetto parochialism but also a culture of value, and the quasi-bohemian life of New York intellectuals in the 1930's and 1940's, with its frantic mixture of idealism and ambition, high seriousness and mere sententiousness. These wry, depressed and insidiously clever stories—"America, America," "The World Is a Wedding," "The Child Is the Meaning of This Life"—were put together in a form that Schwartz was making his own: longer than the story but shorter than the novelette, with little visible plot but much entanglement of relationship among characters, stylized dialogue replacing action or drama, and a major dependence on passages of commentary, ironic tags, deflated epigrams, and skittish ventures into moral rhetoric.

The risks of this kind of story were very considerable. To an unsympathetic reader, Schwartz's stories could seem ill-fitted, self-conscious, excessively parochial in reference and scope. Some of the inferior ones are precisely that: manner becoming merely mannered, an adept mimicry of itself. But this hardly counts, since a writer must be judged by his strengths, not the necessary failures along the way.

One charge frequently made against Schwartz's work, however, merits a closer look. The "tougher" literary people of his time—and it was then very much the fashion to be "strict" and "severe" in judgment—often said that Schwartz's work suffered from self-pity. They were sometimes right, but in the main they lacked the patience to see that in stories about the kinds of people Schwartz was describing self-pity is a necessary theme—how else can you write about young intellectuals, at once lost in the coldness of the world and subsisting on dreams of later achievement and glory? Schwartz had the rare honesty to struggle with this out in the open, struggle with it not merely as a literary theme but a personal temptation, so that in his best work he could control or even transcend it. A good many other, less honest writers learned to mask their self-pity as comic heartiness or clipped stoicism. But no one reading "America, America" or "The Child Is the Meaning of This Life" is likely, I think, to suppose that the self-pity which plagues some of the characters is unresistantly shared by the author.

The stories Schwartz wrote in the years between "In Dreams Begin Responsibilities" and *The World Is a Wedding* (1948), capture the quality of New York life in the 1930's and 1940's with a fine comic intensity—not, of course, the whole of New York life but that interesting point where intellectual children of immigrant Jews are finding their way into the larger world while casting uneasy, rueful glances over their backs. These were stories that helped one reach an emotional truce with the world of our fathers, for the very distance they established from their subject allowed some detachment and thereby, in turn, a little self-criticism and compassion. (Not too much, by the way.) Sliding past the twin dangers of hate and sentimentalism, Schwartz's best work brought one to the very edge of the absurd, I mean to that comic extremity in which the characters of, say, "New Year's Eve" and "The World Is a Wedding" were wrenched almost to caricature even as it remained easy to identify their "originals." It was as if ironic distancing, even ironic disdain were a prerequisite for affection, and thereby one could gain through these stories a certain half-peace in contemplating the time of one's youth. The mockery Schwartz expended upon the New York intellectuals and would-be intellectuals can be caustic, even bitter and, to be honest, sometimes pretty nasty; but it is not dismissive, it does not exclude anyone, it does not relegate to the limbo of the non-human. Finally, Schwartz's voice here is sad and almost caressing, as if overcome by the waste of things.

What is more, this comedian of alienation also showed a gift for acceptance, a somewhat ambiguous reconcilement with the demands and depletions of common experience. Schwartz's work gained its fragile air of distinction partly from the fact that he avoided the pieties of both fathers and sons, established communities and floundering intellectuals. I am not speaking here about Schwartz the person. As a writer he came to see, especially in "America, America" and "The Child Is the Meaning of This Life," with the eyes of both fathers and sons, or perhaps from a distance greater than either could manage, as if he were somehow a detached student of the arts of misunderstanding.

In the early stories (more disturbingly in the later ones) there was also a strong awareness of the sheer foolishness of existence, the radical ineptitude of the human creature, such as reminds one a trifle of Dostoevsky's use of buffoonery in order to discharge aggressiveness against both readers and characters. The *persona* of buffoonery, which goes perfectly well with a sophisticated intelligence, brings with it some notable dangers, but at its occasional best it enabled Schwartz to catch his audience off guard, poking beneath the belt of its dignity, enforcing the shared ridiculousness of. . . I guess, everything.

By the time Schwartz published *The World Is a Wedding*, he had developed his own style. Some years ago I tried to describe this style, and since I can't now do any better I beg the reader's pardon for quoting myself: "it seemed to be composed of several speech-layers: the sing-song, slightly pompous intonations of Jewish immigrants educated in night-schools, the self-conscious affectionate mockery of that speech by American-born sons, its abstraction into the jargon of city intellectuals, and finally the whole body of this language flattened into a prose of uneasiness, an anti-rhetoric."

An anti-rhetoric is of course a rhetoric. But more important: In his stories dealing with immigrant Jewish families Schwartz may have begun by using language as an affectionate and deliberate mimicry of immigrant speech, but very soon, I think, he yields himself to it almost entirely. Yielding himself, *he simply writes that way.* It becomes his language. The world is a wedding? Then turn back shyly, ambivalently to the past—though not quite yet with ceremonies of marriage.

It is in "America, America," as the "young writer of promise," listens to his mother, Mrs. Fish, tell the story about the neighbors, the Baumanns, that all of Schwartz's themes come to fulfillment and his literary voice strikes it characteristic note. Hearing his mother, recognizing the intuitive wisdom and depths of experience out of which she speaks, Shenandoah Fish experience a revelation of how smug he has been in his judgment of the Baumanns and all the people like them, how unearned and unworthy has been "the irony and contempt" he has shown them. It is this humane readiness to see both links and breaks between the generations that helps to make this story so rich a portrait of immigrant life.

He reflected on his separation from these people [the immigrant Jews], and he reflected that in every sense he was removed from them by thousands of miles, or by a generation . . . Whatever he wrote as an author did not enter the lives of these people, who should have been his genuine relatives and friends, for he had been surrounded by their lives since the day of his birth, and in an important sense, even before then . . . The lower middle-class of Shenandoah's parents had engendered perversions of its own nature, children full of contempt for everything important in their parents . . .

Shenandoah had thought of this guilt and perversion before, and he had shrugged away his unease by assuring himself that this separation had nothing to do with the important thing, which was [his] work itself. But now . . . he began to feel that he was wrong to suppose that the separation, the contempt, and the gulf had nothing to do with his work; perhaps, on the contrary, it was the center; or perhaps it was the starting-point and compelled the innermost motion of the work to be flight, or criticism, or denial, or rejection.

Of dismay and disintegration, chaos and ugliness, waste and malaise there was more than enough in the life, sometimes the work, of Delmore Schwartz. Yet there is something else in his poems and stories, so rare in our time and so vulnerable to misuse and ridicule that I hesitate to name it. What complicates and enriches Schwartz's comedy is, I think, a reaching out toward nobility, a shy and aspiring spirituality, a moment or two of achieved purity of feeling. Surely this is what his friend, the art historian Meyer Schapiro, must have had in mind when he wrote the concluding lines of a poem about the death of Delmore Schwartz.

The poet's work, wrote Schapiro,

> . . . has the beauty of his honest thought,
> Of gravest musings on the human state,
> On thwarted dreams and forced deformities
> And ever-resurgent hopes of light.

GEORGE KONRAD:
THE TRAFFIC OF SUFFERING

Beneath the lowest rung of society live the speechless. They are the broken and deranged, the flotsam and the *lumpens,* all those helpless people who have signed a separate peace with reality and now choose not to confront regulations, skills, responsibilities. The hierarchy of class crushes them, but they do not form part of it. They are the waste of modern life, and they are kept going, sometimes kept down, by agents of the state whom we call social workers.

Modern literature has noticed them not as "cases" but as creatures. They appear as tragic buffoons in Dostoevsky, rasping comic voices in Céline, grotesques in Nathanael West's *Miss Lonelyhearts,* stumps of life in Hubert Selby's *Last Exit to Brooklyn.* But never, to my knowledge, have they been evoked with such grating clarity as in *The Case Worker,* a brilliant novel by a new writer from Hungary. With this one book George Konrád, himself a social worker in Budapest, strides to the forefront of contemporary European literature.

Becaue it is an original book, one grasps at straws of comparison. The claustrophobic atmosphere of unfeeling bureaucracy and torpid streets—a faint echo of Kafka? The bizarre gaieties of the deformed—perhaps like Grass? A fixation upon sensory assault—doesn't it remind one of Smollett? Such comparisons come to mind only to be dismissed: Konrád speaks in his own voice.

He speaks as a case worker, a fairly decent and competent bureauc-

189

rat whose job it is to record the pleas, the lies, the revelations of his "clients" and then send them to some home, or to another office, or back to the street. A humane man, he is also a policeman regulating "the traffic of suffering." Who can cope with the battalions of misfits, the regiments of victims? "My interrogations make me think of a surgeon who sews up his incision without removing the tumor." Something lies imbedded in the nature of things that is radically terrible, not so much evil in purpose or end, as gratuitously malformed. The case worker does his job in Communist Budapest, but except for the absence of drugs, it seems very much like capitalist Manhattan.

The narrator makes no accusations and places no blame. He speaks in a rhetoric of dispassionate grief. He is not indignant: who can imagine these shattered "clients" being stirred to revolt? He is not sentimental: who can suppose them to be models of innocence or morally admirable? They stink, they cheat, they lie—quite like successful people. Thrust into the endless web of their troubles, the case worker is shaken, implicated, drawn to their fumbling, stained by their need. He must record everything, because he is "a burden bearer without illusions, specifically of the complaining type."

The Case Worker is constructed as a chain of vignettes, quite as if the narrator were thumbing through his files and stopping at an especially vivid or wretched case. There is the old man "standing on a chair with his pants down, he is blowing kisses out of the window"; mistaken for a common exhibitionist, he is freed on the case worker's recommendation, and the next day he strangles a child who had run away from home. There is the asthmatic widow who can't breathe at night, but has never been so happy as with her "half-witted son . . . in the darkness of the room" where he pounds his drums for entertainment. There is the senile couple: "both of them have false teeth, and after depositing them in glasses of water for the night, they shout lisped insults at each other." There is the apartment of another client: "A black lace brassiere hung from the window fastening; in a corner two stringless tennis racquets, on a shelf an alcohol stove, an illustrated horoscope, some old lottery tickets with a rubber band around them, and a cheese bell with two white mice inside." There are, at doorways, "unwashed milk bottles . . . tattered boots." And everywhere, "the smell of poverty, that yellow star."

The Case Worker offers rather little of such traditional novelistic materials as story and characterization. It has a plot of sorts, with the narrator becoming involved with an idiot 6-year-old child whose parents have killed themselves. The case worker abandons his job and family, moves into a moldy room with the child, cleans it, feeds it,

plays with it. "This child," barely able to communicate its desires and reeking of urine, "has become my fate."

What is the case worker searching for? Not solidarity with the oppressed, nor any response that can be socially defined. He has been seized by a persuasion of interchangeability among men. "I search for my fellow man, always certain that the chosen one, my brother, is the one who happens to be coming toward me." This quest for the bottom condition of life fails, as it must, and at the end he is again a case worker, almost adjusted, regulating "the traffic of suffering."

It is a powerful book, and it gains its power from Konrád's gift for the suddenly snapped picture, as if taken through a slightly over-focused camera. The graphic prose carries one from paragraph to paragraph, with no expectation of pleasure or accumulation of suspense, yet a need to share in the fated journey of a mind seeking to reach its limits.

There are losses in this kind of fiction, and the very success of this novel helps to define them. The vignette, the prose snapshot, the virtuoso passage cannot yield us that experience of a sustained narrative that Lionel Trilling has described as "being held spellbound, momentarily forgetful of oneself, concerned with the fate of a person who is not oneself but who also, by reason of the spell that is being cast, is oneself, his conduct and his destiny bearing upon the reader's own." No; in reading *The Case Worker* we are not held spellbound, we are not forgetful of ourselves, since the author is trying for other effects— the effects of a kind of ratiocinative blow, almost a cringing before the extreme possibilities of existence. But what saves the book from mere shock is that Konrád believes overwhelmingly in the moral significance of other people's experience, and writes out of the conviction that the world, no matter how terrible, is still the substance of our days.

The materials of this book are of a kind that in recent years have often become the special property of documentary movies—we have even been told that the old-fashioned printed word cannot match the film for vividness. But *The Case Worker* shows, if anyone doubts it, that language remains the greatest of human powers.

THE PLEBEIAN REALISM OF JAMES HANLEY

There are people who deliberately seek out the front rows of movie theatres. Risking headache and distorted vision, they find pleasure in the claustrophobic immersion that sitting close to the screen provides them. Something like this engulfment in a rush of images comes to mind when one tries to describe the fictional world of James Hanley.

This Irish-born novelist has been writing now for about half a century. No one has ever quite used the English language with such bruising abrasiveness, nor quite worked out the same vision of human existence. In 1927 T. E. Lawrence found in Hanley's fiction a "blistering vividness"—and, especially if one stresses the adjective, that will do as a preliminary description. Trying to place Hanley, one thinks of Gissing or Dreiser or Bennett, but soon such comparisons collapse.

Hanley has never won a large public and in the United States he is barely known. Perhaps for understandable reasons. He yields nothing to sentiment or fantasy; and while not difficult in the way avant-garde writers can be, he demands a highly charged attention. He has perfected a gritty, plebeian realism that leaves one emotionally exhausted yet persuaded that here is a writer of high integrity and considerable achievement.

Hanley's new novel, *A Dream Journey*, is one of his best, a study of two people, Clem Stevens and his mistress Lena, as they slip into middle age. The book focuses on their shared realization of failure, their sufferings during the London blitz in World War II, and, nevertheless, their clinging together with such a fierce absoluteness as to make the word "love" seem a mere trifling.

A *Dream Journey* is set in the grubby precincts of lower-middle-class England, a shabby neighborhood stumbling into decay. As in some of his earlier novels, the characters are loners, people sliding off the margin, grappling for a bit of space. Hanley turns repeatedly, in book after book, to the theme of exhaustion, the exhaustion that comes from the sheer fact of having managed to hang on for a certain number of decades. Consciousness turns in upon itself, becoming obsessive and clogged. Yet Hanley's characters, with an underdog stoicism, cling to their days, still wanting to taste a bit of life's stuff or pursue some end they know is beyond their reach. The career of human will is Hanley's great theme, the will to keep blundering through circumstance and time.

Clem Stevens is a painter who possesses energy, intelligence, devotion—everything but a large talent. He knows this, and it drives him wild. Supporting him both in life and its necessary delusions, Lena has stopped caring whether Clem is talented, for she has surrendered herself entirely to enabling him to keep struggling toward a goal that both know he will not reach.

They live on the top floor of a rotting house. They see almost nobody. They drink a lot. Through wonderfully poised scenes of confrontation, Hanley renders their final days. The customary attitudes of the novelist—either covering up too much or uncovering too much—Hanley leaves far behind. Life taken in close-up has no need for judgment or pity: it has moved toward that heroism of endurance which these ordinary people can improvise as casually as they drink their tea.

A long middle section of the novel takes Clem and Lena back to the years of the blitz. As the Nazi bombers race over London, Clem and Lena drag one of his large canvases, his "masterpiece," down into the cellar and then back up again. Here Hanley steps back a little from his main figures, allowing the story wider focus, to take in the life of the entire building. He shows a fine assortment of English plebes in their kindliness, their nuttiness, their grave limitations, as they too scurry into the cellar, trying to keep a bit of decency through nights of fear.

Clem dies in a fire, apparently set by himself, which also consumes some of his pictures. The dazed yet clear-headed Lena says: "I knew he was a failure," but "you don't walk out on a person because they turn out to be second-rate. There's more to a man than that." And a constable sent to investigate remarks to himself: "Perhaps they didn't like the world at all."

No easy charms, no moral assuagements, no velvety phrasing. All we get from Hanley is a hammering scrutiny of life's damage and an unassertive respect for the people who must sustain it.

Hanley's novels demand to be read slowly, in order to protect oneself from his relentlessness. It's like having your skin rubbed raw by a harsh wind, or like driving yourself to a rare pitch of truth by reflections—honest ones, for a change—about the blunders of your life.

Hanley piles rough slab of language upon rough slab. The usual connectives and transitions are often dropped, the usual "rests" between units of speech denied us. Words rub against one another, bleeding in friction. The effects are accumulative, not local. Sentences can seem ugly, paragraphs like a shapeless rockpile; but the book as a whole is a work of beauty, a capture of truth.

Inevitably there are also serious flaws in this sort of prose. Overfocused language can lead to incoherence, and at times one wants to beg for a shift in voice, an easing of pressure. What keeps Hanley from being a great writer (though he is a very fine one) is the absence of that copiousness of tone, perspective and voice one finds in the masters. By comparison, he seems rigid, stiff.

Still, even those readers who will find his work too oppressive are likely to acknowledge its worth. Reading Hanley, I found myself thinking about the sheer silliness of recent fashionable criticism about "the death of the novel." A Parisian critic is said to have called for "breaking the back of the novel." Well, I should like to see him try it with Hanley. It would be like beating a giant with a feather.

THE POETRY OF ISAAC ROSENBERG

Isaac Rosenberg is one of the few distinguished poets to have come out of England during the 20th century. Born in 1890 to impoverished Russian Jews in London's East End, he suffered the usual cramped years of immigrant youth—though, unlike most American or English writers coming out of this milieu, he rarely shows in his work any signs of strong affection for, or embittered rebellion against, the world of his parents.

In adolescence Rosenberg began to write verse and study painting. His gifts for both were large, but raw and untutored; patrons ranging from wealthy assimilated Jews to kindly Georgian poets, helped him; but a boy who must go to work at 14 cannot learn properly. "You mustn't forget," he wrote later, "the circumstances I have been brought up in, the little education I have had. Nobody ever told me what to read . . ."

From the very start, Rosenberg was totally committed to an idea of himself. His struggle for articulation, that comfort of speech which native patrician writers could take for granted, absorbed his entire being. Perhaps in consequence, he seems to have been without external charm or playfulness; even, one suspects, without the bumps and creases of personality. His work shows the stamp of night-school culture, but often, thereby, a grotesque originality; he wrote English as if it were a new language. To become an artist meant for him a radical sundering from his environment, not as the familiar sentimental or sullen rejection of Jewishness, since Jewish motifs flourish in his work, but as a decision to transplant himself into the great tradition of English poetry. Keats staring into the sweet shop became a Whitechapel boy staring at Keats.

Sent to the Somme as a private in the First World War (the other English "war poets" were officers, gentlemen), Rosenberg fell in battle on April 1, 1918. Before his death he had completed a group of poems about army life, "Trench Poems," which seem to me without equal, for their kind, in English poetry.

Rosenberg would be praised in the '20s and '30s by T. S. Eliot and F. R. Leavis; first-rate critical pieces by Marius Bewley (*Masks and Mirrors*), Denys Harding (*Experience into Words*), and Dennis Silk (in *Judaism*, Autumn, 1965) would follow; recently Joseph Cohen has written the most complete account of Rosenberg's life; but the poems themselves—all together filling a small book and the best of them a few pages—have never held the attention of readers as have the war writings of Rupert Brooke, Siegfried Sassoon and Wilfred Owen. No glamorous fatality hangs over Rosenberg's head: he was just a clumsy, stuttering Jewish doughboy.

Rosenberg's early poems are thick with the language of Shakespeare and Keats, also with pre-Raphaelite decoration. These speak more of an overmastering intent to become a poet, a need to overcome a scrappy education through fierce appropriations, than they do of the usual borrowings and discipleship. The style of these early poems ranges from heaving rhetoric to romantic lyricism, but what marks Rosenberg as a significant writer at this point is just those barbarisms of phrasing such Georgian friends as Gordon Bottomley and Edward Marsh found hard to take. The early Rosenberg is always driving himself to say more than he has to say, because he thinks poets must speak to large matters. Later he learns that in a poppy in the trenches or a louse in a soldier's shirt, there is enough matter for poetry.

I find it a cause for wonderment that Rosenberg escaped from or banished the immigrant Yiddish culture in which he was formed. An early "Ballad of Whitechapel" reads like a bad translation of the "sweatshop" Yiddish poets starting to write in London and New York during the 1890s; it is one of the few instances where Rosenberg is content with pathos. He seems to have decided not to confront directly that tract of adolescent experience which has obsessed so many Jewish writers. Though the sensibility of humanist *Yiddishkeit* enclosed his youth, he simply ignored it in his work. When he does turn to Jewish motifs, they are drawn from Biblical sources but in a manner oddly abstract, even mythical. His verse play, "Moses," ranges from a surplus of rant to glimmers of sublimity; it launches a vision of Jewish rebirth (Moses, he said, "symbolizes the fierce desire for virility and original action"); but it is less the projected rebirth of a nation than a summoning of energies for self-assertion. For Rosenberg's poetry—this helps distinguish it from the other "war poets"—is marked by a strong prophetic urge which he could never quite bring under control or into focus. At best, it leads him to a recognition that he is living in a moment of historical disintegration. The prophet straining to break out in his poems, half ancient thunderer and half modern seer, can be heard in these lines of "Moses":

> I am sick of priests and forms,
> This rigid dry-boned refinement.
> As ladies' perfumes are
> Obnoxious to stern natures,
> This miasma of a rotting god
> Is to me.
> Who has made of the forest a park?
> Who has changed the wolf to a dog?

In the four or five years before going into the army, Rosenberg had begun to write poems in which this sense of historical disintegration, as acute in its way as that of D. H. Lawrence, would be realized through images not always coherent or settled but very powerful in fragments, stanzas, lines. Never having mastered the art of writing a good poem, he was preparing himself to write a few great ones.

One of the most astounding of these earlier poems is "The Female God," where his gifts for intense dramatism and expressionist phrasing come into mature play:

> We curl into your eyes—
> They drink our fires and have never drained.
> In the fierce forest of your hair
> Our desires beat blindly for their treasures.
>
> In your eyes' subtle pit,
> Far down, glimmer our souls.
> And your hair like massive forest trees
> Shadows our pulses, overtired and dumb.

This seeming submission to, or even celebration of, feminine substantiality is followed by two weak stanzas (like most self-taught writers, he often had trouble with his middles), and then redeemed by surprise, a ferocious denunciation of all that had been put forward at the outset:

> You have dethroned the ancient God,
> You have usurped his Sabbath, his common days,
> Yea! every moment is delivered to you,
> Our Temple, our Eternal, our one God.
>
> Our souls have passed into your eyes,
> Our days into your hair,
> And you, our rose-deaf prison, are very pleased with
>   the world,
> Your world.

The fury that men have felt in our time, and no doubt before it, at what they see as their entrapment by "the feminine principle," the suffocating dampness of sensual need, is here enlarged to a kind of metaphysical vision. The "female god" who has dethroned the ancient masculine God, comes to seem "rose-deaf"—"rose": lovely, enchanting; "deaf": unresponsive, imperial.

About Rosenberg's Jewish poems I can only say here that he anticipated what may be a course for poets in the future. Once milieu and memory are exhausted, Jewishness can take on the strangeness of a fresh myth, or at least a myth rediscovered; the Bible loses its tyranny of closeness and becomes a site to be ransacked. Rosenberg wrote as if he were *free* to do what he wished with Biblican materials, not exactly a common condition among Jewish writers, and while "Moses" and "The Unicorn" are failures, they point to major possibilities. In "The Jew" he compressed these possibilities into eight lines:

> Moses, from whose loins I sprung,
> Lit by a lamp in his blood
> Ten immutable rules, a moon
> For mutable lampless men.
>
> The blonde, the bronze, the ruddy,
> With the same heaving blood,
> Keep tide to the moon of Moses,
> Then why do they sneer at me?

Except perhaps for the last line, "The Jew" shows Rosenberg's gift for packed phrasing: "a lamp in his blood," the moral vision carried by the race; the commandments as "moon," not sun, because the moon reflects and moral life requires reflection; and the wonderful play in the fourth line twisting the terms of the previous two.

Finally Rosenberg's talent came to fruition in the "Trench Poems." In the letters he sent home from the trenches, Rosenberg gripes as much as anyone else, but in the poems it is as if he himself were no longer there, no longer afflicted and imperiled. Hating the war, calling the soldier's life "slavery," he nonetheless proposed to "saturate myself with the strange and extraordinary new conditions of this life, and it will all refine itself into poetry later on." From a merely human point of view, it is both impressive and chilling: as if all experience must finally be put to the service of poetry. Yet that does seem to have been Rosenberg's idea: "Iron are our lives/Molten right through our youth," he wrote in the poem, "August, 1914," and from the "iron" he made his handful of great poems.

In the best of the "Trench Poems"—"Returning, We Hear the Larks," "Dead Man's Dump," "Break of Day in the Trenches" and "Louse Hunting"—he focuses upon a commonplace event, a lull in the fighting, the weariness after a dangerous moment. Some men have come back, in "Returning, We Hear the Larks," from a night mission:

> Sombre the night is.
> And though we have our lives, we know
> What sinister threat lurks there.
>
> Dragging these anguished limbs, we only know
> This poison-blasted track opens on our camp—
> On a little safe sleep.

"A strange joy" follows, for the night is "ringing with unseen larks" and "music showering on our upturned list'ning faces." The conclusion is overpowering in its acceptance of the sheer arbitrariness of survival:

> Death could drop from the dark
> As easily as song—
> But song only dropped,
> Like a blind man's dreams on the sand
> By dangerous tides,
> Like a girl's dark hair for she dreams no ruin
>   lies there,
> Or her kisses where a serpent hides.

In "Break of Day in the Trenches," the poet pulls "the parapet's poppy/To stick behind my ear," and then encounters "a queer sardonic rat." He speaks directly: "Droll rat, they would shoot you if they knew/Your cosmopolitan sympathies." The rat and the poppy become symbols of the intermingling, the indistinguishability of existence and perishing, and the poem ends:

Poppies whose roots are in man's veins
Drop, and are ever dropping;
But mine in my ear is safe,
Just a little white with the dust.

There are depths upon depths, pain after pain, in those lines, but let me hurry on to "Louse Hunting," perhaps the greatest of the "Trench Poems." In its Goya-like dark brilliance, it must be quoted entirely:

Nudes—stark and glistening,
Yelling in lurid glee. Grinning faces
And raging limbs
Whirl over the floor on fire.
For a shirt verminously busy
Yon Soldier tore from his throat, with oaths
Godhead might shrink at, but not the lice.
And soon the shirt was aflare
Over the candle he'd lit while we lay.

Then we all sprang up and stript
To hunt the verminous brood.
Soon like a demon's pantomime
The place was raging.
See the silhouette agape,
See the gibbering shadows
Mixed with the battled arms on the wall.
See gargantuan hooked fingers
Pluck in supreme flesh
To smutch supreme littleness.
See the merry limbs in hot Highland fling
Because some wizard vermin
Charmed from the quiet this revel
When our ears were half lulled
By the dark music
Blown from Sleep's trumpet.

Reflecting upon these poems I have found myself turning back to T. S. Eliot's doctrine of the impersonality of poetry. "What happens [in a poem]," writes Eliot, "is a continual surrender of [the poet] as he is at the moment to something which is more valuable. The progress of an artist is a continual self-sacrifice, a continual extinction of personality."

Rosenberg seldom reached, perhaps he did not live long enough to reach, that middle plane of achievement which entails the tokens of a formed *persona*. In most of his poems he fell short of a distinct poetic personality, and in a few went beyond it. In his early poems there is a false or assumed personality, a Whitechapel Keats; in the "Trench Poems" there is a transcendence of mere personality: no individual voice, no complaint, no sadness, no opinions, no irony, no rebellion, indeed, an utter submergence of the grief that must lie behind the poems, quite as if some drained being were writing, rather than a mere afflicted man. This saturation in the life available to him, this submission to what little he could have, enabled Rosenberg to achieve the moral poise of an absolute dramatism, that creative faith in the value of rendering which is really beyond argument.

Rosenberg began with the common stock of Romantic diction, and then, as I hear it, borrowed heavily from Hardy. There are some lines from "Dead Man's Dump" describing corpses on the battlefield—

> Burnt black by strange decay
> Their sinister faces lie,
> The lid over each eye,
> The grass and colored clay
> More motion have than they . . .

—which share the rhythm and diction of Hardy's "Transformations." In the end, however, one should acknowledge a margin of originality in Rosenberg's language, a fusion of ill-heard and thereby, at times, recharged poeticism with harsh urban speech. In a few poems, a moment of the world is held by the grip of truth.

PRIVACY FOR JOYCE?

In 1909, at the age of 27, obscure, impoverished, struggling to gain a foothold as a writer, James Joyce heard a rumor that his wife, Nora, had been unfaithful with an old Dublin friend. The rumor left him distraught. In August he wrote to Nora: "Is Georgie my son? . . . Were you f——— by anyone before you came to me?" Joyce was soon reassured that his wife had been faithful, but the incident set loose, or disarranged, his erotic imagination and in a group of letters that autumn he poured out his anxiety. "O take me into your soul of souls and then I will become indeed the poet of my race. "

The soul of souls counted, but Joyce also had a realistic awareness of its dependence on the body. He felt, apparently, that the momentary estrangement between his wife and himself could be used to create a closer sexual bond, and for that, more would be needed than an appeal to her somewhat conventional soul. He decided to shock Nora into an excited recollection of their sexual life, dwelling with fierce detail on their pleasures, moments of violent play, shamefaced fantasies. Knowing the reticence Nora had inherited from the culture of Irish Catholicism—a reticence from which he himself was by no means free—Joyce chose the most obscene images, the most "dirty" words he could think of. Through language he called "ugly, obscene, and bestial" he wanted to shake Nora into a fervor of sexuality. His usual lyricism would not suffice: it was too tender, too becalming. He therefore set out to shock her—apparently, with some success.

Withheld until now from publication, the several obscene letters and passages form the most "sensational" aspect of Richard Ellmann's new selection of Joyce letters. In the long run, what will be most appreciated about this book is that Ellmann, Joyce's distinguished biographer, has arranged the letters so that they yield a coherent and affecting portrait of a great writer. But right now it seems unavoidable that the newly-printed letters of 1909 will rouse the most attention.

Obscene language can be an enormous resource of the imagination, but only if used sparingly, as a reserve for moments of crisis. Joyce knew this—it is notable that except for the outbursts to Nora in 1909 there is not an obscene word in any of the letters in this book. The obscenity of the 1909 letters is not ugly, as Joyce felt or pretended to feel when apologizing for them to Nora, and it is not beautiful, as some of our "swingers" are likely to say. The obscenity is something else: it is effective, it is powerful as a token of extreme feeling. It does precisely what Joyce wanted it to do: stir, arouse, perhaps unnerve. It escapes, thereby, the tone of vulgarity far more than letters of genteel titillation might.

Precisely because one responds strongly and sympathetically to the young Joyce trying to lure his wife through a last resouce of language, one finds oneself wondering whether these letters should have been made public at all. (This is not the kind of question a sophisticated literary man is supposed to allow himself, but there it is.) To Joyce as man and writer these letters do no damage whatever, and what they describe are things most human beings have done or wanted to do. Still, the mere fact of their publication causes uneasiness. What Joyce would have felt at seeing these letters in print, we do not know; I think he would have been distressed.

It will be said, of course, that all letters are personal and that publishing any of them can be regarded as a violation of personal rights. No doubt; but the problem I want to raise here is not the "principle" of publishing letters, it is the moral and esthetic appropriateness of publishing letters so utterly *intimate* in character. Joyce's early tribute to Ibsen can also be regarded as a personal letter, yet common sense urges a distinction between making public that letter and the 1909 letters to Nora.

The arguments in favor of publication have considerable force— everything pertaining to a genius ought to be known, once you start withholding material on grounds of privacy there is no clear guidance as to where you stop, sooner or later it will all come out anyway, etc. Yes; and that is why I am not so much criticizing Mr. Ellmann for giving us these letters as regretting the fact that he has. I regret it not because the letters diminish Joyce but because their appearance in print seems still another instance of that relentless undermining of privacy which is one of the most disturbing features of American culture.

Somewhere, even if we cannot always defend it with strict logic, a line ought to be drawn between what the world has a right to know and what is really none of its business. And even the dead ought to have some rights.

This matter apart, let me hasten to add that Mr. Ellmann has put together a splendid collection. Starting with the young Joyce who leaves Dublin because he finds it spiritually asphyxiating, the letters chart a life in which commitment to art takes on a sacred exaltation yet remains free of any posturings of aristocratic superiority. Joyce's strategy of "silence, exile, and cunning" led him to years of wrechednes—one is repeatedly shaken to read letters to his brother Stanislaus asking for a small loan, otherwise there will be no money for food or rent.

"I cannot enter the social order except as a vagabond," writes the young Joyce, and the fortitude with which he bears this vagabondage leads one to remember a phrase from his early letter to Ibsen: "You walked in the light of your inward heroism." Sometimes irritable, sometimes despairing, Joyce kept true to his course.

If his career is set against the present moment of literary exhibitionism, it takes on an exemplary character. And not only for his courage as a writer, but for his touching vulnerability and humaneness as a person. There are lovely bits of humor, a parody, for example, of "The Waste Land" ("Hurry up, Joyce, it's time.") There are repeated instances of personal strength: his steadfast refusal to give up the struggle to help his mentally-ill daughter Lucia; the kindness he could show to other writers, such as Italo Svevo; the little-known fact that in 1940 he was helping Jewish refugees escape from Europe. What we gain from this book is a portrait of the artist as a young man and then as he ripens into age—the artist as a kind of hero, utterly without the gestures or pretensions of romantic heroism, and thereby all the more heroic.

Postscript

When I wrote this piece I hoped it would provoke some strong expressions of agreement and/or disagreement. It provoked neither. Some people must have thought I was a hopeless prude, others that I was saying something obvious. But the problem I was raising seems a serious one, and as the industry of literary biography becomes increasingly efficient and rationalized (through not necessarily more interesting) the problem will become still more serious. Right now, the one sure way for a writer to know that private papers of the sort he might not want to show his closest relatives will not be published after his death, is to burn them.

LILLIAN HELLMAN AND
THE McCARTHY YEARS

There are writers with so enticing a style that, in their own behalf, they must stop themselves and ask: "Is what I am saying true? Charming yes, persuasive also; but *true*?" This has, or should, become a problem for Lillian Hellman. Her three recent memoirs recalling her life with Dashiell Hammett and, in *Scoundrel Time*, her 1952 clash with the House Un-American Activities Committee (HUAC), all make attractive reading. By the same token, however, Miss Hellman has reached a point where she risks mythologizing her own life, transfiguring the story of a taciturn Dash and the peppery Lillian into a popular literary romance.

But let that pass, and let us turn to the claim of Miss Hellman and her admirers that in her latest book she provides an accurate and balanced record of the McCarthy years. My contention is that she does not. What she provides is half the story, a vivid and useful half, but no more.

Nothing, to be sure, in her book is as false and certainly nothing as vulgar as the Introduction Garry Wills has written for it. Yet, nuance and sensibility apart, Miss Hellman and Wills hold pretty much the same view of the early 1950s. Quickly summarized, it is this: The U.S. was seized in those years by an ideological fever, whipped up by Cold

War reactionaries. America, says Wills, had fallen "in love with total war"; American intellectuals, says Miss Hellman, grew fearful that the spread of Communism might bring to an end "their pleasant way of life." Now that the Nazis were smashed, a new scapegoat was needed and for this the Communists were ready at hand. The dirty work was done by congressional inquisitors, the intellectual support given by anti-Communist liberals and radicals. The ADA, sneers Wills, did "the Committee's [HUAC's] kind of work in a more sophisticated way."

This view of the McCarthy years is simple, self-serving, and untrue. It starts from a premise always dear to those who would deny the reality of Communism as problem or threat: the premise that there is a single, undifferentiated, and necessarily reactionary "anti-Communism." Thus, writes Miss Hellman, the anti-Stalinist intellectuals have not yet found it "a part of conscience to admit that their Cold War anti-Communism was perverted, possibly against their wishes, into the Vietnam War and then into the reign of Nixon, their unwanted but inevitable leader." It is an astonishing sentence, with gaps in the argument through which battalions of historical complications could march.

• It assumes the existence of a unified body of intellectuals, all holding the same views about Communism, McCarthyism, etc. But even within the ranks of "the New York intellectuals," whom Miss Hellman seems mostly to have in mind, this was untrue.

• It is preposterous as history. Complicated chains of events, as well as unforeseeable accidents, intervened between the McCarthy years and the Vietnam War; events and accidents that could more plausibly be assigned as causes of that war than could the McCarthyite inquisition. Equally preposterous is the claim that Nixon as leader was "inevitable." What about the many intellectuals who did *not* follow Nixon, either evitably or inevitably? What about the possibility that the events of the late 1960s created a backlash from which Nixon profited? Suppose that in a few crucial states, like California, voters inclined toward the New Left had voted for Humphrey—might not Nixon have been defeated and not become our "inevitable" leader? Miss Hellman has wandered into a swamp of determinism/freedom that more experienced historians know it is wise to avoid.

• The shoddiness, in any case, of Miss Hellman's argument can be revealed by proposing an equivalent: "The uncritical support given Stalinist Russia by people like Dashiell Hammett and other literary people led, possibly against their wishes, to a whitewash of Gulag

Archipelago and the murder of millions, and for this the fellow-traveling intellectuals must inevitably be held responsible." I imagine Miss Hellman would be outraged by such an argument, insisting we must make discriminations as to kinds of support, degrees of involvement, and the nature of motives. Well, let her try to imagine as much for others.

Except as a rhetorical device for dull-witted reactionaries, on the one hand, and bashful fellow-travelers on the other, there was no such thing as a monolithic "anti-Communism." Opposition to Communism by demagogues like McCarthy rested on reactionary opinions and a fear privileges might be lost; opposition to Communism by liberals and radicals rested on libertarian opinions and a fear freedoms might be lost. In political methods and outlook, Joe McCarthy was a lot closer to the Communist Khrushchev than to the anti-Communist Norman Thomas.

That "anti-Communism" was exploited by the McCarthy hooligans does not mean there was no reason for serious people to worry about Communism as a threat to freedom. The Soviet Union had just gobbled up Eastern Europe—but Garry Wills sees only the "aggressive" foreign policy of Harry Truman. If Miss Hellman and Wills want to provide a balanced picture of this historical period, they must point not only to the failures of American policy, real and grave as these were, but also to the reasons that led many of us to fear that the Communist movement in Europe had gathered a dynamic of expansion threatening political freedom.

At the least, a few simple facts! Though Wills carries on at length about foolishness spewed by Ayn Rand before HUAC in order to ridicule the very idea that there was any ground for concern about Communism, he says nothing, nor does Miss Hellman, about the discussions then being carried on throughout the world on this matter by such people as Ignazio Silone, George Orwell, Nicola Chiaromonte, Willy Brandt, Norman Thomas, and many others. Really, to think you can dispose of any point of view by invoking Ayn Rand!

Still more—and here we come to a *feat*—both Wills and Miss Hellman talk about the early '50s without so much as mentioning the event that sent shivers through the hearts of intellectuals, and not theirs alone. Imagine writing about this period, imagine discussing the response of intellectuals to Communism, McCarthyism, and all the rest, without even mentioning the 1948 Communist coup in Czechoslovakia. It would be like writing a study of the upheavals in the late 1960s without mentioning the Vietnam War! For it was the coup in Czechoslovakia that persuaded many people that there could be no lasting truce with the Communist world. I don't know whether Garry Wills is old enough to remember that event, or has troubled to read anything about it, but Lillian Hellman must remember it.

There were, to be sure, intellectuals who buckled under the McCarthyite assault (it was not, by the way, a "terror": people could speak, write, agitate against it without fearing a knock on their doors at 4:00 in the morning). Other intellectuals allowed their hatred of Communism to deflect them from an adequate resistance to McCarthy. As instances of the latter, Miss Hellman cites *Partisan Review* and *Commentary*. She is largely unfair about the first, largely right about the second. *Partisan Review*, as she notes, printed in 1954 a violently anti-McCarthy and free-swinging attack by myself on conformist intellectuals; the piece was written at the suggestion of Philip Rahv, then its leading editor; and it could hardly have gotten into the pages of *PR* behind the backs of the editors. What seems to me true is that the magazine didn't take a sufficiently bold lead in rallying intellectuals against McCarthyism; but that is something very different from what Miss Hellman says. As for *Commentary*, it was then controlled by intellectuals hurrying rightward (a fate that seems to befall that journal periodically) and its record on McCarthyism was, let us say, shabby. Two of its leading editors, Elliot Cohen and Irving Kristol, while not giving their approval to McCarthy, went to some lengths to dismiss the idea that the Wisconsin demagogue constituted a serious threat to American liberties. Kristol wrote: "there is one thing the American people know about Senator McCarthy; he, like them, is unequivocally anti-Communist. About the spokesmen for American liberalism, they feel they know no such thing. And with some justice." Miss Hellman is right to attack this wretched stuff, but by no stretch of polemic could it be called typical of what intellectuals in America at large or in New York in particular were then saying.*

Surely she must remember, as Wills might have troubled to find out, that there were old-fashioned liberals like Henry Steele Commager and Roger Baldwin and old-fashioned Socialists like Norman Thomas who combined a principle opposition to Communism with an utter rejection of McCarthyism. Thomas fought for the liberties of the very Stalinists who had supported the prosecution of Trotskyists in Minneapolis under the notorious Smith Act. Pick up the first issue of *Dissent* in 1954 and you'll find an opening piece—either by Lew Coser

---

*It was not even typical of all the editors of *Commentary*, since as Nathan Glazer recently wrote in that magazine, he did attack McCarthyism in its pages during the early 1950s when he was one of its editors. But his attempt retrospectively to exonerate the magazine from Miss Hellman's charges seems to me, on this point, feeble.

or myself, I forget which—attacking McCarthy as a bum and criticizing some of the *Commentary* people for their waffling.

The same holds for ADA. Perhaps some people in that group had bad records in the early 1950s. There were cowards everywhere in scoundrel time. But as it happens, a hero of Miss Hellman's book is Joe Rauh, the lawyer who represented her before HUAC. Everyone who knows ADA also knows that Rauh has been one of its two or three central figures from the moment of its birth. If Garry Wills is so intent upon pillorying ADA, shouldn't he at least ask how he can reconcile the charge that ADA did "the work" of HUAC with the fact that this leading ADA figure emerges in the Hellman book as a staunch defender of liberties? Didn't Wills read Hellman or Hellman Wills?

Wills is equally feckless in writing about the once-famous Waldorf Conference in 1949, of which Miss Hellman was a prominent sponsor. In the name of peace, this gathering was organized by "the Cultural and Scientific Conference for World Peace," a group Wills neglects, somehow, to characterize politically. In fact, it was dominated by Communists and their friends, and represented the last hurrah of the fellow-traveling intellectuals in the U.S. Its overwhelming stress was to blame the developing Cold War on the U.S.

Wills tells us that U.S. footpads and intellectual auxiliaries joined at this conference to harass lovers of peace. "Guardians of liberalism" like Mary McCarthy and Dwight Macdonald went to the sessions "in order to disrupt them." The composer Shostakovich, who was one of the Russian delegates, "was, in the name of freedom, publicly insulted for not being free."

False, every word. In 1949 Mary McCarthy and Dwight Macdonald were anti-Stalinist, independent radicals—to speak of them as "guardians of liberalism" is gratuitously patronizing. Nor did they disrupt the conference. McCarthy, Macdonald, and Robert Lowell asked questions of Shostakovich (who looked as if he wanted to be anywhere but where he was) and of the Russian culture commissar Alexander Fedayev (who looked as if he'd like to get these American wiseguys back home, he'd teach them to ask questions!). The questions concerned the fate of Russian writers persecuted by the regime and, in the case of Lowell, the sufferings of conscientious objectors in the Soviet Union.

Now, to someone trained in a GPU school all this might have seemed "disruptive." But to Garry Wills, so severe in his judgments about standing up for freedom?

In her own essay Miss Hellman is more charming and certainly writes better than Wills. She has earned the right to be proud of her record in defying the HUAC bums, though her explanation of why some of her friends, like Clifford Odets, lost their nerve and gave names to the Committee is very disturbing. "The children of timid immigrants [Jewish immigrants?—I.H.] are often remarkable people: energetic, intelligent, hardworking; and often they make it so good that they are determined to keep it at any cost." Are we to infer that the children of bourgeois German Jews or starchy Protestant Americans have proven themselves to be rocks of fortitude in resisting tyrannical authority? And as for that remark about "timid immigrants," Miss Hellman ought to look at a recent book called *World of Our Fathers*, where she can learn just how "timid" many of those immigrants were.

Miss Hellman's main target is finally the intellectuals, those—mostly unnamed—who failed to stand up or stand up strongly enough to McCarthy. "Up to the late 1940s," she had believed that "the educated, the intellectual lived by what they claimed to believe: freedom of thought and speech, the right of each man to his own convictions." Well, as I've indicated, a number of American intellectuals did just that. Yet before Miss Hellman grows so furious with the others, those who caved in and those who wobbled, oughtn't she to be asking the same *kind* of questions about the people with whom she collaborated politically over the years, signing statements, organizing the Waldorf Conference, sponsoring the Progressive party? How can it be that someone who believed in such splendid things didn't trouble to ask friends and collaborators whether *they* lived by "freedom of thought and speech, the right of each man to his own convictions"?

Miss Hellman doesn't ask such questions, she isn't inclined to make things hard for herself. She is riding high these days—and no one, really, should begrudge Lillian Hellman her success, for she is a gifted writer. Still, I find myself disturbed by the way she clings to fragments of old dogmas that, at other and more lucid moments, she knows she should have given up long ago. "Most of the Communists I had met," she writes, "seemed to me people who wanted to make a better world; many of them were silly people and a few of them were genuine nuts, but that doesn't make for denunciations. . . ."

No individual should be harassed or persecuted, or denounced to the cops, for holding even the most obnoxious opinions. But what about judgments of the opinions themselves and of the public consequences of holding them?

Most of the Communists Miss Hellman met may have wanted a better world, but the better world they wanted came down to a soul-destroying and body-tormenting prison: the Moscow trials, the Stalin dictatorship, the destruction of millions during the forced collectivization, and a systematic denial of the slave camps in Siberia. (Do you really think we didn't know about Gulag Archipelago until Solzhenitsyn published his remarkable book? He offered new material, but the essential facts were known as far back as the late 1930s—and were violently denied by many of the people with whom Miss Hellman worked at the Waldorf Conference and the Progressive party.)

A final point and we are done. On her next-to-last page Miss Hellman writes that the intellectuals whom she has attacked have a right to criticize her for "taking too long to see what was going on in the Soviet Union. But whatever our mistakes, I do not believe we did our country any harm."

Dear Lillian Hellman, you could not be more mistaken! Those who supported Stalinism and its political enterprises, either here or abroad, helped befoul the cultural atmosphere, helped bring totalitarian methods into trade unions, helped perpetuate one of the great lies of our century, helped destroy whatever possibilities there might have been for a resurgence of serious radicalism in America. Isn't that harm enough?

Scoundrels there were in the 1950s, as in all other times, and Lillian Hellman has pointed to some of them accurately. But she would have done both her readers and herself a greater service if she had been more precise—and more comprehensive—in her pointing.

LIONEL TRILLING:
SINCERITY AND AUTHENTICITY

The Italian novelist Ignazio Silone once remarked that most writers keep telling the same story over and over again: it is the story that releases their controlling sense of existence, their springs of anxiety and dilemma. Critics may seem to enjoy greater possibilities for dispersing or disguising their deepest interests, but that is probably a mere illusion. Those who are truly engaged with the movements of their own minds also keep telling the same "story," returning to a single question or group of questions.

For several decades now Lionel Trilling has written on a wide range of topics, yet in most of his criticism there keeps breaking out a dispute of his inner mind, so that in reading his essays one becomes witness to a drama of self-recognition. An essay of perhaps a decade ago, "On the Teaching of Modern Literature," brought this dispute to a sharpness unusual for a critic who generally prefers the canny pleasures of the tangent. In that essay Trilling exposed a dualism of response that many other literary people feel but few care to state. There is the Trilling who teaches, writes about, and defines himself culturally through the modernist masters, writers of the oblique, perverse, complex, problematic. This Trilling responds to the violence, the moral chaos proudly thrust forward, the refusal of simple virtues or verities, the negation of worn or indeed any certainties, all of which we know to be the glory of our literature.

But another Trilling makes himself heard, a little weary with the suave virtuosities of the first one, more and more ironic toward the performance of ironies that has become the set-piece of the "advanced" critic, falling back with some didactic bravado on the moral assurances of the 19th-century writers. This second Trilling seems to wonder—he cannot suppress the heresy, and then finds relief in venting it, since that defines *his* authenticity—whether the whole modernist enterprise will turn out to have been a brilliant detour of Western culture from which, at great cost, we may have to find a path of return.

Whereupon the first Trilling has his answers, for he knows how conclusive have been the historical imperatives behind modernism and he will not brook a retreat into limp traditions that we can still name but do not really possess. He is a resourceful man, this first Trilling, and he finds himself suspicious of his "archaic" alter ego.

From our quarrels with others we make rhetoric, said Yeats, and from our quarrels with ourselves, poetry. He might have added, criticism too, first-rate criticism, from our quarrels with ourselves. Lionel Trilling's *Sincerity and Authenticity*, is deceptively modest in scale, though tremendously ambitious in reach. It leaps, without pretense of transition, from one crucial moment to another in the history of Western culture; it offers no explicit conclusions or theses in the course of sketching the turn from sincerity to authenticity as guiding cultural norms—a method bound to trouble minds like my own, captive to at least the illusion of historical continuity and thematic connection. But *Sincerity and Authenticity* is a wonderful book, precisely in its tentativeness, the way it perches at a given historical moment to dramatize through variations a deep, abiding theme.

Novelists and poets, familiar in the Trilling cast, are brought in to testify; so too philosophers like Hegel and Diderot; ideologues like Rousseau, Marx, and Sartre; and, of course, Freud. One can read the book for its recurrent pleasures of local insight: a clever section on Oscar Wilde's defense of the truth of masks as against the self-deceits of sincerity; a moving passage in which Trilling asks himself whether the enormous moral credence, tantamount to a religious yielding, which some of us have placed in literature may not prove to be undone by a "proliferation of art" transforming it into a trivial commodity; and an uncharacteristically fierce polemic against Sartre and Sarraute for the haughtiness with which in the name of authenticity they attack figures, indeed people, like Emma Bovary.

Trilling begins by remarking that there are moments in history when the assumptions of moral life suddenly become subject to intense scrutiny and radical transformation. One such moment, crucial to the whole subsequent experience of Western civilization, occurs as the post-Renaissance concern with the value of sincerity, "the avoidance of being false to one's own self." The "congruence between avowal and actual feeling" becomes in Europe a passion, even a craze, toward the end of the 18th century, by no means confined to the intelligentsia. Yet this has certainly not always been a crucial or even recognizable norm of conduct. As Trilling puts it:

We cannot say of the patriarch Abraham that he was a sincere man. That statement must seem only comical. The sincerity of Achilles or Beowulf cannot be discussed: they neither have nor lack sincerity. But if we ask whether the young Werther is really as sincere as he intends to be, or which of the two Dashwood sisters, Elinor or Marianne, is thought by Jane Austen [in *Sense and Sensibility*] to be the more truly sincere, we can confidently expect a serious response in the form of opinions on both sides of the question.

In time, however, the cult of sincerity, with its program for harmony within the self and *thereby* without, gives way (I would think with the rise of modernist literature) to a celebration of the inharmonious state of authenticity. Indeed, authenticity is usually regarded as possible only to those who have discarded the delusion of wholeness, and in whom the relation between me and myself is not harmonious. This relation must also be, for the program of authenticity, close to self-contained, so that the inner, fragmented struggle for definition or re-creation is uncontaminated by social constraints. A similar expectation operates in regard to the work of literature:

[It] is itself authentic by reason of its entire self-definition: it is understood to exist wholly by the laws of its own being, which include the right to embody painful, ignoble, or socially inacceptable subject-matters. Similarly the artist seeks his personal authenticity in his entire autonomousness—his goal is to be as self-defining as the art-object he creates. . . . When, in Sartre's *La Nausée*, the protagonist Roquentin . . . permits himself to entertain a single hope, it is that he may write a story which will be "beautiful and hard as steel and make people ashamed of their existence."

Now, all this may seem abstract and unanchored, as in summary form it must, but Trilling takes pains to show the interweaving and diverging paths of his two categories as they are embodied in the movement of Western culture—or at least, he shows some crucial points along the graph of their development. Perhaps the clearest exposition appears in a chapter called "The Honest Soul and the Disin-tegrated Consciousness," devoted mainly to Hegel and Diderot. Start-ing with a text that has long fascinated him, Diderot's *Rameau's*

Nephew, Trilling contrasts the *Moi* of that great dialogue, Diderot himself, the "honest soul" who lives for the moderate virtues of sincerity, with young Rameau, the *Lui*, scoundrel and scapegrace who boasts of his crimes in order—quite as if he were our contemporary—to solicit admiration for the candor, the shining authenticity, with which he confesses them. Hegel, entranced by Diderot's book, uses the epithet "honest" in its

old condescending sense, implying a limitation both of mind and power. The "honesty" of Diderot-*Moi*, which evokes Hegel's impatient scorn, consists in his wholeness of self, in the directness and consistency of his relation to things, and in his submission to a traditional morality. Diderot-*Moi* does not exemplify the urge of Spirit to escape from the conditions which circumscribe it and to enter into an existence which will be determined by itself alone.

And again:

I have remarked the obvious connection between sincerity and the intensified sense of personal identity that developed along with the growth of the idea of society. Sincerity was taken to be an element of personal autonomy; as such, it was felt to be what we might call a progressive virtue. But considered in the light of Hegel's historical anthropology, it must be regarded in the opposite way, as regressive and retrospective, standing between the self and the disintegration which is essential if it is to develop its true, its entire, freedom.

For Hegel, anticipating many writers of our own moment, feels that only by cracking the facade of coherence, integrity, and sincerity of "the honest soul" can the reality of fragments (as we might call it) be reached.

The opposition so beautifully dramatized by Diderot appears, in somewhat different variants, as the two sides of Rousseau, who speak both for "honest consciousness" and "disintegrated consciousness," with particular reference, as Trilling is quick to underscore, to the problem of the moral value of art. In another chapter called "The Heroic, the Beautiful, the Authentic" Trilling is at his most brilliant, but incomplete and difficult, as he contrasts the pedagogic intent of narrative with the heroic gesture of tragedy, the traditional view that beauty inheres in the design of art with that "settled antagonism to beauty" which authenticity, as a tacit polemic against historical continuity, brings to bear upon art.

In his concluding essay, "The Authentic Unconscious," Trilling touches on the contemporary implications of his study. There is a discussion of Freud, which I find deeply absorbing but finally recalcitrant—when we reach the point where a segment of the ego is said to overlap the unconscious, it becomes hard to share Trilling's patient readiness to follow step by step the journey of the master. More accessible by far is an amiable, even touching polemic against Herbert Marcuse, with whom Trilling nevertheless finds some ground for kinship, since it turns out that Marcuse, though prophesying in his more utopian writings "the virtual end of necessity, discovers in it a perverse beneficence—upon its harsh imperatives depends the authenticity of the individual and his experience." Marcuse, as Trilling notices with a sly friendliness, "*likes* people to have 'character,' cost what it may in frustration. He holds fast to the belief that the right quality of human life, its intensity, its creativity, its felt actuality, its weightiness, requires the stimulus of exigence." Anyone who has ever had an encounter with the author of *Eros and Civilization* can testify to the keenness of this description.

With R.D. Laing, Trilling is harsher, and rightly so, since Laing has a much simpler mind than Marcuse. Laing is ready, at least in his writings, to go all the way into the chaos of the "disintegrated consciousness," and it is with regard to Laing's frivolous evocation of madness that Trilling reaches the conclusion of his book:

Perhaps exactly because the thought [that "alienation is to be overcome only by the completeness of alienation"] is assented to so facilely, so without what used to be called seriousness, it might seem that no expression of disaffection from social existence was ever so desperate as this eagerness to say that authenticity of personal being is achieved through an ultimate isolateness. . . . The falsities of an alienated social reality are rejected in favor of an upward psychopathic mobility to the point of divinity, each one of us a Christ—but with none of the inconveniences of undertaking to intercede, of being a sacrifice, of reasoning with rabbis, of making sermons, of having disciples, of going to weddings and to funerals, of beginning something and at a certain point remarking that it is finished.

Sincerity and Authenticity is essentially beyond summary, because its value consists largely in detailed nuance and variation. Let me try, instead, to push the distinction between sincerity and authenticity to a point of high focus, perhaps overfocus, in ways that Trilling might not always approve, and with the end of bringing into the glare of the explicit some of the implications I gather from his book.

Sincerity involves aspiration, an effort to live by a moral norm; authenticity directs us to a putative truth about ourselves that depends on our "essential" being, "beneath" and perhaps in disregard of moral norms—though it demands that we drive toward that "essential" being with an imperiousness that is very much akin to traditional moralism. Sincerity implies a living up to, authenticity a getting down into. Sincerity is a social virtue, a compact between me, myself, and you;

authenticity is an assertion, a defiance, a claim to cut away the falsities of culture. It takes two to be sincere, only one to be authentic. Sincerity speaks for a conduct of *should;* authenticity for a potential of *is.* Sincerity is a virtue of public consciousness, authenticity a repudiation of its bad faith. Sincerity implies a recognition of our limits, authenticity asserts the self as absolute. We are to be persuaded toward sincerity, but stripped, shocked, and shamed into authenticity. And—though Trilling avoids these linkings—sincerity strikes me largely as an attribute of Romanticism, authenticity as a straining of modernism.

Now, in truth, there are no such sharp distinctions between the two, nor is it mere carelessness that allows us in ordinary speech to use them, at times, interchangeably. For as Trilling shows, historically there has been a slide from one to the other, and the compartments of discourse are not always respected in the development of actuality. What the passion for sincerity and the search for authenticity share, and what makes them first cousins within the family of modern sensibility, is their common if tacit dismissal of the premise of objective truth. To be true to oneself replaces being true to the truth. Authenticity is a brilliant if often destructive bastard offspring of sincerity, and sincerity a token of that "psychology of exposure" through which the 19th century unmasked itself, or thought it was unmasking itself. The triumph of literary modernism is signalled by a shift from impersonal truth to personal sincerity, from belief in objective law to search for unimpeded response. The first of these involves an effort to apprehend the nature of the universe; the second an effort to apprehend the nature of our inner being. Sincerity becomes a defense for men losing religious belief, authenticity the term for destroying absolutes, systems, moral claims. Nor is it an accident that the quest for the reality about our selves should eventually lead to a nagging, violent attack upon the self—just as the desire of the "honest soul" to be faithful to the commonplace virtues has led, through the cunning of history, to a modernist contempt for ordinary consciousness, ordinary life, ordinary people, all dismissed as "inauthentic" (or "two-dimensional"). One of Trilling's most forceful passages is a comment on Nathalie Sarraute's dismissal of Emma Bovary:

. . . this poor, doomed Emma, although inauthenticity certainly does touch her, is not a being of no actuality or worth whatever. . . . She has a degree of courage, although of an imprudent sort, an attractive presence, a sexuality which is urgent when once it is aroused, an imagination which kindles to the idea of experience . . . and a will to overcome the nullity of her existence. . . . Mme. Sarraute [cannot] give the forlorn creature even a wry compassion. A similar harshness of judgment informs Mme. Sarraute's fiction, beginning with her first book, *Tropismes,* a work which induces us to wonder why this gifted and imperious author should choose as the objects of her fierce discernment such *little* and, so to speak, merely incidental persons as she depicts. . . . Why does she descend from the height of her privileged state of being to make explicit her disgust at the nothingness of these persons who, as the title of the work proposes, are not persons at all?

Apart from the issues it raises, *Sincerity and Authenticity* is a deeply interesting book by reason of making clear the controlling concerns of a writer who has been one of the two or three most influential American critics during the past thirty years. Trilling refers at one point to Nietzsche's injunction that we "look below the surface of rational formulation to discover the *will* that is hidden beneath, and expressed through, its elaborations." If we make this effort in regard to Trilling himself, two observations come to mind.

First, his deepest interest in literature is not the critical act narrowly conceived, the description or analysis of a work and judgment of its merits—though he has often performed this act with force and delicacy. His deepest interest is in searching for the animating biases, the all-but-unspoken modulations of sentiment and value which give shape to a moment in cultural history. In an earlier time he might have been called a philosopher or historian of "moral consciousness," when that term did not carry the aura of faint depreciation it now does and when "moral" would have been assumed to include a range of experiences for which we have since found other names.

Perhaps my description of Trilling's central concerns may be clarified if I mention the school of critics who take a no-nonsense delight in ascribing recurrent turns of action and qualities of feeling in literary works to the shaping presence of "conventions." It is a "convention" that heroes behave as they do in epics, that sonnets often deal with romantic love, that Gothic novels are set in haunted castles. But to say this, while useful, is only a beginning. For the "convention" is a patterned, sometimes calcified record of historical turmoil and cultural innovation; the conduct of romantic heroes in 19th-century writing often follows a convention set in Goethe's *The Sorrows of Young Werther*, but for that fixing of premise and style to be possible there had first or concurrently to take place a revolution in sensibility. Now, what fascinates Trilling and comprises, I think, the main burden of this work is the way a major work of art "comes out of" (I use quotation marks because we do not really know how that happens) the seedbed of a culture and then how the major work helps to define the very terms of the influence exerted upon it. How or why does a given moment of historical consciousness find it so hard to yield to the attractions of physical pleasure? How or why does another moment turn away from the quest for transcendence and accept the small change, if small change it be, of quotidian contentment?

In his role as historian of moral consciousness Trilling is far from systematic. He relies very heavily on the premise, shared with F.R. Leavis, that the major text is a decisive instance, and his work is steadily open to the criticism of compacting the history of "consciousness" into a realm too self-contained and insufficiently complicated by mere events.

Second, we see in *Sincerity and Authenticity* the guiding norm, the goal, the working of *will*, to recur to Nietzsche's phrase, that inspires Trilling's work. It is a sense of life which makes Freud deeply congenial to him, and many recent cultural prophets uncongenial. Freud's "imagination of the human condition preserves something—much—of the stratum of hardness that runs through the Jewish and Christian traditions as they respond to the hardness of human destiny. Like the Book of Job it propounds and accepts the mystery and the naturalness—the natural mystery, the mysterious naturalness—of suffering." In advancing this austere vision Freud "had the intention of sustaining the authenticity of human existence that formerly had been ratified by God." Nietzsche too had wished for some such sustenance, as he "dreaded the 'weightlessness of all things,' the inauthenticity of experience, which he foresaw would be the consequence of the death of God." It is a wonderful if all-but unglossable phrase, that "weightlessness of things" dreaded by Nietzsche quite as if he had foreseen California. And as Trilling invokes it in behalf of his own sense of authenticity, he gains one's assent—yes, we know what he is trying to suggest here, we share his underlying uneasiness and urge to historical salvage. Until another question comes to mind: is not the very category of authenticity too coarsened in tone, too abrasive and lacerating in its effects, too inextricably associated with impulses toward dismissal and contempt? Might there not be some point in easing that self-assault, at one time liberating and later a mere complacent mimicry, which has been one of the less happy directives of modern culture? If *Emma Bovary, c'est moi*, and if she merits the compassion, even the sliver of respect, that Trilling would give her, might there not be some benefit in a similar indulgence for the rest of us? In short, would there not be some value if human beings, especially those who pride themselves on their cultivation, were to learn to like themselves a little once again—and authenticity be damned?

A MAN OF LETTERS

Almost everyone looked up to him. Writers and critics looked up to him, both those for whom he served as mentor and those ambitious enough to take him as model. So, too, did a company of cultivated readers who knew that regularly Edmund Wilson would come bearing gifts: Read Kipling, even if you detest his politics; read Ulysses Grant's memoirs, even though he was a brute of a general and a dolt of a President; read Agnon, read Dawn Powell, read Pushkin (hopeless as he sounds in English translation), read the Haitian novelist, Philippe Thoby-Marcelin. The whole sweep of world literature seeemed in Wilson's grasp, to be sifted, judged, protected. He could sometimes be difficult, even haughty, but in his work he was profoundly the democrat, eager to share every pleasure of literary discovery.

His career took on a heroic shape, the curve of the writer who attains magisterial lucidity in middle age and then, in the years of decline, struggles ferociously to keep his powers. One doesn't customarily think of writers as heroes, nor are heroes always likable. But in Wilson's determination to live out the idea of the man of letters, in his glowing eagerness before the literatures of mankind, and in his stubborn insistence upon speaking his own mind, there is a trace of the heroic. He didn't trim, he didn't court, he remained the same writer in and out of popularity, and he fought hard for what he thought was true.

Letters on Literature and Politics, Wilson's large collection of public letters—the more intimate ones may come later—holds fast to a credo he sent a friend in 1917, when he was all of 23: "My single aim has been literature." Except for a few dozen on politics, the letters are remorselessly literary, ranging from an appreciation of "The Waste Land" written the year the poem came out to an amusing remark 30 years later that he may yet have to read the whole Talmud, since "there seems to be no other way of really finding out what is in it."

Wilson's sheer willfulness in fulfilling the career he had set for himself is staggering. Reading these letters can make a reasonably prolific writer feel he has been wasting his years in idleness. For the general reader, whoever that may be, this collection could turn out to be intellectually claustrophobic, too much of a very good thing. But for anyone interested in literature or the literary life in America these past 60 years, the book is simply a treasure, a feast.

Not that the letters themselves are always distinguished or charming. Whatever it is that we value in great letter writers—a new voice, rapid shiftings of tone, sudden flares of bravura, keen notice of the surrounding world, quick rises into playfulness and drops into passion—is only occasionally present in Wilson's letters. They tend to be brusque and compact intellectual communications. Many read like miniature essays, echoes of work just completed or anticipations of work soon to be undertaken. There is some humor: Wilson thinks of selling his *Axel's Castle* to the movies, "with Adolphe Menjou as Proust and the Marx Brothers as Joyce." But too often Wilson's humor strikes one as facetious, bear-like. There are occasional personal remarks startling in their abruptness and brevity (in a 1938 letter he remarks: "I'm married to a girl named Mary McCarthy"—and then off he goes into talk about his next book).

Wilson's breadth of learning comes through more impressively than even his admirers might suppose. There are incisive remarks on a very wide range of writers whom he never got to in his essays: Virgil's high austerity, Defoe's gift for impersonation, Gibbon's "enormous scope," which reminds him of *Das Kapital.* He finds studying languages "a great relaxation"—he's not joking—and at the end of his life regrets he can't plunge into Chinese. He is the great literary taker-in and giver-outer. When these letters are cut off from the story of his life and his more personal writings, they seem a little distant, chilling. But wait: I mean that as praise at a time when "the personal" has become a license for all sorts of exhibition and cheapness.

There is plenty of feeling, but not bubbling on the surface; it lies behind the words, measured and serious. In 1919 Wilson wrote an injunction to F. Scott Fitzgerald meant to amuse but also to stiffen:

"No *Saturday Evening Post* stuff, understand! clear your mind of cant! brace up your artistic conscience . . . forget for a moment the phosphorescences of the decaying Church of Rome! . . . Concentrate in one short story a world of tragedy, comedy, irony, and beauty!!! I await your manuscript with impatience." Years later Wilson wrote another friend, the poet John Peale Bishop: "I'm sorry you're feeling exhausted—but come! Somebody's got to survive and write."

Wilson knew the miseries of the literary life; he had himself experienced a "sort of nervous breakdown" in 1929. And when he tried to console still another writer in trouble, the poet Louise Bogan, he fell back upon the stoical creed of hard work that sustained him for half a century: "give literary expression to your internal conflict and ranklings. . . . Once you get the expression out of your system in a satisfactory literary form, you can thumb your nose at the world." Well, at least for a while.

Wilson could be a scold. A 1938 letter to Malcolm Cowley is a classical denunciation of the latter's defense of the Moscow Trials; it ends with a wisecrack about Cowley's poor taste in praising Hemingway's "Popeye-the-Sailor novel" (*To Have and Have Not*) and "best wishes," of a sort, "for a return to health." When Wilson heard that his old friend Allen Tate had converted to Catholicism, he lashed out with a fierce yet considered attack, ending with the hope that "becoming a Catholic" may give Tate "peace of mind." (One would like to see the reply of the hot-tempered Tate.) To the editor Maxwell Perkins Wilson sent a letter in 1939 complaining, justly enough, that Scribner's had been miserly with advances to him, while it had squandered on Thomas Wolfe "money and attention like a besotted French king with a new favorite." And to his lifelong friend John Dos Passos, become conservative in his late years, Wilson burst out in 1964: "I never expected to see you develop into such a hot-air artist. How can you take Goldwater seriously?"

Yet it's notable that all of these people, though bridling under Wilson's blows, did not break with him, or did not break for very long; they knew he took ideas seriously and that the ferocity with which he lit into them was a sign that he took them seriously too.

Wilson had his cherished blind spots. The two best American poets of his time, Frost and Stevens, meant little to him. He sadly underestimated Hardy's poetry. And in 1942 he wrote that he "never could read Hazlitt." *Inconceivable*—not to be able to read Hazlitt!

More important is the evidence these letters provide of Wilson's gradual surrender, in his late years, to a sort of zoological materialism, a reductive biological determinism, which found expression in the preface to *Patriotic Gore* and mars some pages of that great book. In the preface Wilson had written that the affairs of humanity, the conduct of nations, seemed to him increasingly to resemble "the voracity of the sea slug" which "ingurgitates" all the smaller creatures within reach. This view of things can never be entirely resisted by anyone living in our century, for it releases a wish we all sometimes have to be done with the whole bloody mess of human history. Isolating the murderous element in the historical record, it distracts attention from those moral and social forces which also enable men to act somewhat in accord with a human standard—not least of all in their judgment of the times when they act like sea slugs. The Mencken-like, almost misanthropic view to which the aging Wilson gave way was partly a result of his feelings of disgust with post-war America; and, of course, there was plenty of reason for disgust. Yet Wilson's own later work, and the letters surrounding it, also testify to a more complex and modulated view of the human enterprise.

There is finally something harsh, even truculent, about Wilson's career, as if he is steadily driven to see it through images of embattlement and siege. Despite a strand of rhetorical overstatement, he was, I think, largely right in seeing the literary life as he did. American culture, he wrote in 1923, is overwhelmed with "an enormous mass of diluted intellectual goods," and this judgment, with stacks of supporting evidence, he extended and deepened each decade. It reflected both his basic response to our culture and something so relatively minor as his attitude toward publishers, most of whom, as Daniel Aaron remarks in his introduction to this book, "he regarded as Henry Adams did Congressmen." I recall once, in talking with Wilson, that his face grew flushed with feeling as he said that every self-respecting writer ought to die owing advances to publishers.

Wilson did not romanticize "the plight of the artist" nor often yield to self-pity. He was a fighter. All through his career, and not only during his radical phase in the 1930's, he took a sharply critical view of American civilization. He saw the serious writer not merely confronting the corruptions of commercial society—that was an old story, almost to be taken for granted. Other temptations, both gross and subtle, had a way of sneaking up. And if you wanted to be a serious writer, you had to fight every inch of the way: fight against the lures of the world, against vulgar popularization, against silly fads, against academic somnolence, against elite snobbism, and perhaps most of all, fight against your own weariness and weakness.

At the end of his life, when a tank of oxygen had to be kept in his bedroom-study because of his cardiac condition, the 75-year-old Wilson tacked up on the wall behind the oxygen a Hebrew motto. In English it means, "Be strong, be strong."

OCTAVIO PAZ: MEXICAN MODERNIST

The perception of distance can be a tricky problem. Here is Octavio Paz, a Mexican writer of striking gifts and postures, virtuoso of several genres, at home with French surrealism, American poetry, German romanticism, Marxist polemic. He seems very much the modernist writer as we have come to know him in the 20th century: sophisticated, mercurial, ambitious, self-dramatizing. A familiar type, a splendid instance.

Look a little harder and the contours start to blur. The "other" Paz is a man from a neglected country and a provincial culture, a Mexican who had to *decide* to go to Paris in order to "insert myself into the history of modern poetry." Throughout his writing there is a mournful contemplation of Aztec recesses of his country's past, as also of the speechless Indians of its present (the "meek panthers" as another Mexican poet, Alfonso Reyes, calls them). Both in poetry and prose, Paz's work has a rhetorical bravura, a love for the high dramatic stance, which may be satisfying to Latin readers but seems a little too grand in English. So Paz no longer figures as our intellectual cousin, he now emerges as a writer from a far territory, speaking from the outskirts of history.

No American critic—especially if, like myself, he reads Paz through the roughened lens of translation—can engage such a writer without severe risks of misapprehension. Yet these risks are worth taking, if only as a way of starting up some connections. Seeing him in both closeness and distance, we shuttle between worlds, from the Paz who shrewdly remarks about the surrealist master André Breton that he regarded the idea of sin "as a stain on man's dignity" to the Paz who plunges into discussion of Mexican writers—Velarde, Teblada, Ceruda—about whom, alas, we are likely to be ignorant.

The struggle to integrate his multiple *personae*, to find a common term between, say, a Parisian cafe and Mexican village, is a central preoccupation for Paz's work. It is not a struggle that can ever quite succeed. For to succeed fully would be a self-betrayal, a drop into mere synthesis, at a time when his true obligation as a writer is to keep grappling with his plural selves, align them with some humor, and rest uncomfortably with the contradictions that form his life.

By and large, that is what Paz does in his *Alternating Current*, a high-pressured gathering of essays. The sheer range of the book is evidence of his determination to bring the world to Mexico and perhaps even Mexico to the world. Everything tempts Paz, as if modern culture were still young, still fresh, and he writes about literary theory, Mexican fiction, European poetry, Sartre, Oriental thought, drugs, McLuhanism, the politics of "the third world." I shall return to this book, but first a few penciled lines toward a literary portrait of Octavio Paz.

His masterpiece is a book put into English a dozen years ago: *The Labyrinth of Solitude, Life and Thought in Mexico.* A venture into historical anthropology, or that riskiest of all genres, the evocation of national character, this book roams through the phases of Mexican past and present seeking to define the outrages, violation and defeats that have left the Mexican personality fixed into a social mask of passive hauteur. Indian past, colonial exploitation, *caudillo* bombast, brutalities of generals, religious fanaticism: all contribute to the Mexican face. Describing with a caustic sympathy the traumata of a wounded people, Paz studies Mexican resignation, hermeticism, sadism, the cult of the bleeding Christ, the adoration of death, delusions of *machismo,* the elevation of stylized contemplativeness over acts of personal will, postures of stoicism, the fiesta as national release, whatever it is that makes a Mexican move "through life like a man who has been flayed." At once brilliant and sad, *The Labyrinth of Solitude* constitutes an elegy for a people martyred, perhaps destroyed by history. It is a central text of our time.

With Paz's poetry one had better be a little more cautious. His theories about poetry, drawn mainly from French sources and developed in the first section of *Alternating Current*, are familiar, even too familiar: the celebration of the word severed from mere reference and become an icon or sacred object in its own right. But at least in Paz's longer poems, what strikes one forcefully is the dominance of Latin rhetoric, a facility in gestures of excess. In a long poem like "Solo for Two Voices," a North American reader searches for points of connection, and some do appear: passages suggesting Whitmanesque self-transformation, a kind of protean slipperiness meant to project possibilities for renewal of experience, and other passages sounding a more erotic, even "primitive" ground-note, as if Paz were searching for bits of salvage in the Mexican dust.

"Memory is a root in the dark" runs a splendid line in "Solo for Two Voices." And then: "Feed on the dark/Feed on forgetfulness:/Not what you say, what you forget/Is what you say. . . ." Here the voices of Octavio Paz achieve a strong fusion; but in the main—collages of imagery, nervous, rapid, disjointed—the long poems resist the grasp of at least this reader, perhaps because they need more time for psychic settlement, perhaps because there is just too steep a chasm between cultures.

At some moments—it's almost certainly a cultural misunderstanding—Paz can sound like a Latin, more excitable Wallace Stevens: "There is a motionless tree/There is another advancing/A river of trees." Or in these lines, perhaps only the first two of them:

> I saw the world resting upon itself.
> I saw the appearance.
> And I named that half-hour:
> Perfection of the Finite.

The short poems are more ingratiating, and one doesn't need to grope, in reading them, for tenuous connectives. Paz appears here as a poet of wit, control and a readiness to drop his many-colored cultural costumes in order to attend the beat of his inwardness. "Touch" is characteristic:

> My hands
> Open the curtains of your being
> Clothe you in a further nudity
> Uncover the bodies of your body
> My hands
> Invent another body for your body

Or, in the same manner, minus what I'll call Latin American, boom-boom, there is "Friendship," in which Paz attends not history s but his private silences:

It is the awaited hour
Over the table falls
Interminably
The lamp's spread hair
Night turns the window to immensity
There is no one here
Presence without name surrounds me

With Paz's political writings, we re-enter the familiar terrain of modern controversy. As a young man Paz worked for the Spanish Republic during the Civil War years, then helped edit a radical paper in Mexico City, and a bit later, in revulsion against Communist authoritarianism, had a brief encounter with the Trotskyist opposition. During the sixties Paz served as Mexican Ambassador to India; but when police in 1968 gunned down students in Mexico City, he resigned his post as a protest against this outrage.

Paz is not, in any narrow sense, an ideological man, but neither is he a dilettante jotting down mere fancies. In writing about politics he shows solid historical knowledge and a fine moral seriousness; he speaks with an authority akin to that of European writers like Silone and Orwell, who also declared themselves men of the left while insisting that liberty is the absolute precondition for a bearable existence.

In a little book called *The Other Mexico* Paz develops his political thought with verve and lucidity. He traces the convolutions of the Mexican Revolution over the past half-century and concludes that, for all its notable achievements, it has declined into the opportunism and rigidity of "a political bureaucracy set up in a state party and composed of specialists in the manipulation of the masses." What Mexico needs most of all is a democratic ventilation so that both free ideas and quickened blood may start to flow.

Paz then moves beyond the Mexican setting, to a theoretical consideration of "the third world"—his most valuable contribution to contemporary thought. Stressing the need for radical change in the "underdeveloped" countries, he nevertheless dissociates himself from the Fidelistas, Fanonists, Guevarists and Maoists, all of whom advocate or would accept revolutionary-bureaucratic dictatorships. Paz understands that liberty of speech, press, and political association is not just the luxury for intellectuals that some pseudo-realistic American professors, both left and right, suppose it to be; it is a necessity for burgeoning social groups within the poor nations seeking to assert themselves, and a necessity for those nations themselves as they undertake self-critical programs of economic modernization.

Let me quote a crucial passage from Paz's essay, "Olympics and Tlatelolco": "Whatever the limitations of Western democracy (which are many and grave . . .) there can be no political life without freedom of criticism. . . . The young fanatics who recite the catechism of Mao—by the way, a mediocre academic poet—commit not only an esthetic and intellectual error but also a moral one. Critical thinking cannot be sacrificed on the altars of accelerated development, the revolutionary idea, the leader's prestige and infallibility, or any other mirage, . . . Every dictatorship, whether of man or of party, leads to the two forms that schizophrenia loves most: the monologue and the mausoleum."

All of the themes I have noticed, as well as many others, come into play in *Alternating Current.* Paz's criticism, of a kind seldom undertaken by his sober contemporaries to the north, consists of an epigrammatic philosophical dramatism, with a high quotient of generality and not much effort at textual detail or expository sequence. At its best, this can be strikingly effective, as in a one-page essay comparing Kafka's cockroach with Apuleius's ass, or a piece about the fiction of Carlos Fuentes whose "humor . . . carnal, corporeal, and ritual [is] as incongruous as an Aztec sacrifice in Times Square." (Though if you must have an Aztec sacrifice, what better place these days than Times Square?) But sometimes Paz's criticism becomes a relentless hammering of displayed brilliance, a little wearying in its emission of insights and formulas; one wishes for moments of quiet conversation.

While Ambassador to India, Paz grew absorbed with Oriental thought, Hindu Tantrism and drugs; and he writes with apparent sympathy for the idea of grace through pharmacy, reporting that during a religious festival in India he took "a variety of hashish called bhang." Drugs "snatch us out of everyday reality, blur our perceptions, alter our sensations, and in a word, put the entire universe in a state of suspension." One's heart sinks: no, not this worn-out rhapsodizing of the vacuous. But an essay later: "The first encounter with mescaline ends with the discovery of an 'infinity-machine.' The endless production of colors, rhythms, and forms turns out in the end to be an awesome, absurd flood of cheap trinkets. We are millionaires with vast hoards of fairgrounds junk." Paz can sometimes put his mind aside, but not really for very long.

Full of energy, curiosity, intelligence, still eager to taste the goods of this world, and loving, as he says, nothing "more than verbal perfection," Octavio Paz is an intellectual-literary one-man band who performs everything from five-finger sonatas to full-scale symphonies and even electronic music, all in *Alternating Current.*

TRIBUNE OF SOCIALISM

W.A. Swanberg has written an old-fashioned biography of Norman Thomas, and mostly the book is the better for it. No strands of political theorizing, no dips into Freudianism, no lumps of sociology. All is narrative—the story of a splendid man told simply and with a controlled affection.

Swanberg has understood that a lifelong devotion to the poor and the exploited is not something that needs—in the style of current sophistications—to be "explained." The kind of life Norman Thomas led is always a possibility for us, and the biographer need only show it forth as an exemplary instance. If this book has some pedestrian pages, if it rarely breaks into eloquence or profundity, the story it tells is nevertheless a deeply moving one.

The pedestrian pages come at the start, in sketches of Thomas's early years in a high-minded Presbyterian family. The earnestness of young Norman preparing for the ministry, his search for a social vision that might give substance to his ethical-religious sentiments, his turn to pacifism in World War I and then to a larger social rebelliousness—these are described with a shade too much detail and stolidity of tone. But once Thomas shifts in the early 1920's from Social Gospel to Socialist Party, trying to pull together a movement ripped apart by Government persecution and Communist defection, the story comes entirely to life.

Ferociously energetic, endowed with a loud crackling voice, quick in debate and wonderfully free of the public man's self-importance, Thomas now became both the leader of his floundering party and an all-American circuit rider. He ran for office again and again, speaking at street corners, union halls and universities, and touring the country in a beat-up car with his wife Violet, a patrician lady who gave her heart to her husband and his cause. (In one campaign they barnstormed through New England for 10 days—at a grand cost of $55.45!) Old-party spokesmen learned to avoid Thomas in debate: he knew more, he talked faster, and—miracle of American miracles!—he came out with comely sentences and coherent paragraphs.

Wherever there was injustice, Thomas spoke up. Boss Hague in Jersey City tried to institute a vest-pocket fascism? Thomas was there to challenge him, suffering rough treatment and jail. Gov. Paul McNutt of Indiana proposed informally to repeal the Bill of Rights? Thomas was there to say it couldn't be done. Some of Mr. Swanberg's best pages concern Thomas's one-man crusade to help the Southern Tenant Farmers' Union, formed in 1934 by desperately poor share-croppers in Arkansas. Thomas kept going down there, risking his neck, defying vigilante terrorists, winning the affection of farm workers who had never before dared speak for their rights. And up North, Thomas kept needling Secretary of Agriculture Henry Wallace (later the fellow-travelers' darling) to do something for the Arkansas sharecrop-pers, but Wallace steadily refused to meet with him and, instead, made a shameful speech saying the trouble in Arkansas was due to "Com-munistic and Socialistic gentlemen" who "have gone in to stir up trou-ble."

In the late 1930's, Thomas tangled with President Roosevelt (who nevertheless seems to have liked him). He tried to persuade the Presi-dent that his embargo on arms to Loyalist Spain was enabling a major fascist victory in Europe, but as Thomas caustically reported, Roosevelt "in his own inimitable way changed the subject."

As a man who tried to bring together the imperatives of morality and the devices of politics, and as leader of a small socialist party who felt keenly the intellectual crisis that socialism was undergoing throughout the world, Thomas made a lot of mistakes. He let himself be exces-sively influenced by the sectarian-academic Marxists of the 1930's. He came too close to the isolationists during the years before World War II.

Thomas was a superb tribune for socialism, but an indifferent party leader. Partly this was due to his temperament, which drew him more strongly to the rostrum than the desk. But mostly it was a result of overwhelming, perhaps insoluble, problems that the socialist movement was facing in the mid-30's and later.

The failure of the German Left to fight against Hitler's seizure of power seemed to the young radicals gathered near Thomas evidence that social democratic reformist policies were futile and that more militant methods were needed. Thomas half agreed, though he also sensed that in the United States revolutionary policies could only lead to the hermeticism of the sect. The right-wing Socialists, the Old Guard that was dug into the Jewish garment unions, welcomed F.D.R.'s New Deal as a partial fulfillment of the demands they had long been making. Thomas half agreed, though he also argued that the New Deal provided no more than minor palliatives to a sick society.

Meanwhile, the Communists had turned rightward and were barraging the Socialists with appeals for a "united front." The Old Guard distrusted the Communists on principle, and often with good reason, while the left wing Socialists felt that the threat of fascism warranted at times the risk of limited blocs with the Communists. Thomas saw justice in both views, so much so that some of his friends, on both left and right, made the mistake of seeing his intelligence as indecision.

Retrospective widsom (in which we're all rich) suggests that the Socialists might have supported New Deal reforms as far as they went while not abandoning their basic critique of our society. Or it might have been possible to recognize the ned for militant struggle against European fascism while also grasping that American circumstances did not lend themselves to the revolutionary outlook.

But Thomas suffered from the defects of his virtues. He wasn't single-minded or devious enough to be a strong party leader; he couldn't content himself with easy formulas, left or right. The result was that his party, which had grown encouragingly in the early 1930's, was destroyed by splits and defections. The Old Guard settled into a passive friendship with the New Deal; the left-wing got cut up in a romance with the Trotskyists; ordinary members quit in disgust. Thomas remained, loyal to the end, but increasingly a leader without followers.

Yet it was in these last years that he reached his peak as a public man. Aging, sick, lonely, he was always on call, always ready to speak, write, debate, picket, organize. He rethought some of his ideas, writing a friend that "various grim experiences, including the record of the Russian Revolution, make me far more doubtful of easy collectivist . . . alternatives," and his socialism now consisted of a rather loose democratic egalitarianism. His mind grew more subtle, he cut away the barnacles of dogmatism.

And hs kept his sense of humor. A lady told him he'd been running for President since she was a little girl. "Madam," he replied, "I've been running for President since I was a little boy." Once, as Mr. Swanberg tells it, "Thomas made histrionic use of his aches . . . he seated himself at the far end of the platform so that when he was introduced he limped very slowly to the podium, cane in one hand . . . then turned to the audience and rasped, 'Creeping Socialism!' "

Among those who had abandoned him politically, it became the custom to honor him with sentimental tributes, sometimes even speaking of him as a saint. He was nothing of the sort. The few of us who remained his political friends in the 1950's and 60's knew him as something more than saint—we knew him as a passionate, troubled, eager, sometimes irascible man. He could be impatient with fools, especially the sort who bored him with elaborate introductions when he gave a speech. He could twist your arm if he wanted you to do something for a cause. He could be sharp and sour: after debating William F. Buckley Jr., he did a very funny imitation of Buckley's self-adoring superciliousness. His sight failed, but his voice kept booming out. ("I'm a tottering wreck, and it's annoying.")

Here he is, close to the end, as Dwight Macdonald describes him speaking at a SANE rally against the Vietnam War:

"So now he is 82 and he has to be helped to the speaker's stand, but once there, in the old, familiar stance, facing the crowd—they are on their feet applauding, calling out to him—he takes a firm grip on the rostrum, throws his head back, and begins to talk in a voice that is quavering . . . . For ten minutes he baits the President, modulating from irony to polemic to indignation to humor to fact to reasoning, speaking in a rapid businesslike way without rhetorical effects . . . .

"He winds up briskly, professional brio, as how many times, how many times? We get to our feet again to clap, to cheer timidly, to smile at one another as members of the same family do when one of them acquits himself well in public. The old man endures the applause politely for a reasonable time, then begins to make his way back to his seat. . . ."

Norman Thomas was the only great man I have ever met, and if I never meet another I will not feel deprived.

Postscript

I'm not sure this piece fits into the scheme of this book. But it gives me pleasure to say these words of tribute to a wonderful man, and so I say them.

THE HOLOCAUST
AND MORAL JUDGMENT

On October 4, 1943, Heinrich Himmler, head of the Nazi SS troops, spoke in confidence to his *Gruppenführer* (lieutenant generals). The plan for "the extermination of the Jews," as he frankly labeled it, was well advanced, and despite some soft-hearted Germans who claimed to know an "A-1 Jew" who ought to be spared, the Nazi élite forces would not be deflected from their course. They alone, he said, knew what it meant "to see a hundred corpses lie side by side, or five hundred, or a thousand." In public "we will never speak of it," but the destruction of the Jews would forever remain "an unwritten and never-to-be-written page of glory."

The Nazis were seldom this candid about the "Final Solution," their code name for the mass murder of millions of human beings, but from the beginnings, writes Lucy Dawidowicz in her distinguished book, *The War Against the Jews,* an incipient version of this objective had been central to their program. The "Final Solution" was more than an outburst by the hoodlums of Europe; it was the realization of a totalitarian ideology: the elimination of the polluting stranger, the defiling alien. To have burned mountains of flesh in so scientific a way as the Nazis learned to do, was to move beyond spontaneous sadism and into the gross fantasia of one of those systems of pseudo-thought which have been the curse of our century.

Books about Nazism are endless, and so too about anti-Semitism, but

234

Mrs. Dawidowicz's book comes to us as a major work of synthesis, providing for the first time a full account of the holocaust not merely as it completed the Nazi vision but as it affected the Jews of eastern Europe.

It is a work committed to the sovereignty of fact; free of metaphysical decoration; and emerging out of an awareness that no theory about the holocaust can be as important as a sustained confrontation with the holocaust itself. Austere and disciplined, this book comes to seem an exemplar of that Jewish belief—or human delusion—that somehow there may still be a moral use in telling what it meant to live and die in the 20th century.

Mrs. Dawidowicz begins at the point in the 1880's when "the idea of mass annihilation of the Jews had already been adumbrated" in Germany. Anti-Semitism festered not merely among cranks but at the centers of *Kultur:* in the universities, among the German nationalists, and in the churches, where echoes were heard of Luther's injunction, "next to the devil thou hast no enemy more cruel . . . than a true Jew." Even the liberal-spirited Social Democrats were sometimes infected with the stereotypic notion, inherited from the young Marx, that "the Jew" was a huckster whose god was money.

The Nazi movement as it emerged in the 1920's could thus draw upon many strands of German tradition while adding a special tone of gutter fanaticism, that fevered hatred one associates with the atmosphere of postwar Europe. At first Hitler's rantings against the Jews were dismissed as mere bait for the masses, but Mrs. Dawidowicz argues forcefully that, on the contrary, anti-Semitism was the Nazis' deepest, most "authentic" persuasion. The evil they preached was worked-out and remarkable for its absoluteness; it bore the stamp of our century.

Once in power, the Nazis pursued their two major goals—a German expansion eastward and the destruction of the Jews—with a coherent intensity. Brutalities of the street matched formalities of legalism; the murderers felt obliged to specify with finicky niceness precisely who was and was not a Jew; and their propagandists linked the internal terror with an external "crusade," the drive against the Jews with the drive for *Lebensraum.* Meanwhile, the agency that would unite all these strands of Nazi policy—the black-shirted SS—began "to assert its hegemony with regard to the Jews over all state and party institutions."

Throughout the war, the SS insisted that the "Final Solution" be given first priority. The SS commandeered trains for shipping Jews to the death camps at a time when the German army badly needed those trains for the eastern front. And from the Nazi point of view, the SS had a kind of gruesome logic: nothing mattered more than killing Jews.

This book forces one to reconsider earlier theories about Nazism, especially the Marxist theory that it was essentially devised as a last-ditch defense of German capitalism. Portions of the upper bourgeosie did help finance the Nazis and later profited from their success; but it now seems clear that Nazism had a dynamic and a meaning all its own, one that transcended the usual thrust of class interest. Melding irrational blood-lust with bureaucratic finickiness, the Nazi movement brought together ideology and terror in a "permanent" fusion that often seems like a parody of the Leninist world-outlook: schematic, planned, totalistic, brooking neither qualm nor distrust. André Malraux spoke of "le retour de Satan," a vast explosion of the hatreds and phobias gathering beneath the crust of civilization; and while hardly sufficient as a theory of Nazism, his insight penetrated more deeply than most theories.

In the summer of 1941 Hitler gave the signal for the "Final Solution." Adolf Eichmann proposed "killing with showers of carbon monoxide while bathing," but it was discovered that Zyklon B, a cyanide gas, was more effective. Clouds of smoke emerging from crematoria became a familiar sight on the German landscape. At Auschwitz "the red sky could be seen for miles."

In Mrs. Dawidowicz's severely controlled narrative there are chapters on the camps as total institutions, the pitiful efforts of the German Jews to maintain a fragment of dignity, and the close relation between German foreign policy and race. The most poignant pages are those dealing with the holocaust in eastern Europe—and here the mind becomes numb. Let me quote a passage at random, by no means the most horrible:

"In Czestochowa, on a frosty night in January 1940, the police surrounded a densely populated Jewish area . . . Thousands of half-naked men and women were assembled in a large square and beaten to bleeding. Then they were kept standing for hours in the biting frost. Others—especially young girls—were taken into the synagogue . . . forced to undress, sexually shamed, and tortured."

In her concluding chapters Mrs. Dawidowicz writes about the victims with an objectivity that comes to seem indistinguishable from compassion: those Jews who, in accord with their pacific and religious traditions, tried to survive by submitting, and those, like the socialists and Zionists who tried to organize an underground resistance. There are chapters rich in detail, but almost unbearable to read, about the efforts of the Jews to maintain an inner cultural life (illegal schools, concerts, political discussions) in the ghettos of Poland.

Even about the much-despised *Judenräte*, the Jewish local authorities sometimes set up by Nazi decree and sometimes meant to thwart the oppressors, Mrs. Dawidowicz writes with objectivity and compassion. Some *Judenrät* officials were driven by fear—"hunger broke down traditional canons of morality." Others were scoundrels. Most were confused and tormented people who tried both to accommodate and resist, to surrender victims and save others. "I, Gens," said the police chief of the Vilna ghetto, "lead you to death and I, Gens, want to save Jews from death . . . I render the account of Jewish blood and not the account of Jewish honor. With the thousands that I hand over, I save ten thousand."

The account of Jewish honor was finally rendered in the Warsaw uprising of April, 1943. With a handful of revolvers and grenades, the Jewish youth fought to the death, quite aware that nothing else could await them, almost joyous that this last act of defiance remained to them. And there Mrs. Dawidowicz ends her narrative.

In reading this book one finds oneself returning to a question much discussed, perhaps too much discussed, in the last 20 years: the alleged passivity of the European Jews as they were being slaughtered by the Nazis. From the materials amassed here it becomes utterly clear that, even as politically-conscious Jews did engage in more underground activity than has commonly been supposed, there was no possibility whatever for effective resistance. No matter what they might do, it could only be a farewell of the doomed. Without arms, drained by starvation, inexperienced in military crafts, subjected to a system of brutality beyond description, and distrusted, sometimes even betrayed, by other European nationalities that were also being oppressed by the Nazis, the Jews of eastern Europe were simply unable to hold back the "Final Solution."

A few behaved badly; more were heroic; most, like ordinary people at all times, tried to survive, then to protect their children, and finally to brace themselves for death.

Who, then, dares set himself as judge? Who can say what the "right" conduct should have been? Bend before the murderers in the hope of surviving? Sacrifice the old and sick in order to save the young? Or embark on hopeless gestures of resistance that would bring ghastly reprisals upon thousands of innocents?

The moral norms by which we hope to live are meant for common circumstances, but also for extraordinary ones, those in which we find it difficult to satisfy the requirements we set for ourselves. But beyond these two spheres, the ordinary and the extraordinary, there arise situations so extreme that it becomes immoral to make moral judgments about those who have had to confront them. When flesh has been seared and bones have been broken, when not even a memory remains of the common restraints of civilization, what point is there in speaking about heroism or the lack of it, resistance or the lack of it?

The minimal fragment of freedom which is surely a precondition for moral conduct, that fragment which allows us the slender persuasion of being able to make a choice, has been destroyed. The only remaining question is the ability of a living creature to endure physical torture—and that soon ceases to be a moral issue. It becomes inappropriate, even obscene, to speak either in praise or dispraise of those who perished. They need only be remembered.

This book can hardly be "recommended," since reading it yields neither pleasure nor relief—it is an experience of unbroken suffering. From the suffering of the world, as Kafka says, "you can hold back, you have free permission to do so, and it is in accordance with your nature, but perhaps this very holding back is the one suffering you could have avoided."

LITERATURE AND LIBERALISM

It is now a quarter of a century since Lionel Trilling remarked upon the difficulties faced by educated Americans in reconciling their political ideas with their literary tastes. Most of "us," he wrote, "are in our social and political beliefs consciously liberal," yet the writers we most admire—and he named the great figures of European modernism—"are indifferent to, even hostile to, the tradition of democratic liberalism . . ."

The problem was aggravated for Mr. Trilling by the fact that those works of recent American literature presenting themselves as "patently liberal" could seldom excite our deepest loyalties. We could not gain from them "the sense of largeness, of cogency, of the transcendence which largeness and cogency can give, the sense of being reached in our secret and primitive minds." Mr. Trilling was referring here to the damage wrought by fellow-traveling ideology, but still more, he was deploring a tendency of liberal writing to congeal into set formulas such as the simplistic notion that "the life of man can be nicely settled by a correct social organization, or short of that, by the election of high moral attitudes."

In these reflections Mr. Trilling was consciously echoing the complaint that John Stuart Mill had made a century earlier. Mill had felt dismay at seeing his favored ideas turn rigid and life-denying, and in his resulting confusion had gained unexpeccted nourishment from the poetry of Wordsworth and the prose of Coleridge. Neither Wordsworth's poetry nor Coleridge's prose won Mill's full intellectual acquiescence, yet he valued them for what Mr. Trilling calls "a sense of variousness and possibility," that richness of feeling that the dry, overly programmatic liberalism of the utilitarians could not yield.

The passage of a quarter of a century has not lessened the force of Mr. Trilling's argument, though one might add that his judgment of liberalism could be made with equal strength against other systems of contemporary thought: against Christianity, Marxism, and conservatism, which have all become sterile or sentimental. What has characterized the literature of our lifetime has been an absence of sustaining belief, or more to the point, an absence of even provisional belief, the kind that writers can conditionally employ or seriously pit themselves against. And since the dominant intellectual tendency of twentieth-century America has been one or another kind of liberalism, the result of this breakdown has been to arouse scorn, irritation, and boredom with the claims of liberalism.

Our literature and our thought have never, to be sure, been aligned in a simple flow of harmony: it is naive to suppose that such an untroubled relation could ever exist. Even with regard to the Christian centuries, it is only popularized history that proposes an untroubled, "organic" relation between belief and imagination. Once we take a closer look at particular Christian works we find them complicated by tension, heresy, perhaps even a masked skepticism. Nevertheless, later generations may pardon us for supposing that our own time is one in which, partly as a consequence of the exhausting fanaticsms of fascism and communism, there has occurred a radical sundering between belief and imagination. Sometimes a sundering so extreme, that serious writers have been provoked into feeling that imaginative survival depends on a refusal of all beliefs.

It has not always been so. Whatever criticisms we may wish to make of twentieth-century liberalism, it is desperately useful to remind ourselves that liberalism in its heroic phase—toward the end of the eighteenth and a good part of the nineteenth century—enabled and perhaps even inspired a large portion of Western literature. Being utterly obvious, this proposition has been mostly ignored; and largely ignored, it might now have some freshness and force. What I have in mind is liberalism not as a mere program for social change or a political movement advancing that program; what I have in mind is liberalism as a new historical temper, a turning of minds to openness of idea and variousness of sentiment.

Liberalism in its heroic phase constitutes one of the two or three greatest revolutionary experiences in human history, comparable with the ethic of the Old Testament and the word of Jesus in its power to transform the imagination. Whether or not a given writer calls himself a liberal or can be said to "reflect" the outlook of liberalism, matters hardly at all. What does matter is that the richness and multiplicity of modern culture would simply have been impossible without the animating liberal idea. The root terms and values of modern literature would be inconceivable without the thought of the Enlightenment or the new image of human potentiality cast up by Romanticism—and both the Enlightenment and Romanticism, with whatever complications, contribute to liberalism in its heroic phase. The very idea of "the self," a central convention of modern literature, simply could not have come into being had there not been the earlier, fructifying presence of liberalism. The dynamics of plot that characterize the nineteenth-century novel, based as these are on new assumptions about mobility and freedom, are quite inconceivable without the shaping premises of liberalism.

To say this isn't, of course, to suggest that literature of the modern era has no other or older sources; it is only to account, somewhat, for distinctive new energies. "The deepest driving force of the liberal ideas of the Enlightenment," writes Karl Mannheim, "lay in the fact that it appealed to the free will and kept alive the feeling of being indeterminate and unconditioned. . . ." Without such feelings, how could the modern novelist so much as have conceived of a *Bildungsroman*, with its progress through society and growth of the self, or of an escape from the locked frames of social role and class perspective? I don't mean to suggest that these typical patterns of modern literature have no analogues in earlier, more traditional literatures; only that the moral and psychological contents we recognize as distinctively our own depend crucially on that complex of ideas and impulses we identify as liberalism. And insofar as these truisms are actually true, they hold for writers as various in opinion as Dickens and Dostoevsky, Zola and Lawrence, Proust and Dreiser, all of whom respond to, find sustenance in, turn sharply against, and express disgust with the values of a liberalism they cannot escape. Even the conservative counter-Enlightenment, which coexists with major portions of modernist literature, is able to reach definition because of privileges that liberalism had secured as rights.

It is a great moral and imaginative power, this liberalism that begins to blossom in eighteenth-century Europe. It promises a dismissal of intolerable constraints; it speaks for previously unimagined rights; it declares standards of sincerity and candor; it offers the promise that each man shall have his voice, and that each voice will be heard. For the whole of European and American literature from, say, the last third of the eighteenth century, liberalism helps release energies of assertion, but, more important, energies of opposition—opposition to privilege and vulgarity, to the imprisonment of the body and denial of the spirit. If the nineteenth-century novel is frequently organized as a comedy of conflict between fading aristocracy and oncoming bourgeoisie, that novel takes emotive sharpness from the vision of human possibility that, more than any program, is the great contribution of classical liberalism.

For how could Julien Sorel make his gesture without the strain of liberalism in Stendhal's outlook? Or Pip break past the accumulated snobbisms of his England without the strain of liberalism in Dickens's outlook? Or Jude Fawley stumble toward his vision of the ennobled life without that strain in Hardy? And how, for that matter, could a writer like D.H. Lawrence, self-declared enemy of liberalism, suppose himself to be moving beyond its limits had not the luxury of that option been provided by liberalism?

Nor is it only for its energizing role of opposition that liberalusm matters here. With some nineteenth-century writers liberalism also becomes the substance of a deeply serious and humane moral vision. What Mill invokes in his essays, George Eliot realizes in her fiction. Eliot, it is true, brings to her novels affections for English country life and received churchly pieties that contribute to that fullness of spirit we admire in her work. But what is distinctive in her work is the transfiguration of liberal opinion into moral sensibility. Respect for all living beings, belief in human potential, appreciation of differences among us that go deep and differences that merely amuse, and an awareness of the need for compassionate solidarity in facing the terribleness of life—these values are realized in George Eliot's work, values of liberalism made warm and vibrant.

But need we suppose that such values are unique to liberalism? I certainly would not wish to claim a monopoly of virtue for any political outlook. Yet it must be said that over the past two centuries it has been mainly liberalism, at least liberalism in its times of early freshness, that has done the most to advance such values. Perhaps it is in the nature of liberalism that it can gain social strength only when allied with other world-views, say, the ethical substance of Christianity or the political promise of democratic socialism. George Eliot's outlook has often been summarized as a "religion of humanity," as if thereby to acknowledge the still-vibrant residue of faith that sustains her novels. And that seems to me very well, for a true liberalism makes no demand for exclusiveness or even hegemony. It is always to ready to welcome amiable partners.

Liberalism proves to be enabling for literature, especially the novel, in still another and more distinctively "literary" way. It provides an organizing principle through which nineteenth-century novelists can bound their worlds; it helps them locate the jostling plurality of groups and interests that comprises modern society; and it improvises linkages between the increasingly irksome and repressive actualities of our life and those unsubdued yearnings for transcendence that linger among sensitive people. *Jude the Obscure* seems a crucial instance, the pathos of its leading figures being inseparable from those visions of a truthful life that reached Hardy through writers like John Stuart Mill. But even when we turn to a novelist like Trollope, less fine-grained than either Eliot or Hardy and sometimes marred by that English complacency that takes the guise of heartiness, we find that his actions and characters are focused through the lens of a whiggish liberalism—it is his way of comprehending the world in which men must live and act.

Torn from the rib of John Locke, America presents a more complicated relation between literature and liberalism. When Locke says, "In the beginning all the world was America," he is saying more about America than "the beginning"; he has in mind, one supposes, that America began as an idea of Europe. Whatever may be reformative in European culture, and a modest part of whatever is revolutionary, finds a locus of desire in the *idea* of America. That our national experience diverges from this idea everyone has noticed, and the act of making that discovery soon becomes an essential part of the national experience. Through the cautions of our historians and the pain of our history, we have come to recognize as mere foolishness any claim for America as pure emanation of liberal virtue—there is plenty in our origins and still more in our development that is anything but liberal. Nevertheless, America as a distinctive civilization does emerge at least partly out of a Europe enlivened by the ferment of liberal thought. And this holds for both our institutions—the republic itself, our civil freedoms, the development of the party system—and our myths—America as a new Israel, the second chance for a fallen humanity.

Even in so illiberal a culture as New England Puritanism one can already see some of the reformative European energies at work. If the Puritans, in Perry Miller's striking phrase, regarded themselves as embarked on an errand into the wilderness, it was an errand shaped both by the changes under way in Europe and by the Nature they encountered in America. In its "incessant drive to learn how and how most ecstatically . . . to hold any sort of communion" with the unsullied Nature of the New World, this errand would be gradually transformed by the wilderness itself. Miller traces, from the early Puritan divines through Jonathan Edwards and then to the heretical Emerson, a continuity of search "to confront, face to face, the image of a blinding divinity in the physical universe"; but what is here most striking is how the Puritan errand was transformed by the wilderness it sought to transform, how that Nature that was to be graced by God's mission came to be seen as the source of grace. And in this change one can see the course of American myth itself, to be intertwined with our institutions as both complement and contrast.

This relationship between institutions and myth is crucial for an understanding of what happens to the sentiment of liberalism in nineteenth-century America—I say "sentiment" because the fate of liberalism in nineteenth-century America seems very much to be a gradual diffusion from original doctrine to shared feeling. "The great advantage of Americans," writes de Tocqueville, "is that they have arrived at a state of democracy without having to endure a democratic revolution." There is really no long-settled weight of reactionary traditions to throw over or guard against. Except perhaps when railing against the decadence of Europe, which soon becomes a kind of popular sport, liberalism in America cannot define itself as a force of opposition, a movement intent upon breaking down the barriers of the past. For the past is far away, across the ocean, or it lives secretively within the present, afflicting the consciousness of those who suppose it a sign of freedom that they wish to be rid of the past. The very prevalence of liberal assumptions, shared in part even by the more conservative thinkers among the Founding Fathers, seems to remove or lessen the need for a highly focused articulation of the liberal idea. What all accept, none feels obliged to argue. The major political groupings are to be distinguished not by whether they favor or reject the premises of a liberal polity, but by the degree of fervor or caution with which they advance them.[1]

The one large exception, of course, is to be heard among Southern ideologues trying to justify slavery. But even there it seems to be mainly a defensive impulse, a scraping together of bits and pieces of argument in behalf of the "peculiar institution." Slavery is a cancer in the body politic, but it does not radically deflect American thought from its democratic course. One can see a certain appropriateness in Henry Adams' description of America in the 1820s: "Except for Negro slavery, it was sound and healthy in every part. Stripped for the hardest work, every muscle firm and elastic, every ounce of brain ready for use, and not a trace of superfluous flesh on his nervous and supple body, the American stood in the world as a new order." Not the least interest of this passage is that it centers on that moment in the national experience when social reality and cultural myth are probably more harmonious than ever before or since.

It is a moment, as we also know, of rather severe social conflict. The Jacksonian upsurge represents an effort to extend the social promise of the republic; yet whatever terms we may wish to use for it—populist, plebeian, petty bourgeous—we aren't spontaneously inclined to think of it as an instance of liberalism. Nor of anything contrary to liberalism. It seems a phase in the transformation of received liberal values into that quasi-religious ethos of democratic individualism that dominates nineteenth-century American experience.

But let us turn back for a moment, to the Founding Fathers, and ask ourselves what the authors of *The Federalist Papers* might have made of Locke's sentence, "In the beginning all the world was America." I imagine a dialogue between Madison and Hamilton. With a touch of asperity, Hamilton remarks that in trying to work out the foundations for a new republic they aren't, after all, composing by-laws for paradise—which by its very nature wouldn't require any. And Madison replies, yes, he had already suggested as much in a controversial *Federalist Paper;* yet it would be well for Mr. Hamilton to remember that Locke's remark had been a shrewd one, since without acknowledgment of the paradisal yearning in the imagination of our fellow Americans, we would hardly be in a position to work out the foundations of a new republic.

Hardheaded men, these Founding Fathers were proposing a political experiment largely in accord with Locke's prescription for a limited constitutional government; they believed in imposing restraints upon the very government to which they yielded powers; they were not romantic about either the New World or its inhabitants. Yet their entire enterprise presupposed *some* romanticism, some sense of the hold America had established upon the European imagination (otherwise, why would Lafayette have bothered to help?) and thereby on the American too. That romanticism seems to have been present, if only as a force to be confined, in the awareness of men like Madison and Hamilton. The former writes in *The Federalist Papers* a classical statement of the doctrine of countervailing powers:

Ambition must be made to counteract ambition. . . . It may be a reflection on human nature that such devices should be necessary to control the abuses of government. But what is government itself but the greatest of all reflections on human nature? If men were angels, no government would be necessary. . . .

And Hamilton touches on the same theme in a more caustic style:

Reflections of this kind [in behalf of a balance of power] may have trifling weight with men who hope to see realized in America the halcyon scenes of the poetic or fabulous age; but those who believe we are likely to experience a common portion of the vicissitudes and calamities which have fallen to the lot of other nations . . . etc., etc.

Now what seems most striking about these passages is the polemic against unspecified opponents, those who might suppose men to be angels or want to see realized in the New World halcyon scenes. Who could they be? Jeffersonians, no doubt, but also, perhaps, a good many Americans wearing no political tag. Writing such polemics, Madison and Hamilton were responding to something urgent and authentic in the American imagination, something they too must have felt if only in order to repudiate. And the question that must be faced is this: Could the principles upon which the American government was founded and the expectations that had arisen with the beginning of American settlement be reconciled? Can one bring together the worldly realism of *The Federalist Papers* with the Edenic nostalgia coursing through American literature?[2]

Much depends on what we mean by "bring together." Reconciling into a unity—no. But that the worldly realism and Edenic nostalgia could coexist in some subterranean relation of complicity and tension, I take to be a fact. The mundane workability of the republican arrangement enabled our literature to rise to that imaginative autonomy that distinguishes it in the nineteenth century. There is a close relation between the constraints of power built into the American system and the soaring of the American imagination toward visions of bliss where nature and spirit, individual and society find an ultimate harmony. The sturdiness and roominess of a stable liberal polity allow literature the freedom to "transcend" it and even oppose it in the name of higher values.

At least insofar as it yields itself to visions of democratic transcendence, the literary imagination of nineteenth-century America finds release through two channels: the thought of the Emersonians and the fiction of those writers who summon, through fables of solitary friendship, brief and fragile versions of anarchic community.

In Emersonian thought a major driving force is the wish to find a religious sanction for democratic sentiment, or, perhaps more accurately, to find a strategy for elevating democratic sentiment to religious emotion. The young Transcendentalists of the 1840s proposed, in Emerson's words, "to cast behind you all conformity, and acquaint men at first hand with Deity." And the best place, as it turned out, for making that acquaintance was within the self.

Emerson and his friends, in what amounted to a restatement of an old Christian heresy, raised the *I* to a quasi-divine status, so that man would now be seen not merely as a being like God but as a being that shares directly in the substance of divinity. Lending an air of sanctity to the persuasions of individualism, this outlook provided a new vision of man for a culture seeking to define itself as a new home for man. The culture that had arisen on the site of mankind's second beginning was declared, not yet a paradise, but a paradise in potential—or of potentiality.

All this was very stirring and served our literature wonderfully well. Not only did it stimulate Whitman to his vision of democratic man as one who exalts the glories of the autonomous self while, out of sheer exuberance, shuffling a supply of replaceable selves, it also provoked Hawthorne and Melville to their various embodyings of dissent. But—I repeat a point essential to my argument—even as the Emersonian view of man was released by the creation of a liberal polity, it is also a view that in crucial respects diverges from the assumptions of that polity.

The point may be illustrated by turning to Thoreau. For most of his life, though apparently less so toward the end, he looked upon freedom as an absolute state of being, which might be reached by men who shook off the torpor of convention and penetrated the roots of self. He was openly contemptuous of those who saw freedom as an arrangement between authority and citizens that necessarily involved social constraints. His vision of freedom was asocial; except by way of preliminary it did not depend on collective effort or established government; it was a state of being that each man could reach for himself, perhaps to be described as a romantic equivalent to the religious state of beatitude.

Now this is a powerful vision, and it has a permanent value, especially for those of us who reject it in principle because we accept the limits of a liberal society. Thoreau, however, cared rather little about such a society or its limits; his commitment to an absolute selfhood—at its least attractive, a private utopia for anarchic curmudgeons—implies an antipathy not only to the idea of government but to the very nature and necessary inconveniences of liberal government. Ultimately derived from liberalism, the Emersonian ethos has here been driven toward an antiliberal extreme.[3]

A somewhat similar pattern can be seen in major fictions written by Americans in the nineteenth century: Cooper, Twain, Melville. In their work the wish to break past the limits of society—perhaps even the limits of the human condition—manifests itself through images of space. They chart journeys not so much in order to get their heroes out of America but to transport the idea of America into a new and undefiled space. The urge to transcendence appears as accounts of men who move away, past frontiers and borders, into the "territory" or out to sea, in order to sustain images of communal possibility. For the enticements of space offer hopes of a new beginning, so that, for a time, an individual hero can be seen as reenacting, within or beyond society, the myth upon which the society rests but that it cannot fulfill. And in America this start is seen not so much as the liberal idea of reordering the social structure, but as a leap beyond the edge of society itself—a wistful ballet of transcendence.

A special kind of politics is at stake here: not the usual struggle among contending classes nor the interplay and mechanics of power, but a politics concerned with the *idea* of society itself, a politics that dares consider whether society is good and—still more wonderful question—whether society is necessary. These are the questions ultimately posed by the stories of Natty Bumppo and Chingachgook, Huck Finn and Nigger Jim, Ishmael and Queequeg—stories in which the search for transcendence shifts its locus from God to friendship and friendship becomes an emblem for an apolitical politics. A literature that on any manifest level seems hardly to be political at all, becomes the one to raise the most fundamental problems in political thought: what is the rationale for society, the justification for the state?

And if we agree for a moment so to regard nineteenth-century American writing, we discover running through it a strong if subterranean current of anarchism. Not anarchism as it is known to Europe, but anarchism as a social vision arising in preindustrial America, encouraged by the apparently secured triumph of the liberal polity and thereby resurgent fantasies of paradisal fulfillment.

Anarchism here signifies a vision of a human community beyond the social calculation of good and evil, beyond the need for the state as an apparatus of law and suppression, beyond the yardsticks of moral measurement, beyond the constraints of authority. It envisages a community of autonomous—one might almost say, Emersonian—persons, each secure in his own self. What is novel here is the assumption that because of our blessed locale we could find space in which to return, backward and free, to a stateless fraternity supposed to be anterior to and surely better than the liberal polity.

The oppressive system of laws, oppressive because they are laws, gives way to a self-ordering discipline of persons in a fraternal relationship. While this relationship is seen as enabled by and perhaps only possible within an unsullied nature, it is not so much the thought of pastorale that excites the major nineteenth-century American writers as it is a vision of human ease and comradeship being fulfilled within pastoral that excites the major nineteenth-century American writers most difficult that can be faced in political thought, is imaginatively dissolved: a solution as inadequate as it is entrancing.

But even as the dream of paradise is lodged deeply in the imaginations of our nineteenth-century writers, they must live in a society Madison helped to form, Jackson to reform, and the expansion of

American business to transform. The conviction that injustice and vulgarity grow stronger is shared by many of our nineteenth-century writers—a conviction that, finally, an America is being created that frustrates both the dream of a new Eden and the political idea of a liberal democracy. Neither in practice nor thought can our writers find a way of coping with this disenchantment. In their bitterness with the social reality and their growing sense of helplessness before it, American writers seek to get round the intractability of what they encounter. They summon poignant images of utopia—fragile, evanescent—on the borders of the forest, on rafts drifting down the Mississippi, on ships ruled by monomaniacal captains. Whatever they cannot change, they will turn away from, clinging meanwhile to the anarchic vision that seems all the more beautiful as it reaches into the distance of lost possibilities.

In the career of Herman Melville this pattern takes on a tragic and archetypal character. Speaking of the "democratic parable" as a major theme in Melville's work, Harold Kaplan has summarized its development:

In its first step . . . the theme criticizes the obtuse tyrannies of cultural forms and exhibits the primary value of the person, equipped with nothing much more than the strong impulse to life. But it is equally critical in its second step, as it exposes the resourcelessness of mere freedom and the destructiveness of nature. . . . On its third level of understanding, it combines negatives and positives in order to safeguard freedom against the threat of order, and order against the threat of freedom.

Melville's early writings, up to and including *Moby Dick*, are suffused with visions of anarchic bliss. How deeply the paradisal dream remained lodged in his imagination we can gather from a poem, "To Ned," which he published in 1888, three years before his death. It is a poem addressed to Richard Tobias Green, Melville's companion in the South Pacific adventures recorded in his first book, *Typee*. The tone is nostalgic: "Where is the world we roved, Ned Bunn?" In the Marquesas that Melville and Ned had known in their youth, they "breathed primeval balm/From Eden's eye yet overrun," but now the author must marvel whether mortals can twice, "Here and hereafter, touch a Paradise." One can only envy a man who supposed he had touched it once.

Taipi as a tempting if also threatening Arcadia, the comely friendship between Ishmael and Queequeg before they submit to Ahab's compulsive authoritarianism—these are stages in Melville's celebration of a roaming freedom that leads, and perhaps must lead, to a final, saddened recognition of "the resourcelessness of mere freedom and the

destructiveness of nature." The early books—though with clear anticipations of the doubts and cautions that will crowd the later ones—
release Melville's distaste for those "forms," those arthritic regulations
that in *Billy Budd* finally achieve their dubious victory. The young
Melville exudes a plebeian hopefulness; he is utterly American in his
democratic impatience with liberal constraints. Even in *Billy Budd*
there is much social irony—muted, wary, despairing. Billy is an ar-
chetype of innocence, imaginable only as a creature of a utopian yearning so intense and yet so untenable in the life we must lead that
Melville's mature imagination has no choice but fondly to destroy him.
Billy Budd reflects Melville's weary disenchantment with the radical
utopianism, the anarchism of his youth; by the time he came to write
this story Melville could do no more than be the Abraham to his
imaginary Isaac, sending to the sacrificial altar the boy who in gesture if
not speech summoned the dream of his youth. He had come round,
one might say, to a resigned perception of liberal necessities, those
limits and injustices entailed by the mere fact of society.

Less stark yet rather similar in direction is the turning of the later
Whitman, especially in his essays, "Democracy" and "Personalism,"
written in the late 1860s and fused into "Democratic Vistas" in 1871. In
these prose writings we can still see Whitman the Emersonian, clinging to "sovereignty and sacredness of the individual" and finding "in
the absolute Soul" of "each single individual something so transcendent" that it "places all beings on a common level." But there is also a
new Whitman fumbling his way toward a stance of liberalism, trying to
cope with a noisy mass culture and justifying his adherence to democracy not "on the ground that the People, the masses, even the best of
them, are . . . essentially sensible or good," but simply because democracy seems "the only safe and preservative" mode of political life.
These linked vocabularies speak of a tension between two styles of
thought: the earlier quasi-religious democratic individualism and the
emerging liberalism of the post-Civil War years. This liberalism—what
I would call modern or social liberalism—tries to bring together a
traditional liberal concern for personal rights and liberties with a belief
that the very government long regarded as suspect must now actively
reign in the excesses of industrial capitalism.

It is a liberalism that carries an air of puzzlement and disenchantment, a liberalism signifying a reluctant surrender of myth and dream.
Emotionally still attached to the more innocent varieties of democratic
faith, the writers who, like William Dean Howells, begin to move
toward social liberalism (or socialism) seem to understand that they are
being swept up as part of a reaction to American failures. The
liberalism to which they now turn implies that America must share the

destiny of other nations, the burdens and failures of history; it is a politics of making do.

From the high-minded individualism of E. L. Godkin, the editor of the *Nation* in the 1880s and 1890s, to the progressivism of Herbert Croly, who founds the *New Republic* in 1914 as an explicit advocate of a strong national government that is to serve as a kind of social umpire—this is to put into political terms what I have been trying to sketch as a shift of literary sentiment. The progressivism of a man like Croly, linked with the career and vagaries of Theodore Roosevelt, is by no means a simple matter, but it moves toward the essentials of twentieth-century American liberalism: an impatience with "the energetic and selfish individualism" that Croly saw as the heritage of the Jeffersonian past; a belief in the need for a strong reforming, central government; a commitment to social change that would right the imbalances cast up by *laissez faire*. This is a liberalism that accepts society as a given, struggles to tame large secondary institutions like the corporations and the trade unions, and cares more about controls and limits than transcendence and myth. It may not deny the uniqueness of the American tradition, but it insists that any effort to cling to the views or language of Jefferson, Jackson, and Emerson is simply self-deluding.

In twentieth-century American writing—we will merely glance at it—the influence of social liberalism is obviously large, though I doubt that any serious reader would challenge my impression that the influence of Emersonianism remains considerably larger. In the work of almost every significant novelist following Dreiser, the criticism of commercial values that liberalism develops as a major theme, finds both echo and embodiment. A writer like Frost who clings to a brittle native individualism, seems driven in his inferior work to mere ideological posturing—there is an ungainly willfulness in that New Hampshire mask of his. In the early Hemingway traditional American individualism has been burnished to a fine stoical defense, later to yield to a grudging recognition of those communal sentiments prompted by liberalism. In the work of Fitzgerald an exquisite balance is struck between the American democratic myth and the later liberal critique. *The Great Gatsby* brings together the theme of utopian yearning (that receding green light) and the theme of social waste, as if to span two eras of American understanding. And even in the work of William Faulkner, a professed opponent of liberalism, its influence remains powerful. A book like *Light in August* stems from a conscious, if despairing, adherence to traditional Southern values, but the energy of anger, the thrust of violence represented by Joe Christmas suggests that the liberal critique of modern society had registered on Faulkner's imagination—registered against his will, perhaps, but powerfully nonetheless, since he was a deeply honest writer who could not help acknowledging truths not his own.

I have flitted past some of the major figures of twentieth-century American writing, but if one considers the names of other, scarcely less distinguished writers, the influence of social liberalism seems equally evident. For Edmund Wilson liberalism takes on a rockier cast, it figures as a residual integrity. Only, by the late 1920s, it seems to have failed. He lurches briefly "leftward," toward Stalinism, then for a time toward the fragile groupings of the anti-Stanlinist radical intellectuals, and finally into a stance of personal opposition, a truculent resistance to the cant of our time—all of these being developments that reflect an original bafflement and disappointment with the liberal heritage. For a writer like Robert Penn Warren, self-consciously emerging as a Southern figure, liberalism at first seems emotionally thin, much too rationalistic, excessively interlocked with the mechanism of the industrial city; yet in his deepest feelings, in his instinctive sympathies for underdogs and his growing awareness of the claims of the blacks, he too has been deeply affected by the liberalism that, in theory, he may still declare himself to reject. And so it goes for a great many American writers in our century: For those who may sneer at liberalism, as John Dos Passos did in the late 1920s when, for a little while, he became a contributor to the communist *New Masses;* for those who declare liberalism to be philosophically superficial, as Lewis Mumford has from time to time, and as, in a different way, the Southern writers have frequently done; and for those who have attacked it for timorousness, an unwillingness to move toward a radical social program. Yet what seems remarkable is that it is liberalism, in its large American orbit and its continued hold upon the language and limits of our politics, that remains the central force—central morally, intellectually, politically—toward which so many of our writers have had to orient themselves, sometimes in affection, sometimes repulsion, sometimes an uncomfortable mixture of the two.

Still, things are very different from what they were in the "classical" moment of American romanticism a century earlier. The relationship between liberal belief and literary work is at best uneasy and tense; there is mutual influence, but also incomplete sympathy and entangled opposition.

In the past, then, there were times when liberalism and literature could strike up a fruitful intimacy, sometimes marriage and sometimes liaison. This usually occurred when liberalism had become clenched into a force of opposition to entrenched privilege or power, or when, in unexpected security, it had become diffused into a quasi-religious myth or mystique. The second of these options now seems unavailable: this is hardly an age for a Whitman. The first is being reenacted in the world of Eastern Europe where the most courageous writers gain their energy from the vision of a liberalized society. Some of these writers, to be sure, do not think of themselves as liberals; others, like Solzhenitsyn, now declare themselves to be opponents of liberalism, scorning it in ways that remind one of Dostoevsky and Tolstoy. But the logic of their situation, as social and moral critics of the authoritarian state, presses them to offer as a vibrant counterimage the possibility of a society where men are free to speak, and dissidence will not lead to the camps. No matter what Solzhenitsyn's formal declarations or later ideological turnings, his two major novels, *The First Circle* and *The Cancer Ward*, rest upon this vision as it might enable his Nerzhins and Rubins and Sologdins to live as free men. When struggling for elementary rights in the claustrophobic spaces of authoritarianism, the liberal vision can again take on historical urgency and moral force.

But with us in the West, where liberalism is more or less accepted as the common ground of public life and where, by now, it has taken many bruises, many stains, it has to accept a decidedly more modest relation to the life of culture. It probably has to forgo tragic and heroic themes, since precisely its public virtues—doubt, hesitation and irony—make those themes largely inaccessible. But comedy remains a major possibility, especially if the writer touched by liberalism can turn upon its snobbisms and affectations, while still finding in it some strands of virtue. If we glance at the greatest work of fiction composed in English during our century, we find at its center a roly-poly pacific Jew, a small figure of tolerance, muddle, and affection, a creature quite the opposite of the hero, a man liberal almost by default, as if he could not be anything else. Yet in these comic limitations there are values to be honored, a precious sediment of civilization.

Between liberalism and literature there must now be a relation of uneasiness, suspicion, disaffection. Modernist literature has strained toward extreme instances, impatience before compromise and commonplace, and a vision of the agonistic, the ultimate. Modernist literature has shown little taste or capacity for "balance." The legend of modernist literature has inclined the great writers of the last century to see themselves as heroes, acknowledged or neglected, while liberalism, except when summoning men to resist tyranny, works on a smaller scale. By now liberalism does not have much glamour and it feels decidedly uneasy before the allurements of transcendence. But when we look back at the murderous intoxications of our century, we may find it in our hearts to feel kindlier to these moderate virtues.

If, then, we finally turn again to Mr. Trilling's complaint against liberalism—that it "has not been able to produce a body of literature which can strongly engage our emotions"—I think it reasonable to say that he was perhaps asking too much from liberalism, demanding from it powers that at this point in history it cannot have. Liberalism (and in some European countries, one might add, social democracy) is now committed to a defense and extension of the welfare state, and whatever the practical uses of this politics may be, it is not likely to yield large images of dramatic possibility or heroic challenge.

The great virtue of liberalism is that it creates the conditions that enable writers to take a measure of its failings, to rail against its deficiencies of vision, to cry out that a merely tolerable world is not enough. They are right: it is not enough. But let them also be certain that in so crying out, they do not repeat the terrible mistake of a good many writers sixty and seventy years ago, which was to help create an intolerable world.

Postscript

This essay was written as an introduction to a collection of literary work—poems, stories and essays—which had first appeared in *The New Republic.* I began with the idea of discussing the role of that magazine in twentieth century American culture, but almost unawares the piece turned into a more general discussion of the relation between literature and liberalism.

[1]The term "liberal" as a political designation that large numbers of Americans, especially educated ones, apply to themselves, is rarely to be found (so far as I can discover) in nineteenth-century American usage. "Liberal" as qualifying adjective, as in "liberal Christianity" or "liberal sentiments," yes; but "liberal" as a substantive political category, no.

[2]This question as well as a few of the following paragraphs, are borrowed from an earlier essay of mine, "Anarchy and Authority in American Literature."

[3]The point has been nicely argued by Heinz Eulau: "Thoreau was incapable of recognizing those distinctions of degree which are politically decisive. He could not recognize them because he fell back, again and again, on the principle of individual conscience as the sole valid guide in political action . . . [But] individual conscience as a political principle was too obviously in conflict with the democratic principle of majority rule, even for Thoreau. . . . His only way out was, once more, a paradox: 'Any man more right than his neighbors constitutes a majority of one already.' Consequently, Thoreau had to postulate a (by democratic standards) curious distinction between law and right, with the explanation that one has to have faith in man, that each man can determine for himself what is right and just. Hence, no conflict is possible, so the argument goes, because law is law only if identical with right. Thoreau could not demonstrate, however, that there is, in case the majority is wrong, an objective criterion for assaying the correctness of an individual's or a minority's judgment."

Books Discussed

Below is a list of books discussed in *Celebrations and Attacks,* alphabetical according to author, and with date of publication following.

Anderson, Quentin. *The American Henry James.* 1957.
Babel, Isaac. *The Collected Stories.* 1955.
Baker, Carlos. *Ernest Hemingway: A Life Story.* 1969.
Chambers, Whittaker. *Witness.* 1952.
Chase, Richard. *The Democratic Vista.* 1958.
Dawidowicz, Lucy. *The War Against the Jews.* 1975.
Du Bois, W.E.B. *Autobiography.* 1969.
Eliot, George. *Letters* (edited by Gordon Haight). 1954-55.
Ellison, Ralph. *Invisible Man.* 1952.
Faulkner, William. *The Town.* 1957.
　　　　　　The Mansion. 1959.
Fiedler, Leslie. *Love and Death in the American Novel.* 1960.
Hanley, James. *A Dream Journey.* 1976.
Hellman, Lillian. *Scoundrel Time.* 1976.
Hindus, Milton. *The Crippled Giant.* 1950.
Jewett, Sarah Orne. *The Country of the Pointed Firs.* 1896.
Joyce, James. *Selected Letters* (edited by Richard Ellman). 1975.
Konrad, George. *The Case Worker.* 1974.
Lessing, Doris. *The Golden Notebook.* 1962.
Mailer, Norman. *Barbary Shore.* 1951.
Malamud, Bernard. *The Magic Barrel.* 1958.
O'Connor, Flannery. *Everything That Rises Must Converge.* 1965.
Paz, Octavio. *Alternating Current.* 1973.

Pirandello, Luigi. *Short Stories* (edited by Frances Keene). 1959.

Poggioli, Renato. *The Theory of the Avant-Garde.* 1968.

Power, Crawford. *The Encounter.* 1950.

Robbe-Grillet, Alain. *The Voyeur.* 1958.

Roth, Philip. *Goodbye, Columbus.* 1959.

Salinger, J.D. *Raise High the Roof Beam, Carpenters* and *Seymour An Intro-duction.* 1963.

Schwartz, Delmore. *In Dreams Begin Responsibilities* (reprint). 1978.

Singer, Isaac Bashevis. *Satan in Goray.* 1955.

Stewart, John L. *The Burden of Time, The Fugitives and the Agrarians.* 1965.

Swanberg, W.A. *Norman Thomas, The Last Idealist.* 1976.

Trilling, Lionel. *Sincerity and Authenticity.* 1972.

Tuckerman, Frederick. *The Complete Poems* (edited by N. Scott Momaday). 1965.

Williams, John. *Stoner.* 1965.

Wilson, Edmund. *Letters on Literature and Politics, 1912-1972.* 1977.

Wright, Richard. *Eight Men.* 1961.